A Theology for the Earth:
The Contributions of
Thomas Berry and Bernard Lonergan

RELIGIONS AND BELIEFS SERIES

The series includes books bearing on the religions of the Americas, the Bible in its relationship to cultures, and on ethics in relation to religion. The series welcomes manuscripts written in either English or French.

Editorial Committee

Robert Choquette, Director

Margaret Dufour-McDonald

David Jeffrey

In the Same Series

Pauline Côté, *Les Transactions politiques des croyants : Charismatiques et Témoins de Jéhovah dans le Québec des années 1970 et 1980*, 1993

Adolf Ens, *Subjects or Citizens?: The Mennonite Experience in Canada, 1870-1925*, 1994

Robert Choquette, *The Oblate Assault on Canada's Northwest*, 1995

Jennifer Reid, *Myth, Symbol, and Colonial Encounter: British and Mi'kmaq in Acadia, 1700-1867*, 1995

M.D. Faber, *New Age Thinking: A Psychoanalytic Critique*, 1996

André Guidon, *L'Habillé et le Nu : Pour une étique du vêtir et du dénuder*, 1997

Vicki Bennett, *Sacred Space and Structural Style: The Embodiment of Socio-religious Ideology*, 1997

Colin Grant, *Myths We Live By*, 1998

Louis Rousseau et Frank W. Remiggi (sous la dir. de), *Atlas historique des pratiques religieuses : le Sud-Ouest du Québec au xixᵉ siècle*, 1998

RELIGIONS AND BELIEFS SERIES, NO. 10

A Theology for the Earth: The Contributions of Thomas Berry and Bernard Lonergan

ANNE MARIE DALTON

University of Ottawa Press

This book has been published with the help of a grant from the Canadian Federation for the Humanities, using funds provided by the Social Sciences and Humanities Research Council of Canada.

University of Ottawa Press gratefully acknowledges the support extended to its publishing programme by the Canada Council, the Department of Canadian Heritage, and the University of Ottawa.

We acknowledge the financial support of the Government of Canada through the Book Publishing Industry Development Program for this project.

CANADIAN CATALOGUING IN PUBLICATION DATA

Dalton, Anne Marie

A Theology for the Earth: The Contributions of Thomas Berry and Bernard Lonergan

(Religions and Beliefs series; no. 10)

Includes bibliographical references.
ISBN 0-7766-0478-3

1. Human ecology—Religious aspects—Christianity. 2. Berry, Thomas Mary, 1914-   —Contributions in ecological theology. 3. Lonergan, Bernard J. F. (Bernard Joseph Francis), 1904-1984—Contributions in ecological theology. I. Title. II. Series.

BT695.5.D35 1999   261.8'362'0922   C99-900192-2

Cover design: Robert Dolbec
Typesetting: Colette Désilets
Cover photograph: Centrepiece for *Stations of the Cosmic Earth*,
Carolyn Van Huyse-Delaney, Toronto
1985, stained glass, 17" x 32"
Commissioned by Holy Cross Centre for Ecology and Spirituality,
Port Burwell, Ontario. Used by permission of Holy Cross Centre.

The *Stations of the Cosmic Earth*, and this centrepiece in particular, were inspired by the following quotation from Teilhard de Chardin:

"In one manner or the other it still remains true that, even in the view of the mere biologist, the human epic resembles nothing so much as a way of the cross." Pierre Teilhard de Chardin, *Phenomenon of Man*, trans. by Bernard Wall (New York: Harper Torchbook, 1965), p. 313.

ISBN 0-7766-0478-3
ISSN 1480-4700
© University of Ottawa Press, 1999
542 King Edward, Ottawa (Ont.), Canada K1N 6N5
press@uottawa.ca   http://www.uopress.uottawa.ca

Printed and bound in Canada

FOREWORD

I have seldom reflected on the epistemological or critical implications of my writings. Thus it is a special delight to read these pages of Anne Marie Dalton. They give me insights into my own thinking that I have seldom thought about in any conscious manner. It is particularly helpful to have her reflections done in the context of the epistemological and theological work of Bernard Lonergan. She is quite correct in understanding my work in terms of Lonergan's notion of Descriptive Discourse, for my intent has been simply to present and to leave the reader to respond out of whatever background the reader might have.

This century, through most of which both Lonergan and I have lived and worked, can be compared to that of Thomas Aquinas. He was born into a world being transformed in its thinking through the newly acquired writings of Aristotle that came into Christian Europe from the Moslem schools of thought in Spain. Prior to his times, Western thought had been dominated by the Platonism of the Fathers and the Neo-Platonism of Dionysius as these had come down through Boethius and Scotus Erigina. These new writings that came in through the Moslem world, especially through the interpretation of Averrhoes, were so convincing that the Moslem world had become anxious lest they foster rationalism and so draw believers away from faith in the Koran. This led to a sudden withdrawal of support for philosophical studies in the Islamic schools at Cordoba and elsewhere in the Moslem world.

The same question arose regarding reason and faith in the Christian world after the arrival of these Aristotelian writings. Thomas Aquinas was called from Paris to Rome in 1259 to advise church authorities concerning the attitude they should adopt to this issue. After having new translations made from the Greek text, Thomas spent several years writing commentaries on most of these writings. Of special importance were his commentaries on the *Physics*, the *Metaphysics* and the *De Anima*. Consequent on these studies and in the line of traditions that had come down through the earlier Christian thinkers, Thomas made clear his view. There was not only a consonance between the writings of Aristotle and the teachings of faith, but the principles presented in the cosmology of Aristotle provided a remarkably clear and coherent context for an integral exposition of Christian faith. The consequence was his *Summa Theologica*.

Our situation can be compared to that of Thomas Aquinas. We have a new way of understanding the universe, a new cosmology. For the first time, we are able to extend and correct the work of the Greek scientists through new cosmological data based on empirical observation. We see infinitely more than they were able to see. Only recently, however, have we been able to see that the universe is less a fixed entity than a vast complex of astronomical forms that emerged into being some 14 billion years ago and have been undergoing an evolutionary sequence of transformations ever since.

Unlike Thomas we have not been able to assimilate this new vision that is made available to us. The scientists who made these discoveries have indicated that they consider the universe as simply mechanistic in origin and in functioning, however, and this has become a dominant view. We have lost any expectation that significant spiritual insight could come from an intimacy with the universe as divine manifestation. We have failed to seriously engage a new way of understanding the universe, considering it irrelevant or harmful to religious faith. Both my work and that of Lonergan have in different ways responded to this challenge.

Earlier in this century, Teilhard de Chardin, among the most distinguished Christian scholars of high academic credentials in geological and anthropological studies, was unique in his acceptance of this new understanding of the universe. He recognized it as a story, a great evolutionary epic. His work revealed the potential of the scientific account of evolution to be the context for a new and enriched Christian theology that would provide in turn a new rapport between Christianity and the modern world.

While Teilhard had, in my judgment, an excessive admiration of modern scientific technologies and an extreme anthropocentrism, I have learned from him three things of special import. The universe has a psychic-spiritual as well as a physical-material dimension from the beginning; the universe story and the human story are two aspects of a single story; and there is need to move from an excessive concern for redemptive processes to a new concern for creation processes.

From Thomas I learned that the universe entire is the primary purpose of both creation and redemption. If the human is the immediate purpose of redemption, the more comprehensive purpose is the entire order of things. Such indeed is what he says in His *Summa Contra Gentiles* where he tells us that "The order of the universe is the ultimate and noblest perfection in things" (SCG,II,46). Also in the *Summa Theologica*, he says the "the whole universe together participates in and manifests the divine more than any single being whatsoever" (ST,I,47,1). Thomas gets a scriptural basis for his thinking from the Genesis statement after each day of creation that God says that it is "good," whereas after the sixth day, God says of the whole of creation that it is "very good."

In my writing one would find only marginally any attempt to explain the coherence of my thinking with Christian belief. What I have tried to provide is a comprehensive understanding of contemporary scientific thinking about the universe as an integral evolutionary process. My basic proposition is that the universe, in the phenomenal order, is the only self-referent mode of being. All other beings, including humans, are universe referent in their origin, in their activities and in their fulfillment. My writings are intended to deal primarily with the phenomenal world. On occasion, however, I do indicate what I see to be a more spiritual or mythic role of the universe. The universe can be seen as divine manifestation or as the visible expression of the numinous world, or simply as expression of some ineffable mystery more available to the artist and musician than to those engaged in rational or verbal expression.

Also, I understand the individual self as seeking in its deepest desires for completion in the Great Self of the universe. The consequence for contemporary humans of being taken away from immediate experience of natural phenomena and having no adequate referent for the deeper mystery of things is a profound personal loneliness. There is only the world of mechanistic technologies.

This quest for fulfillment in natural phenomena finds expression, I believe, in the delight experienced by children with the sights and sounds and feel of the natural world. This experience is presented by Rachel Carson in her book *A Sense of Wonder*. Carson goes with a child to the seashore and together they look at the wonders of the sky, sea and land; the shapes and forms there confront all their senses. It is quite perceptive of Carson to observe that a child needs an adult to talk with and explain in human language something of the mystery of things. In this process each is enriched with the experience of the other. The adult needs the child as much as the child needs the adult.

There are two ways for an adult to explain things to a child. One is with mythic explanations, such as are handed down to us through the earlier stories of the classical world or through the stories of indigenous peoples. The other is through the more scientific accounts that are now available to us. Apparently the true inner appreciation of things can be communicated only through story form whether mythic or epic. This has led some perceptive scientists to appreciate that the evolutionary story needs to be narrated as epic narrative. An epic is a sequence of heroic deeds, generally with some historical basis, deeds of immense importance that are carried out with more than ordinary, even mysterious power. So the universe needs to be understood in its amazing sequence of transformations to produce the wondrous world about us. The coherent sequence of transformations narrated in understandable, non-technical, even literary language; this is what makes the entry of scientists into the epic form so acceptable to both scientists and to the more general reader.

The epistemological and theological implications of this way of thinking about the universe as we have discovered it through our empirical studies could be most significant in the future. This study of Anne Marie Dalton's can be considered a contribution toward understanding these fields of future studies.

Thomas Berry
August 1998

CONTENTS

INTRODUCTION

Scholars of religion are no strangers to challenges from the modern and post-modern world. In this latter half of the twentieth century, the ecological crisis is perhaps among the more difficult of these challenges. When the very foundations of life itself are threatened, how does one engage in reflection on one's religious faith? Thomas Berry was one of the first and most creative North American religionists to seriously consider the issue of the role of religion in restructuring human-earth relations.

Thomas Berry was born in Greensboro, North Carolina, November 9, 1914. From his own reports, he had an early interest in nature and wilderness. As a young adult, he joined the Roman Catholic Order of Passionists and was ordained to the priesthood May 30, 1942. Berry had a passion for learning and teaching. Despite his Order's first commitment to preaching, rather than to university careers, Berry did gain permission to prepare for an academic career. He completed a Ph.D. in history at The Catholic University of America and went on to China, where he began a study of Chinese languages. Berry's teaching career in the United States of America was in the area of world religions, most of it spent at Fordham University, New York, from which he retired in 1979.

Berry's interest in the ecological crisis came to the fore in the 1960's. For him, however, it was not a passing fad of that memorable decade. It remained a serious and dedicated commitment that consumed his attention and expressed itself in almost all his teaching, writing and speaking from that time until the present. During that time, there was considerable development, refinement and synthesis to his thought, but also an overwhelming consistency in the cultural solution he proposed to the ecological crisis. Berry's proposal was simple but radical; a new story of the universe to inform and reinvent modern culture in all its expressions. At the basis of his contention was the notion that divine-human-earth relationships must be recast. It is both his creativity and his dogged persistence, as it is evidenced in his writings, that compelled this study of his work and its potential contribution to a Christian theology of ecology.

Perhaps the greatest difficulty one faces in constructing a theology of anything in modern times is the fact that Christian theology itself has been flaying about for an identity and a methodological basis since the demise of scholasticism and the encroachment of empirical science on theology's claim to universal knowledge. Where does one find a convincing foundation for a contemporary theology capable of conversing with modern science, the most obvious player to date in the attempt to confront the ecological crisis? This is a problem, given the extremely tenuous nature of the science-religion relationship in modernity. The construction of a Christian theology of ecology calls for a revision of the very way in which we think about what theology is, how one does theology and on what bases it can claim to present any kind of truth or functionality in word or action. No one in our time has met these questions with a more careful and convincing response than the Canadian philosopher-theologian Bernard Lonergan (1905-1984).

Bernard Lonergan took serious account of the philosophical and ideological assumptions underlying the modern rift between science and Christianity, confronted them and rebuilt the foundations of Christian theology. Hence, my decision to use Lonergan's heuristic account of world process and the role of theology within it as the theoretic tool toward a construction of a Christian theology of ecology.

Post-modernism has raised legitimate questions that challenge such thinkers as Thomas Berry and Bernard Lonergan. On what basis can one take seriously the work of a popularizing scholar who proposes the dreaded "grand narrative" as a global solution to the ecological crisis, as Berry does, or the foundationalism of Lonergan?[1] Have we not convincingly deconstructed narratives and uncovered their inherent colonizing and imperialist ideologies? Haven't foundations been shown to rest on still other perceptions and assumptions as equally precarious as the edifices they attempt to ground? A full account of the legitimacy of such questions as well as their own fallacies is beyond the scope of this work. Briefly, however, an apologetic for Berry and Lonergan might proceed along the following lines.

We set aside for the moment the epistemological concerns underlying the deconstructionist objection to grand narrative or narrative of any kind. These are more adequately met within the discussion of Lonergan's work below. In terms of cultural imperialism, it is difficult to sustain such a charge against Berry. Admittedly, Berry's proposed story of the universe, which he argued ought to provide a global context for all human activity, is a grand narrative. However, it allows and even calls for a contextualization within different cultures. The question of how to accomplish any such contextualization continues to be debated in hermeneutical circles without satisfactory resolution.

As a discussion of Berry's writings on world religions will reveal, Berry's own sensitivity to the insights and wisdom of non-Christian religions and in particular to those of primal peoples would seem to indicate his own awareness of cross-cultural problems and to a sensitivity to issues of ideological imperialism.[2] Nevertheless, there remains the question of the importation of Western scientific cosmology into other cultures. While this is already occurring in many ways and no doubt Western science is almost everywhere to stay, the question is whether or not one ought to propose a story that incorporates a Western scientific cosmology into other cultures. This is a vast question that requires extensive investigation both at the empirical level as to what is already the case in particular circumstances and in terms of the compatibility of the meanings and values of this cosmology with cosmological stories of other cultures. It is beyond the limits of these pages to pursue.

The question pursued here is a prior and smaller one. It inquires about the potential effectiveness of the new story in any culture at all and in particular as a potential mediator of Christian meanings and values.

The issue of the possibility and legitimacy of narratives as representative of anything other than human colonization of the world is the same question addressed to foundationalism. Deconstructionism points not only to the radical pluralism of human experience, but ultimately to its unintelligibility. It stands in sharp opposition to classicism and dogmatism. It is, however, its own witness to the impossibility of even conceiving of an uninterpreted world. Deconstruction is itself an interpretation and a grand narrative of sorts.[3]

Moreover, Lonergan was not a foundationalist of the classicist or dogmatic stripe. He offered a third alternative: authentic human performance as a foundation of norms for human knowing, loving and acting in the world. Through a phenomenology of human subjectivity, he uncovered the invariant transcendental structures operative in human knowing, loving and acting. He likewise revealed the constitutive role of culture and society in the human production of meanings of all sorts. The choice of Lonergan's system of thought is, then, an option for meaning over meaninglessness and for the possibility of norms over normlessness. This is not an arbitrary choice, however, since Lonergan's system is pre-eminently convincing.

While Lonergan's explanatory categories are employed, they serve in the pages ahead to explicate the primary focus, which is the proposal of Thomas Berry to meet the ecological crisis. It was Berry who brought together scientific and religious insights to meet the ecological crisis and called for a renewal of theology in the context of the new story he constructed. Lonergan took the methodology of science seriously in providing the heuristic structure for the renewal of theology under any legitimate contemporary horizon.

The first four chapters below trace the genetic development of Thomas Berry's thought. This involves an examination of the influences and sources that inform his response to the ecological crisis. The sources dealt with are those that were an obvious preoccupation in the major phases of his public professional life; namely, the subject of his doctoral dissertation, Giambattista Vico, world religions, Teilhard de Chardin and contemporary scientists. Chapter five examines Berry's proposal to deal with the ecological crisis and the writings surrounding and supporting that proposal. The concluding chapters select and present categories from Bernard Lonergan's work with a view to analyzing Berry's potential contribution to Christian theology.

Finally, it is not even Berry's work in itself that is the horizon of this effort. It is the continuation of his life's passion; namely, the evocation of a religious praxis adequately grounded in traditional, but renewed, religious belief and faith and capable of confronting the destructive presence of humans within the natural world.

Notes

1.   The term "grand narrative" is François Lyotard's, cited in J.M. Bernstein, "Grand Narratives," in *On Paul Ricoeur: Narrative and Interpretation*, ed. David Wood (New York: Routledge, Chapman and Hall, Inc., and London: The University of Warwick, 1991), 102-123.

2.   See Thomas Berry, "The Divine and Our Present Revelatory Moment," in Thomas Berry with Thomas Clarke, *Befriending the Earth*, ed. Stephen Dunn, C.P. and Anne Lonergan (Mystic, CT: Twenty-Third Publications, 1991), 19 and passim.

3.   Cf. J.M. Bernstein, "Grand Narratives," esp. 110.

CHAPTER ONE

THE METHOD AND TRADITION OF BERRY'S CULTURAL HISTORY

Introduction

Berry's first interest was cultural history, a designation he gave his own work and which remained significant. While on occasion he showed his awareness of political and social influences on the topic under discussion, it is clear throughout his work that his predominant focus was the influence of ideas and intellectual/spiritual movements in history. His penchant for tracing ideas across cultures and making syntheses of large amounts of data remained characteristic of his work.

Berry wrote his dissertation on Giambattista Vico. Even a cursory look at the work on Vico is enlightening in clarifying the significance of Berry's self-designation as a cultural historian as well as placing him in a distinctive tradition of thinkers that can best be described as counter-Enlightenment. The historical context in which Berry's work is best understood begins with his interpretation of Vico's contribution and influence. Vico is seen by many to be at the beginning of a line of cultural historians with a distinctive flavour. While there are definite departures and developments in Berry's work, Berry shows a considered preference for both Vico's method and much of his interpretation of history. There are also consistent references in

Berry's writings to a line of thinkers, whom many consider to have inherited the ideas of Vico.

Scholars consider Giambattista Vico (1668-1744) a humanist in the Renaissance tradition. He was a "Renaissance man" in his diverse interests and expertise, as well as in his positive approach to tradition and to the relevance of the classics to his time. He was anti-Aristotelian and looked to the Renaissance Platonists, Ficinus, Pico della Mirandola, Allessandro Piccolominia and Francisco Patrizi, for the metaphysical basis for his own work. Vico was a philosopher, historian, jurisprudent and philologist. Because of the breadth of his interests and also the perceived obscurity of his ideas, there has been a wide range of scholarship on Vico.

Modern scholarship highlights Vico's diverse contributions to present-day concerns. Linguists and rhetoricians claim him for his use of language and rhetoric as an access to the mind of primitive humankind.[1] In his theory of language as a carrier of the truth of tradition, he is seen as a forerunner of Gadamer. Psychologists and anthropologists study his theory of myth. Epistemologists differ over his theory of knowledge. Political philosophers, philosophers of history and theologians all find points of relevance to present-day concerns. This continued relevance serves Berry well insofar as his work finds resonance with many of Vico's ideas. Berry's interpretation of Vico, especially his most recurrent and insistent insights into Vico's theory of history, shows Vico to be a likely early source of Berry's own perception of cultural history. The stated purpose of his dissertation was to systematize Vico's thought on particular subjects. Berry's method (by his own admission) was to collate all the more important texts of Vico that relate to particular problems or themes associated with Vico's work.[2]

The dissertation was divided into three parts, each of which identified one of these particular problems or themes. Part I dealt with "The Obscurity of Vico's Writings"; Parts II and III with his theory of history, under the headings, "Vico's Approach to History" and "Development and Corruption of History," respectively.

Berry's Dissertation on Giambattista Vico

The Obscurity of Vico's Thought

In Part I, Berry declared that, on the one hand, some of the controversy over Vico's work could be overcome by attending to Vico's own words. On the other hand, however, the admitted obscurity of Vico's work had left him open to many interpretations. In accounting for this obscurity, Berry placed particular emphasis on the general intellectual confusion of the times in which Vico lived. Europe's perennial and traditional quest for unity and uniformity was breaking up. It is noteworthy that Berry carried the significance of this theme of the break-up of a kind of Western unity into his later work.

> Europe [at the time of Vico] had not recovered and still has not recovered, from the shock involved in the transition from the Middle Ages to Modern Times. In former times Western society, in its religious, intellectual and political life had a certain tendency toward unity, despite all its inner tensions, which has not been known since that time. We can scarcely remember even the remnant of this harmony in the realms of thought and religion.[3]

Hence, characteristic of Vico's day were the general skepticism of intellectuals, the lack of a principle around which intellectual pursuit could be ordered and the break-up of the medieval synthesis. In Berry's view, this general state of chaos was not only the way in which Vico perceived his intellectual environment, but also the situation to which Vico attempted a solution.

Vico showed considerable discomfort and disagreement with those scholars of his day who seemed to fragment human knowledge. The philosopher Pierre Gassendi and his follower, John Locke, as well as Robert Boyle were among those criticized. He was especially critical, however, of Descartes' proposal of the *cogito* as a principle of certitude and his identification of clear and distinct ideas as exclusive carriers of truth. He strongly disagreed with the Cartesians and anyone else who did not accept tradition as a carrier of truth or who set aside the philosophy of humankind to become preoccupied with a philosophy of nature. This is an important aspect of Vico's thought and one to which we will return. For the most part, Vico was offering a creative response to the confusion he experienced all around him. He felt that the respect formerly afforded the sciences of man and society had waned.

Other features of this discussion of Vico's obscurity included by Berry were Vico's preference for Platonic over Aristotelian philosophy, the latter being much more suited in Berry's view to the synthesis he sought. Finally, Berry mentioned the largeness and utter impossibility of the task Vico set for himself; namely a synthesis of all human knowledge.

Vico's Theory of History

In his treatment of these themes in Parts II and III, Berry drew three significant conclusions to which he continually returned: (1) Vico's theory of history suffers from an intermingling of historical theory, derived from his Platonist philosophy, with historical fact, despite Vico's own purpose of establishing the origin and succession of actual historical events among the gentile nations; (2) Vico was most concerned to relate to the age in which he lived; and (3) Vico's most significant contributions stem from his recovery of primeval history. These conclusions expose Berry's particular reading of Vico as well as further aspects of Vico's thought that remained influential in Berry's own work.

The Effect of Platonist Philosophy on Vico's Thought

While Berry admitted that Vico was genuinely aware of the complexity of history and its "hard realities," he was consistent in maintaining that the projection of a uniform pattern on history overrode his portrayal of historical contingencies. Berry paid very little attention to the significance of Vico's notion of history as a human production, an idea emphasized by others, notably Max Horkheimer and Bernard Lonergan.[4] This latter interpretation, by way of contrast to Berry's, did not emphasize Vico's Platonism and saw in Vico a beginning of modern historical consciousness.

Many scholars maintain that while Vico set out to prove Descartes wrong in his basic assumptions, he shared with Descartes, as well as with Machiavelli, Hobbes and others, the notion that humans can only know what they themselves produce. He insisted further, however, that what humans produce is history. Therefore, history, and not nature, ought to be the prime object of their investigations. Nature is known ultimately only to its creator, God, and not to humans. Because of the way in which Vico shared this principle with Descartes, he is considered *counter-* rather than *anti-*Cartesian.[5]

While Berry was aware of this contribution of Vico's, he was more concerned with establishing Vico's dualistic conception of history in order to refute a Hegelian reading of Vico. Berry gave the clearest expression of Vico's dualism in Part III, "Development and Corruption in History," where he presented the case that Vico kept both a supernatural view of history and a Platonic metaphysics, and that these two factors accounted for his dualism.

The supernatural view alone sees humanity as "under the divine guidance passing through the sufferings of time to its transcendent eternal destiny." This view tends to absorb the human aspect into the transcendent aspect of history. Vico neither denied nor transcended this view, Berry concluded, but "passed to a lower realm of thought," that is, from the consideration of history as a human phenomenon. When he did, however, he was still "caught up in the realm of the Platonic metaphysics." He referred to a passage from the *Autobiography* in which Vico imposed his characteristic divisions on history as he described the uniform succession of development common to all the nations. This is the "eternal ideal of history traversed in time by the histories of all the nations."[6]

While modern historians might look askance at the notion of uniformity presented by Vico, Vico himself saw it as a deepening of history. Philosophy and history work together, each clarifying the other. Philosophy provides the light for the intelligibility of history. Berry supports this reading of Vico's Platonism with statements of Vico, such as Vico's final summary of his interpretation of the frontispiece of *Scienza nuova seconda*:

> The darkness in the background of the picture is the material of this Science, uncertain, unformed, obscure... The ray with which divine providence lights up the breast of metaphysic represents the Axioms, Definitions, and Postulates that this Science [Vico's New Science] takes as Elements from which to deduce the Principles on which it is based and the Method by which it is deduced.[7]

Consistent with this statement, Vico often referred to the place of philosophy (metaphysic) and of divine providence as he described the role of each of the civil institutions represented.[8]

The point here is not to make some judgment as to which emphasis is more correct, Horkheimer's or Berry's, nor to attempt to reconcile them; it is rather to emphasize the nature of Berry's understanding of Vico.

Vico's Concern for the Age in Which He Lived

As mentioned above, Berry saw the intellectual climate of Vico's day to be a significant factor accounting for the obscurity of his thought. Throughout his study, Berry consistently emphasized the fact that Vico was constantly in conversation with his age. This was so in that he both condemned the age in which he lived and extolled it. His condemnations are found mainly in his private letters and, Berry concluded, pertain to moral weaknesses, whereas the words of praise are found mainly in the *Scienza nuova* and pertain to the heights of culture that Europe had attained. Vico carried within himself a sense of foreboding and sadness regarding the corruption of his own age. Commenting on the early writings, Berry observed that despite Vico's belief that divine providence would finally work everything to the good and that there certainly was development in history, "there was always an abyss of corruption ever threatening to engulf human society." Only divine providence restrained that force.[9]

Vico's theory of history was a response to the corruption he saw around him; it had a diagnostic and corrective intent.[10] His descriptions of the cycles of progress and decline were to a large degree intended to alert his own age to the inherent dangers of many of its noticeable trends. Decline, he maintained, was always from within, even where a nation was taken over by another and disappeared as a separate entity. Furthermore, moral decline was a result of confused thought. The intellectual confusion of the scholarship of his day led to moral relativity and hence threatened an age of barbarism. Here Berry pointed out the fallacy involved in seeing Vico as a forerunner of eighteenth- and nineteenth-century disciples of progress. "The very things in which they placed their hopes," Berry wrote, "were the things of which he had most fear." Those things included faith in physical science as redemptive and a neglect of the "philosophy of man," the result of the new rationalism.[11]

It is precisely Vico's critique of the direction his own age was taking, later to be recognized as the seeds of the Enlightenment, that placed him among those thinkers whom Isaiah Berlin considered counter-Enlightenment. Berlin observed that Vico's view "was subversive of the very notion of absolute truths and of a perfect society founded on them, not merely in fact but in principle."[12] In a similar vein, Vico has been designated as a proto-romantic, early to see the very ill effects of the Enlightenment that the romantics would later rail against.[13] Vico did see his new science of the history of the nations as a program of recovery—a recovery of Platonic philosophy, Christian beliefs, the classics and belief in the truth of tradition in general.

Vico's Recovery of Primeval History

Vico criticized those who saw history as a mere chronology, in which events did no more than supply instances or illustrations of truths arrived at by rational, logical and ahistorical processes. He believed that history itself was the truth about human existence. Berry found his clearest illustration of that principle in Vico's recovery of the "dark night of history," one of Vico's images for the earliest ages of humanity. His contribution to the understanding of the "dark night" lies both in the new meaning he discovered there and in the method he used to discover that meaning.

Vico was extremely critical of those who interpreted the early *gentes* according to present ways of thinking and acting. He discovered "truth" in the "vulgar traditions," preserved in the myths, fables, epics and sayings. He argued, however, that this "truth" consisted neither in the actual historical events that the euhemerists claimed were at the base of the fabulations represented by myths and such, nor in the esoteric wisdom that some philosophers claimed was the possession of the ancients. He demonstrated that these fabulous constructions of history revealed the progression of the ideas and institutions that shape the present. The early poetry did not show the advanced state of the wisdom of the early peoples; the wisdom it contained was rather a common-sense wisdom, born of the experience of the senses. The institutions of each age coalesced around recognizable major ideas. These ideas were of a vulgar, common nature, the *sensus communis*, which Joseph Mali understood to roughly estimate what modern social history called *mentalités*, collective images of reality.[14] Common sense, Vico maintained, was not the wisdom of philosophers, but judgment without reflection, common sensibilities of communities or nations or the whole human race about what constitutes the "true" in everyday life.

One illustration that Vico gave of this conception of the "true" in everyday life over time was from the area of jurisprudence. He described three kinds of jurisprudence, each of which was characteristic of one of the great ages of history: divine wisdom in the age of the gods, heroic jurisprudence in the age of heroes and human jurisprudence in the age of humanity. The first two reflected the desire for certainty in everyday life; that is, they simply worked to bring order to the society. Divine wisdom meant interpreting the intentions of the gods; justice was measured according to ceremonial solemnity. Vico found the basis for his claim in such phrases as *iustae nuptiae* and *iustum testamentum* preserved in Roman laws. Heroic jurisprudence rested with the use of correct speech. "The reputation of ancient Roman jurisconsuls," Vico maintained, "rested in their *cavere*, their taking care or making sure." Their clients were cautioned to present their cases in a way that would be convincing. Human jurisprudence, by contrast, Vico said, "looks to the truth of the facts themselves" and bends the law to meet the requirements of equity in each case. Vico concluded:

> Thus divine and heroic jurisprudence laid hold of the certain when the nations were rude, and the human jurisprudence looked to the true when they had become enlightened.[15]

Likewise, Vico outlined three kinds of authority, reason, nature, customs and judgments, each specific to its age.

Vico came to this conclusion regarding the progression of the "dark night of history," as Berry pointed out, through the introspection of his own mind; that was his method. Vico wrote:

> But in the night of thick darkness enveloping the earliest antiquity, so remote from ourselves, there shines the eternal and never failing light of a truth beyond all question: that the world of civil society has certainly been made by men, and that its principles are therefore to be found within the modifications of our own mind.[16]

Thus, it is only with the greatest difficulty that modern humans can understand anything about their early ancestors, he stated. Reminiscent of Descartes' position of doubting all, Vico asserted that he would proceed as if no books had been written on the subject of the beginnings of the gentile nations. He made this statement, it seems, both because of his disagreement with previous and contemporary theories on this topic and because he proposed to find the truth within the experience of knowing itself.

Berry quoted from the eleventh chapter of the first book of *Scienza nuova prima*: "[history's] beginnings ought to be found within the nature of our human mind and in the power of our understanding..." In the same text, Vico described his undertaking as "a true experiment if the things here conceived were identified with the intimate substance of our soul, that is, that we have done nothing else than explained our reason, which needs to be dehumanized in order to forget..."[17] The farther he went back in history, the more primitive became humanity, until he touched the edges of the emergence of the human race in the "dark night" of history. Vico proposed that modern humans can understand these first barely human ancestors because all humans experience the first emergence of thought and understanding basic to the process of humanization.

Reading the myths, epics and sayings preserved in modern languages, and other vulgar traditions in the light of principles derived from the study of "our human mind," Vico concluded that the gentile nations progressed along recognizable lines from the brutish, ignorant, scarcely human giants that occupied the earth after the great flood to his truly civilized and humane European contemporaries. "The nature of people," he wrote, "is first crude, then severe, then benign, then delicate, finally dissolute."[18] (Vico held that the seeds of dissolution were already sown in the society of his day.)

As the "nature of people" changed, the human race passed through three ages as earlier proposed by the Egyptians: the age of the gods, the age of heroes and the age of men. The civilization process adhered in every nation around the founding of institutions, in one place listed as "first the forests, after that the huts, then the villages, next the cities, and finally the academies."[19] Berry captured this notion in Vico's own words:

> All moves in harmony with the nature common to all the nations; their languages have principles common to all; their histories move through a uniform series of developments, a course followed equally by the Romans, Greeks and Asiatics. Each nation has its Jove, its Hercules and its Achilles. All things are determined by their eternal properties to appear in a certain time and manner.[20]

In all cases, ideas followed upon the exigencies of life along the lower level in which humankind mapped out its existence, while at a higher level divine providence moved everything according to the eternal ideal of history.

It is generally agreed, and Berry pointed this out, that Vico left this method of "introspection of our own mind" in its beginning stages. Nor was it the exclusive method he used in describing the course of the nations. He studied the ways of existing groups that he considered earlier stages than European societies of his day, notably the American Indians and the Chinese. It is also conceded, however, that this introspective method of Vico is a very important insight and one that has gained in significance with time. With regard to the method being discussed, Isaiah Berlin made the following claim for Vico:

> ... the claim for Vico that I wish to make is more circumscribed. It is this: that he uncovered a species of knowing not previously clearly discriminated, the embryo that later grew into the ambitious and luxuriant plant of German historicist *Verstehen*—empathetic insight, intuitive sympathy, historical *Einfühlung*, and the like. It was, nevertheless, even in its original, simple form, a discovery of the first order.[21]

It was this same method that led others, such as Tom Rockmore, to see in Vico the beginnings of what is now called "the anthropological turn." In doing so, Rockmore concluded, Vico "made the transition from an epistemological principle to a view of the human being as the real historical and epistemological subject."[22] This claim implies further nuances that lie beyond our purposes here, except to say that it is more than Berry claimed for Vico. At the same time, however, the further claim supports the significance Berry gave to this aspect of Vico's thought.

Summary of Berry's Work on Vico

In summary, then, Berry's study of Vico focused on the confusion that had arisen in attempts to systematically explain aspects of Vico's thought. Berry relied heavily on Vico's own words, allowing Vico to speak for himself. By doing so, Berry showed the fallacy of certain interpretations, notably the Hegelian dialectical reading of Vico. He also maintained, however, that the source of much of the disagreement over what Vico was actually saying lay with Vico himself.

It has been observed that for Vico, "[P]hilosophy is not the thought of gods or heroes; it is thought that arises out of barbarism and the finality of the third age and rises up against it." The barbarism referred to here is Vico's "barbarism of refinement" from which his own age suffered. In that context of his own age, Vico narrated a history of humankind that began in the distant twilight of primal humanity for whom poetry expressed the truth of their existence.[23] The narration was possible only by a reflection on a kind of knowing largely disregarded in Vico's own day.

Berry paid attention to the confusion that inhered in the academic and social milieu to which Vico wished to respond and to Vico's option for a Platonic philosophy as a tool in interpreting history. He also emphasized Vico's rediscovery of the "truth" of the ancient poetic traditions and the kind of knowing by which Vico claimed modern humans could understand their ancestors. These ideas had a recognizable influence on Berry's own methods and conceptions as a cultural historian.

Vico's Influence on Berry

The Nature of the Influence

In a series of talks given in 1989, Berry mentioned Giambattista Vico as one of the major influences on his thought.[24] In his writings, however, Berry actually referred to Vico very rarely and then in only two contexts: the division of history into "ages" and Vico's portrayal of the poetic age of the gods in contrast to the present barbaric age of rationalism. While rarely mentioned directly, both of these ideas became notable features of Berry's own thought. The fact that Berry continues to recognize Vico's overall importance is supported by his reference to Vico in his seminal essay "The New Story," where Vico's *Scienza nuova* is listed with Francis Bacon's *Novum Organum* and Isaac Newton's *Principia* as important emerging new sciences, "new ways of understanding," of the seventeenth and eighteenth centuries.[25]

Despite the scarcity of direct references to content from Vico, Berry's work resonates with that of Vico in two fundamental areas:

(1) Berry's methodology as a cultural historian and (2) the strand of tradition with which Berry identified most frequently.

The word "resonates" appears to be the best description of the relationship of Vico and Berry in these areas because Berry's syntheses of various writers and traditions makes it difficult to determine for sure the precise influence of any of them. Since such syntheses are clearly characteristic of the content of his work, it would seem highly probable the same is true of his methodology. One thing that can certainly be claimed as a basis for comparison is the concern for the major problems of their respective times in history and a desire to offer a corrective.

The Methodology of Berry's Cultural History

How is Berry's methodology as a cultural historian recognizably Vichian? That question is best addressed in terms of a contrast. In the 1940's while Berry was studying at The Catholic University of America, the field of cultural history was largely defined by Arthur O. Lovejoy.[26] In a seminal work, "Reflections on the History of Ideas," Lovejoy described the work of cultural historians as the isolation of "unit-ideas" (such as the idea of the "great chain of being," which he later isolated) from larger conglomerations, sometimes called *isms*, and the investigation of their development often over circuitous routes through history. "Unit-ideas" are often so embedded in the culture, so tied to the societal structures, that they operate almost as habits in the major thought patterns of any particular age.[27] For the most part, Lovejoy traced his "unit-ideas" in the thought of the intellectual elite. Mainstream historians of culture tended to do likewise and dealt with popular culture only in the context of the popularization of philosophical ideas. History for them was a study of the *rational* motivations of human action.[28]

In the 1960's a new breed of cultural historians, now labeled the historians of collective mentalities, emerged in France and gained momentum. These new historians of culture were interested in what they called "the underside of cultural history," the modifications of the human mindset that occurred over time. While these historians did not see themselves in the tradition of Vico, there arose almost immediately a concurrent interest in Vico studies. The similarity between the cultural history of the 1960's and Vico's work was easily recognized. Patrick H. Hutton identified it as a move from a focus on linking "intellectually sophisticated concepts" over history to focus on how thought itself is "shaped by changes in our mindset."[29] For the historians of collective mentalities, as for Vico, the data from which they inferred the changing mentalities that accompanied historical development included the aesthetic images, narratives and practical wisdom of everyday life.

Thomas Berry did not articulate his method of cultural history. His writings contain no rationale for one approach (Lovejoy's or the historians of mentalities) over the other. He was aware of Lovejoy's work and influenced by it in some areas. His self-designation as cultural historian preceded the new historians of the 1960's. Nor are there any references in his work to Lucien Febvre, Jules Michelet or Robert Mandrou, forerunners of the historians of mentalities, credited with keeping Vico's thought alive in the twentieth century. Hence, any similarity to their method is more likely to have originated with Vico.

There is some basis to argue that Berry followed Lovejoy's approach to cultural history in his tracing of certain "unit-ideas," such as the idea of a spiritual journey, through different embodiments in spiritual and philosophical systems,[30] but evidence of a Vichian influence is more basic to his methodology of cultural history. The clearest indication of Berry's alignment with Vico's approach lies not only in his consistent construal of history in terms of recognizable ages, but also in his characterization of these ages in terms of decline followed by psychic change. Furthermore, Berry accepted Vico's thematization of the changes in human ways of knowing and expression from a predominance of intuition, common sense, functionality and poetic speech in earlier ages to a predominance of introspection, rationality and philosophical speech in later ages.[31]

Berry's first delineation of the eras of human history were the four phases: the tribal-shamanic, the religious-cultural, the scientific-technological and the ecological.[32] He associated a predominant mode of human thought and activity with each of these phases. The tribal-shamanic was characterized by a human sensitivity to "the ultimate mystery of the universe" and the accompanying creativity in the expressions of these experiences. It was a period "dominated by psychic power symbols," the time when "the divinities were born in human consciousness as expressions of those profound spiritual orientations that emerged from the earth process into our unconscious depths, then as symbols into our conscious mind and finally into visible expressions." This is roughly equivalent to Vico's age of the gods and is reminiscent of its characterization.

The religious-cultural phase (classical period) developed, Berry commented, "with extensive similarities throughout the Eurasian and Central American regions." This period saw an increased social stratification, sacrificial rituals, articulated theologies and spiritual disciplines in what are now considered the great civilizations of the world. The human psychic change was constituted by a "liberation from the world of phenomena" and entrance into "an absolute mode of being." All aspects of life could be modeled on the image of the Divine.

In this age of the great civilizations, the Western world developed the sense of historical consciousness. While this sense can be traced to the biblical tradition, Berry maintained that until the latter part of this period that tradition was understood in a spiritual fashion within a predominantly spatial mode of consciousness. Then there was a shift in consciousness away from the psychic powers to the physical structure of the universe. There was also a greater awareness of the radical historicity of human life and the accompanying desire to consciously control that process. In this context, the scientific-technological phase, with its concentration on rational and technocratic modes of thinking and acting, took over.[33] While recognizing the positive attributes of this age, Berry's description is akin to Vico's in that he accentuated its negative aspects. Berry used Vico's words in speaking of the barbarism of the present age, when the imaginative and emotive spontaneities are repressed for the sake of rational-technocratic ways of knowing and doing.

One of the characteristics of the emerging ecological age, as Berry saw it, is the re-emergence of the ways of knowing more characteristic of previous ages, but still alive especially among primal peoples, like the native Americans. Like Vico, Berry saw this reclaiming of earlier ways of knowing to be essential to offset the narrowness of vision that accompanied the modern period.[34] Through these newly regained abilities, humans would also regain an intimacy with the rest of the natural world.

The ecological age, as the scientific-technological age before it, is accompanied by a change in human consciousness. It is not merely a rationalistic response to dire circumstances or an attempt at a technocratic "fix."[35] The modification in the human psyche, which occurs in the ecological age, is one in which the human race recovers and reintegrates with historical consciousness something of the cosmic, spatial consciousness of the primal peoples. For Berry, this is possible mainly because there is the knowing of imaginative empathy in the Vichian sense. By this type of knowing, humans can enter into the inner world, the motivations and meanings of history, even ages of their history far removed from their immediate experience. For Vico, language and artistic expression offered the best access to the historical changes of the human psyche. For Berry, myth and symbol offered that access. These myths and symbols, he argued, are identifiable across all world traditions and also emerge from the depths of man's primordial, pre-rational, unconscious self.

Recently Berry used the metaphor "moments of grace" to accentuate the significance of cultural achievements. Here the cultural achievements were not primarily those of an intellectual elite, but those of societies and cultures in general. They were achievements of the sort described by Vico and later considered important by the historians of collective humanities. Berry wrote:

> Such a moment [of grace] was experienced when humans first were able to control fire. When the first gardens were cultivated. When language was invented. Writing and the alphabet. Weaving and the shaping and firing of pottery. Then there are the moments when the great visionaries were born who gave to the peoples of the world their unique sense of the sacred, when the great revelations occurred. So too the time of the great storytellers, of Homer and Valmiki and other composers who gave to the world its great epic tales.[36]

In Vico's discovery of a new significance of the primal ages, Berry found the key that underlies his notion of cultural change. He commented on this contribution of Vico:

> These achievements [modern scientific, industrial, rational] which are sometimes designated as the full realization of the human mode of being, have a certain tendency to disintegrate in the manner that we are presently experiencing. Giambattista Vico ... considered that the eighteenth century was the period when a second barbarism, a barbarism of refinement, erupted in the civilizational enterprise. A new descent into a more primitive state must then come about, a new reimmersion in the natural forces out of which our cultural achievements came about.[37]

Thus, Vico offered a remedy to decline as Berry saw it happening again, this time in the twentieth century.

Berry was not concerned, as Vico was, to create a "new science." Rather, he articulated a vision and attempted to persuade people to think and act in a new way. He did not, therefore, deal primarily with explanatory categories, but with evocative images, metaphors, analogies and narrative. He did not lay out his methodology intentionally and clearly as Vico attempted to do. Yet the assumptions holding together his own performance as a cultural historian seem clearly to be Vichian.

For Berry, as for Vico, the cultural historian characterized the passage of historic eras by their accompanying psychic changes. Accessibility to the nature of these changes was gained only when one assumed that the historical development of the human race is more than a cumulative rational process. Human action is driven by a complex interaction of emotion, practical judgment and communal interaction accessible to each generation on the basis of our common humanity and encapsulated in the enduring language, symbols and artistic expressions of any culture.[38]

Berry did not obviously advert to Vico's place within the history of rhetoric, nor indicate any influence of this aspect of his contribution on his own work. Nonetheless, as will become clearer in the last chapters of this dissertation, Berry's own project relied on the power of rhetoric. While he did not, as Vico did, set rhetoric against science and mathematics, Berry's own praxis on behalf of the ecological crisis was largely rhetorical, in the contemporary recovered sense of that word.[39]

The Counter-Enlightenment Tradition

While there is a clear distinction between the stated intent of Vico's work and that of Berry, there is an important qualification even to that distinction. Vico's new science of the nations was both evaluative and diagnostic. The basic impetus for his work was the perception of his age as deteriorating and the location of the source of that deterioration in the misunderstanding of the history of the nations and the disintegration of the unity of knowledge in his day. His disagreement with Descartes focused on the narrowness of vision resulting from an exclusive emphasis on mathematics and the consequent emerging rationalism to the neglect of tradition, the arts and human history. In Vico's view, civilization was decaying from within.

Berry's work was also evaluative and diagnostic. Even prior to his writings about the ecological crisis, he spoke of the personal, Western and world crisis in which we are presently involved,[40] the alienation of modern humanity, the necessity of global change, the dark side of both modern capitalist and communist societies, as well as the inadequacy of the religious response. His diagnosis was that the present crises result for the most part from the assumptions (both explicit and implicit) that underlie modern development, rationalism, empiricism, neglect of spiritual traditions and entrenchment of religious institutions. For Berry, as for Vico, society is poised between destruction and recovery. What they both offered was a program for recovery, at the level of culture. Like Vico, he, too, claimed that recovery required a refocusing on the spiritual depth and human qualities of the world's cultures.

This attack on the mainstream cultures of their day suggests a second significant area of commonality between Vico and Berry. As

far as their positions vis-à-vis their contemporary cultures are concerned, they belong to a cluster of thinkers, writers and artists who
have been identified as counter-Enlightenment and romantic. Vico is
generally recognized as counter-Enlightenment and a proto-romantic,
whether or not any actual historical link can be established with the
later romantics. The romantics are within the counter-Enlightenment designation and, despite the great diversity and even contradictions among their positions, can be identified especially within a
certain period of European history as having a few dominant traits
reminiscent of Vico.[41]

Vico did not accept the idea of the absolute progress of history.
Although some of the early romantic works present an optimistic
view of history, their works reveal a growing distrust of this idea as
well. Increased knowledge did not increase happiness.[42] Departing
from the classicist notion that truth was something out there to be
discovered, the romantics, like Vico, claimed that truth was a human
production. There was no objective reality, in the classicist sense.[43]

There were other ideas reminiscent of Vico as well. Berlin refers
to the romanticist belief that rationalism was "the thinnest of walls"
separating a civilized humanity from the "raging sea" of irrationality
and emotion.[44] These notions also reflected Vico's notions of the
bestial beginnings of humankind and of the *corso* and *ricorso*.

Unlike Vico, however, the romantics held that nature as well as
history was such that it could be known by human consciousness.
For those concerned with a philosophical vision of the entire world,
notably Goethe, Fichte and Schelling, idealist philosophy in the tradition of the Platonic "soul of the world" provided the basis for the
essential unity that underlay the differentiation one experienced in
both nature and human history. In the romantic philosophy of nature,
a pervasive mind, spirit or soul, a macrocosmic version of the micro-
cosmic human consciousness, was seen to continually invent and
express itself in the multiple and various contingencies of nature and
human history.

In establishing a continuity between nature and history, the
romantics extended the empathetic, imaginative knowing, which Vico
applied to "the dark night" of human history, to nature as well. For
Vico the knowledge of natural forces and the knowledge of history
were sharply divided. Berlin observed of Vico, in comparison with
Herder, Schelling and the romantics, that Vico did not believe in a
continuity between natural processes and human thought and imagination. Humans cannot know the natural processes *per causas* for
they cannot enter into the production of nature as they can the

production of human processes. Vico's view was dualistic.[45] The romantics attempted to overcome this dualism with a conception of nature as a living organism having more in common with humankind than not.

In several of his works, Berry spoke approvingly of a constellation of Western thinkers whose main thrust had been relegated to the fringes of Western thought in the twentieth century. In a discussion of the *anima mundi*, he listed the following such thinkers as having kept that notion alive: Ficino, Pico della Mirandola and Giordano Bruno in their hermetic teaching, the Cambridge Platonists of England, the German vitalists Silesius, Goethe and Schelling, and those they influenced, including Bergson and, through him, Vladimir Vernadsky and Teilhard de Chardin.[46] In *Teilhard in the Ecological Age*, Berry spoke more specifically of the influence of what he called the "mystical-romantic" tradition, which saw the natural world as a manifestation of a spiritual order. The ideal of human culture was a reciprocal relationship with the earth as a mystical entity. Included in this tradition were the Stoics, the Neoplatonists, the medieval Alchemists, the tradition of Jakob Boehme, of Goethe, Schelling, the English and German romantic poets, and the American transcendentalists. He continued: "Out of this background the ecological movement in its more integral form emerged in later generations." Schelling's works, especially *Three Ages of the World* and *Philosophy of Nature*, are mentioned as "fundamental to understanding the broad outlines of this tradition." Schelling, Berry contended "can be considered one of the most pervasive influences in the mystical understanding of the natural world."[47]

In his introduction to the first edition of *Ideas for a Philosophy of Nature*, Schelling laid out the philosophical principles of his understanding of nature. He attributed the origin of his main ideas to the Platonic idea of a world soul. Speaking of the idea of a hierarchy of life in nature, he wrote:

> This idea is so old, and has hitherto persisted in the most varied forms, right up to the present day—(already in the most ancient times it was believed that the world was pervaded by an animating principle, called the world-soul, and the later period of Leibniz gave every plant a soul)—that one may very well surmise from the beginning that there must be some reason latent in the human mind itself for this natural belief. And so it is.[48]

For Schelling, this older philosophy represented a far more adequate notion of nature than did the science of his day.

Schelling proceeded to show how the scientific "reflection" of his day was insufficient to explain nature because "[a]s soon as I separate myself, and with me everything ideal, from Nature, nothing remains to me but a dead object, and I cease to comprehend how a life outside me can be possible." The contemporary reflection can never solve the problem of the relationship of human consciousness to nature, he continued, "whereas the pure intuition, or rather, the creative imagination, long since discovered the symbolic language, which one has only to construe in order to discover that Nature speaks to us the more intelligibly the less we think of her in a merely reflective way."[49] Hence, the emphasis in romantic circles on art, poetry and cultural symbols as expressive of human interaction with nature and therefore of the essence of nature itself.

While Schelling's thinking about nature changed considerably during his lifetime, his concern remained the questions: What is nature such that humans can know it? How is it that the indifferent (or undifferentiated) unity can become differentiated and by what means does it return to harmonious unity? In the works following *Ideas for a Philosophy of Nature*, such as *The Three Ages of the World*, he attempted to reconcile a realist and an idealist view in answering these questions; in Bolman's words, he sought "an intelligible existential world."[50]

While he moved from a pantheist position to one that incorporated a transcendent creator (from Plato to Aristotle, as he himself stated), Schelling continued to maintain the notion of a world soul. What he changed was the understanding of that concept from the exclusively rational interpretation of Plato to a more mystical understanding, which he claimed overcame a dualistic (real-ideal) cosmogony. The world soul is present in the universe and all its parts just as the biblical Wisdom dwells in the creation working from the inside out as deliberately as an artist at work.[51]

The tradition to which Berry referred above and in which he singled out Schelling is not a uniform tradition in many aspects. The commonality shared by those he mentioned and with which Berry identified the deeper strand of the present ecology movement is the world-soul tradition, seeing in nature a spiritual reality that goes beyond the more mainstream Christian notion that creation reflects the attributes of God. The identity of this reality becomes in modern science the issue of whether or not what was traditionally referred to as the world soul can be explained by identifiable material attributes.[52] Even the "world-soul" tradition in itself was not exactly consistent, however, in how its adherents conceived of the spiritual reality of the world.

The Greek idea of the world soul was that of a divine emanation that both infused the corporeal world and enveloped it. Hence, the

Platonic world, for instance, was a living reality, possessing soul, and within soul, intelligence. For Plotinus, it was described as an energy principle, constantly streaming forth from the Divine. The Stoics held that the Logos, the divine ordering principle, which constituted the destiny of the whole cosmos, was a material reality. Within the Greek tradition, generally, the concept "world soul" was the expression of a belief in a primary unifying essence of reality and the location of intelligibility.[53]

In its permutations through history, the idea of a world soul did not always retain its association with intelligibility, but was often understood as a more numinous presence. For the Gnostics, the whole idea of a rational, harmonious principle (*pneuma*) was removed to the realm outside the material world, but the material world held on to the presence of the "psyche," a kind of hapless, emotional presence totally prey to the ills of the world.[54] As William Wordsworth wrote,

> From Nature doth emotion come, and moods
> Of calmness equally are Nature's gifts.
> This is her glory; there two attributes
> Are sister horns that constitute her strength.[55]

Thus, the nature mysticism of the romantics combined both the attribution of wisdom and order to nature as well as an unpredictable emotional quality or moodiness.

Nature could imprint lasting impressions on the soul. It was conducive to meditation. In art and poetry as in philosophy, the romantics were preoccupied with the relationship of the human mind to nature.[56] In like fashion, the American transcendentalists, who were influenced by Wordsworth, Coleridge and other European romantics, maintained "it is not the fact that imports, but the impression of the fact on the mind."[57] For Henry David Thoreau, immersion in wild and primitive nature enabled one to repossess one's soul, to recapture that elemental spirituality that he considered lost in the human society of his day. This latter desire led many of the romantics, as well as Thoreau, to an interest in indigenous peoples, especially the North American natives. They were seen to possess that mystical bond with nature missing in the larger society.

Much of the original contribution of Vico to a theory of history arose from his reinterpretation of the primal peoples and the meaning of their poetic expression. The romantic or transcendentalist tendency was to exonerate the "noble savage" in a way that Vico did not. Yet there is a consistency in that Vico saw in pre-philosophic perception of the world and its poetic expression something that he considered lost in his day and worthy of reclaiming as an antidote for the "second barbarism" of refinement that had occurred. As will become clearer below, Berry was closer to Vico than to the romantics or transcendentalists on this point.

Even before his explicit concern with the ecological crisis, Berry spoke of the relationship between human consciousness and the cosmic evolutionary process. He wrote:

> We now appreciate the more primitive stages of man's awakening consciousness... These stages of human development have left an abiding impress in the depths of the human psyche, just as the various geological ages remain in the very structure of the earth, and as existing primitive peoples maintain the living cultural forms through which the higher development of humanity has passed.[58]

Again Berry did not work out the relationship in explanatory categories, but relied on the assumption that an integral and dynamic relationship did exist; there is an abiding spirit in the world and it comes to self-consciousness in the human. Berry's assumptions about the nature of the universe rested on this tradition, while at the same time he commented that this understanding of nature had not yet reached full intellectual rigour. The vitalist philosophy of Goethe and Schelling, through Bergson and Whitehead, he stated, provided the intellectual basis for a "more functional understanding of the natural community of the earth although this larger understanding has still not been fully set forth."[59]

In his writings on ecology, Berry's major concern was that the mainstream scientific-technological culture had proven to be dysfunctional in terms of human-earth relationship. Berry saw in the enduring Platonic tradition, with its concepts of *anima mundi*, vitalism, spirit of the world and mystical presence in nature, compelling arguments for the respect of nature and a human-earth relationship that was viable for the whole planet. He added a cautionary note, however. The mystical-romantic tradition had a tendency to spiritualize nature to the neglect of the actual empirical natural world. Despite Berry's high regard for the work of Teilhard de Chardin, for instance, he criticized Teilhard for having "little sense of the importance of living forms in the development of the human qualities of life."[60] Hence, Teilhard's failure to see the ecological effects of human technology, which he viewed rather as a continuation of the evolution of the spirit of the world to a grand unification ultimately in Christ. Berry spoke of the natural world (his preferred designation rather than "nature") in much more realistic terms than did his predecessors in the "world-soul" tradition. He discussed the biological interrelationships that make up ecosystems, the communities that comprise bioregions, endangered species and other ecological disasters.[61] His familiarity with the works of contemporary ecologists, such as Joy Adamson, John Lilly and Farley Mowat, as well as with other traditions, such as the natural history tradition, were probably influential here.[62] Yet when Berry returned to questions of the deeper meaning of why we ought to be ecologically responsible, his presentation retained many of the themes and expressions of the tradition we have just outlined. "What is needed," he said, "and what can appropriately be considered here, is the deeper meaning of the relationship between the human community and the earth process." And further,

> [o]ur own presence to the universe depends on our human identity with the entire cosmic process. In its human expression the universe and the entire range of earthly and heavenly phenomena celebrate themselves and the ultimate mystery of their existence in a special mode of exaltation.[63]

He found in the tradition of the romantics an alternative to the mainstream understanding of the relationship of humankind to the rest of the universe.

Though expressed in more contemporary language, many of Berry's concepts become more lucid in light of their historical roots in the Platonic, romantic, and transcendentalist traditions. As indicated above, there are areas in which Berry departed from some of the more mystical-spiritual elements of these traditions. What is consistent in terms of Berry's overall proposal, however, is the Vichian legacy of counter-cultural retrieval of non-rationalistic, non-dogmatic forms of knowing and expression. Especially in his latest writings, Berry departed from the romantics in their more vitalistic tendencies. Nonetheless, he continued to share with them the extension of the form of knowing, *Einfühlung, the feeling into*, from human history alone to include the natural world. Berry insisted that such an affective, aesthetic relationship with the natural world was needed to infuse contemporary culture with the values necessary to confront the ecological crisis.

Summary

The investigation of Thomas Berry's intellectual background rests on the suggestion that his response to the ecological crisis was a creative consolidation of previous ideas around the perceived urgency of the ecological situation. Berry began his career as a cultural historian and it is not surprising that the solution he offered to the ecological crisis was a cultural one. He called for a change of values especially with respect to the way in which humans relate to the natural world. Hope of changing these values, he maintained, lies with the larger context in which contemporary and future humankind will interpret life, make decisions and act. Berry suggested that that larger context is best expressed in a story that provides a functional cosmology. While the source, content and construction of that story will be considered later, this brief discussion of Giambattista Vico and the affinity that existed between his work and that of Berry is revealing.

Vico narrated the succession of the ages of humanity on the basis of the changes in human consciousness, which he perceived to have occurred over human history. He was able to do this because he postulated a kind of knowing based on the premise that humans over all ages and geography share a principle of knowing, namely that humans can know only what they themselves create. History is a human creation *par excellence*. Vico applied this premise first to an understanding of the very early ages of humanity. The poetry and myths of that period revealed to him a truth regarding the development of the human psyche over time. Primitive humans possessed a different sense of relationship to their world, hence different ways of judging and acting.

Berry followed Vico's methodology not only in construing ages of humanity, as many before and after Vico have done. His work also reflected Vico's way of characterizing these ages as representing major changes in the human psyche. Furthermore, he valued myth, symbol and other poetic expressions as truth carriers in the same sense that Vico did. His own vision of the ecological age, in which the cultural values for which he called will be operative, rests on the recovery of ways of knowing inherent in symbol and myth and neglected in the rationalism of the modern world. In that light, he saw "story" as a conveyor of truth and value and a possible source of transformation. Classic stories to which he continued to refer as important conveyors of the significance of a cosmology were Dante's *The Divine Comedy* and Augustine's *City of God*.[64]

Vico is often described as a proto-romantic. He shared with the romantics a counter-Enlightenment stance. Furthermore, some of the more compelling aspects of the romantic tradition rest on his contribution to historical consciousness. Yet the romantics extended Vico's understanding of human history to include also an understanding of nature, although still within a Platonic philosophy for the most part.

Berry followed the romantics in this extension of Vico's philosophy of history. The romantic philosophy of nature, notably that of Schelling, was extolled by Berry as consistent with the deeper aspects of the contemporary ecological movement. Hence, this underlying philosophy was operative, albeit in more contemporary terms and with significant departures, in Berry's functional cosmology.

Other enduring influences on Berry included his study of the great world religions of India and China, as well as the primal religions of Native Americans. The cosmologies he found in these traditions also suggested to the Western Christian tradition alternate ways of viewing the natural world. His familiarity with the work of Teilhard de Chardin offered a comprehensive new appropriation of the strands of the Western tradition discussed above. On the other hand, the influence of contemporary scientific theory and nature writing gave a concreteness and realism to Berry's work that eventually replaced much of the idealism of this tradition. In all of these cases, however, the methodology and key concepts resonant with Vico's insights operated as a framework for the integration of new ideas into Berry's overall vision.

Notes

1.   Cf. Marcel Danesi, "Language and the Origin of the Human Imagination: A Vichian Perspective," *New Vico Studies* 4 (1986): esp. 47-53, and Donald Philip Verene, "The New Art of Narration: Vico and the Muses," *New Vico Studies* 1 (1983): 21-37. *New Vico Studies* provides an overview of the many disciplines that claim aspects of Vico's thought.

2.   Thomas Berry, *The Historical Theory of Giambattista Vico* (Washington, DC: The Catholic University Press of America, 1949). Henceforth, Berry, *Vico.*

3.   Ibid., 19.

4.   Max Horkheimer, "Vico and Mythology," *New Vico Studies* 5 (1987): 63-75. Bernard Lonergan, *Insight: A Study of Human Understanding. Collected Works of Bernard Lonergan, Vol. 3,* ed. by Frederick E. Crowe and Robert M. Doran (Toronto, Buffalo, London: University of Toronto Press, 1992), 258.

5.   Isaiah Berlin, "The Counter-Enlightenment," in *Against the Current* (New York: The Viking Press, 1980), 1-6. See also Joseph Mali, "'The Public Grounds of Truth': The Critical Theory of G.B. Vico," *New Vico Studies* 6 (1988): 60-61.

6.   Giambattista Vico, *Autobiography, Opere* V, 51-52, in Berry, *Vico,* 108-110.

7.   Giambattista Vico, *The New Science of Giambattista Vico,* 3rd ed., rev. and trans. by Thomas Goddard Bergin and Max Harold Fisch (Ithaca, NY: Cornell University Press, 1968), 26.

8.   Berry, *Vico,* 35, 43 and 51. See also, J. Samuel Preuss, "A 'New Science' of Providence: Giambattista Vico," in *Explaining Religion: Criticism and Theory from Bodin to Freud,* ed. by J. Samuel Preuss (New Haven and London: Yale University Press, 1987), 59-60.

9.   Ibid., 151.

10.   Cf. Joseph M. Levine, "Giambattista Vico and the Quarrel between the Ancients and the Moderns," *Journal of the History of Ideas* LXX, 1 (Jan.-Mar. 1991): 79.

11.   Berry, *Vico*, 136. Inclusive language is used in the text with the exception of direct quotations and phrases from authors in which the generic male forms are used.

12.   Berlin, *Against the Current*, 6.

13.   *New Catholic Encyclopedia*, 2nd ed., s.v. "Romanticism, Philosophical," by A.R. Caponigri.

14.   Mali, "The Public Grounds of Truth," 60.

15.   Vico, *The New Science*, 7: 343-344, 937-941.

16.   Ibid., 1: 331, 96.

17.   *Opere III*, 28-29, 64-65, cited in Berry, *Vico*, 72, 73.

18.   Vico, *The New Science* 1: 242, 79.

19.   Ibid., 1: 239, 78.

20.   Berry, *Vico*, 110. Reference to *Autobiography, Opere*, V, 51-52.

21.   Berlin, *Against the Current*, 116.

22.   Tom Rockmore, "A Note on Vico and Antifoundationalism," *Vico Studies* 7 (1989): 23.

23.   Verene, "The New Art of Narration," 35.

24.   Thomas Berry, *Human Presence in the Earth Community*, Tape 5 (Sonoma, CA: Global Perspectives, 1989). Audiotape.

25.   Thomas Berry, "Creative Energy," *Riverdale Papers* I (1976): 2; "Dynamics of the Future," *Riverdale Papers* I (1974): 6; *The Dream of the Earth* (San Francisco: Sierra Club, 1988), 39, 127.

26.   Patrick H. Hutton, "Vico's Significance for the New Cultural History," *New Vico Studies* 3 (1985): 74.

27.   Arthur O. Lovejoy, "The Study of the History of Ideas," Introduction, *The Great Chain of Being* (Cambridge, MA and London: Harvard University Press, 1936 and 1964), 4; prior publication as "Reflections on the History of Ideas," *Journal of the History of Ideas* 1,1(1940): 3-23. Cf. Paul Ricoeur's similar notion of "root-metaphors": "Metaphor and Symbol," trans. by David Pellauer, in *Interpretation Theory* (Fort Worth, TX: TCU Press, 1976), 64-65.

28.   Hutton, "Vico's Significance for the New Cultural History," 74-75. Cf. Felix Gilbert, "Intellectual History: Its Aims and Methods" in *Historical Studies Today*, ed. by Felix Gilbert and Stephen R. Graubard (New York: W.W. Norton & Co., Inc., 1972), 149, 151.

29.   Hutton, "Vico's Significance for the New Cultural History," 73-75.

30.   See Ch. 2 below.

31.   Berry, *The Dream of the Earth*, 39, 40, and passim.

32.   Thomas Berry, "Perspectives on Creativity: Openness to a Free Future" in *Whither Creativity, Freedom, Suffering?: Humanity, Cosmos, God. Proceedings of the Theology Institute of Villanova University*, ed. by Francis A. Eigo, O.S.A. (Villanova, PA: Villanova University Press, 1981): 12. See also Berry, *The Dream of the Earth*, 39. For similar designation of eras as "axial periods," see Karl Jaspars, *The Origins and Goals of History*, trans. by Michael Bullock (New York: Yale University Press, 1953); and as "stages of meaning," see Bernard Lonergan, *Method in Theology*, 262-265.

33.   Berry, *The Dream of the Earth*, 40-41, and "Perspectives on Creativity," 12.

34.   Cf. Berry, "Contemporary Spirituality: The Journey of the Human Community," *Cross Currents* (Summer/Fall 1974): esp. 176. See also Ch. 4 below.

35.   Thomas Berry, "Technology and the Nation-State in the Ecological Age," paper presented at Saint Louis University Conference, March 1981, *Riverdale Papers* VIII, 27. See also *The Dream of the Earth*, 50-69; and "Science and Technology for Development," paper presented to United Nations Conference, London, 1979, *Riverdale Papers* VII, esp. 2-4.

36.   Thomas Berry, Introduction to *The Breathing Cathedral: Feeling Our Way into a Living Cosmos*, by Martha Heyneman (San Francisco: Sierra Club Books, 1993).

37.   Berry, *The Dream of the Earth*, 201.

38.   Cf. Berry, "Contemporary Spirituality," 176, and Thomas Berry with Thomas Clarke, *Befriending the Earth*, 94-95.

39.   Cf. David E. Klemm, "Toward a Rhetoric of Postmodern Theology: Through Barth and Heidegger," *Journal of the American Academy of Religion* LV,3 (1987): 445.

40.   Thomas Berry, "Christian Humanism," paper given at Newman Centers' Annual Meeting, 1968, *Riverdale Papers* II.

41.   For a discussion of the difficulty of defining romanticism, see Arthur O. Lovejoy, "The Meaning of Romanticism for the Historian of Ideas," *Journal of the History of Ideas* 2,3 (June 1941): 257-278. See also Stephen Happel, "Romanticism," in *New Dictionary of Christian Theology*, 2nd ed., edited by John Bowden and Alan Richardson (London: SCM Press, 1983), 512-514; and Lilian R. Furst, *Romanticism* (London: Methuen & Co., Ltd., 1969), esp. 1-13.

42.   Cf. H.G. Schenk, *The Mind of the European Romantics* (London: Constable and Co., Ltd., 1966), esp. 9-14. See also Isaiah Berlin, "The Preface" *op. cit.*, xv.

43.   We are dealing with the general typology of romanticism to which there are many exceptions spanning almost one hundred years. For a brief discussion of romanticism as a typology, cf. Happel, "Romanticism."

44.   Berlin, *Against the Current*, 22.

45.   Ibid., 112.

46.   Berry, *The Dream of the Earth*, 22.

47.   Thomas Berry, *Teilhard in the Ecological Age*, Teilhard Studies No. 7 (Chambersburg, PA: Anima Books, Fall 1982), 13-19.

48.   Friedrich Wilhelm Joseph von Schelling, Introduction [to the First Edition], *Ideas for a Philosophy of Nature*, 2nd ed., trans. by Errol E. Harris and Peter Heath (Cambridge: Cambridge University Press, 1988), 35.

49.   Ibid.

50.   Frederick deWolfe Bolman, Jr., "Introduction," *The Ages of the World* (New York: Columbia University Press, 1942), 3-10, 76.

51.   Schelling, *The Ages of the World*, 164.

52.   Cf. Bernd-Olaf Kueppers, *Information and the Origin of Life*, trans. by Manu Scripta (Cambridge, MA: MIT, 1990). See also Ch. 3 below.

53.   Conrad Bonifazi, *The Soul of the World: An Account of the Inwardness of Things* (Washington, DC: University of America Press, 1978), 2-3. References to Plato's *Timaeus 30, 36* and to Plotinus, *Enneads, III.8.5.*

54.   Werner Foerster, *Gnosis* 1. (Oxford: Clarendon Press, 1972) and Harold Bloom, "Lying against Time: Gnosis, Poetry, Criticism," *Rediscovery of Gnosticism I—The School of Valentinus*, ed. Bentley Layton (Leiden: E.J. Brill, 1981).

55.   *The Prelude*, Bk. XIII, II. 1-4

56.   H.G. Schenk, *European Romantics*, 162-176.

57.   Henry David Thoreau, *A Week on the Concord and Merrimack Rivers* [Thomas Y. Crowell, 1961], cited in Schenk, *European Romantics*, 174.

58.   Berry, "Contemporary Spirituality," 172-173.

59.   Thomas Berry, *Management: The Managerial Ethos and the Future of Planet Earth*, Teilhard Studies Number 3 (Chambersburg, PA: Spring 1980): 6.

60.   Berry, *Teilhard in the Ecological Age*, 29.

61.   Berry, *The Dream of the Earth*, 163-170, and 171-179.

62.   Cf. Berry, *The Dream of the Earth*, 3-4.

63.   Ibid., 10, 18.

64.   Ibid., 129.

CHAPTER TWO

THE INFLUENCE
OF WORLD RELIGIONS

Introduction

Berry's professional career, his teaching and much of his scholarly research and writing, was in world religions, especially the religions of India and Asia. (His writings about North American native religions came later and within the context of the ecological crisis.) Within the field of world religions he remained primarily a cultural historian, interested in the ideas and events that shaped human culture. Later, as his concern turned toward the ecological crisis, his focus became a history of nature and of ideas relevant to the human-earth relationship. Berry commonly referred to himself as a "geologian," conveying his notion that his religious reflections were focused on the earth.[1] Berry's knowledge of world religions provided him with alternatives to mainline Western notions of human-earth relationships. Furthermore, in terms of methodology, his work in world religions reveals a long-standing concern to make theory and scholarship effectively available to a larger public.

There are three identifiable levels at which Berry's writings about the major religions influenced his proposed response to the ecological crisis: (1) the framework, i.e., his motivational project; (2) the general assumptions within which he worked; and (3) the specific insights of the religions themselves, especially with regard to the beliefs about and attitudes toward the universe.

The General Framework:
An Existentialist-Humanist Motivation

Berry's study of world religions was motivated by a desire to understand the contemporary world, especially what he perceived as the inadequacy of present religion in answering the existential needs of humankind. In responding to a question about his involvement in the ecological issue, Berry remarked that his study of the Asian religions was part of a wider desire to "maintain a certain independence," "to test how people found meaning," because "the process [modern Western society] was not working."[2] The existential concern with meaning and the conviction that "the process was not working" did indeed show up in all of Berry's writings about world religions (as well as in other writings). Although he studied and taught the Asian languages and translated texts, this kind of scholarship for its own sake was not primarily characteristic of him. Huston Smith said of his own classic work, *The Religions of Man*:

> Every attempt has been made to keep scholarship in the foundations, essential to the strength of the structure but out of sight, instead of letting it rise in scaffolding which would obstruct the view of the mansions themselves.[3]

The same could be said of Berry's writings in world religions. While his scholarship and expertise were apparent, his works were not primarily technical. They were accounts of how various cultures across successive historical periods found meaning in their existential realities. They were not written exclusively for his academic colleagues.

In the final chapter of *Buddhism*, Berry wrote:

> All the basic spiritual traditions of man are open, clear, direct expressions of the manner in which man has structured his personal and social life in order to give it some higher, transcendent significance. These spiritual disciplines have enabled man to deal with the problem of suffering and eventually to attain some kind of liberation from the afflictions that mark his temporal existence.[4]

In the introduction to *The Religions of India*, he expressed a similar sentiment in a broader context:

> The similarity of the human condition throughout the ages is one of the forces that brings together all the spiritual traditions of mankind and enables them to communicate with one another on the most profound level, even in present times. Modern man has become increasingly conscious of the agonies inherent in the human condition... Other peoples, knowing that they could do

little to alter the human condition externally, built up a spiritual capacity to sustain themselves as they worked toward final triumph over this condition... In many ways he [modern man in seeking external control] has only aggravated his life tension while lowering his spiritual capacity to absorb the afflictions inseparable from his existence as man.[5]

This latter quotation points not only to Berry's contention of an existential basis for the emergence of the different religions, but also to his interest in modern existential questions.

As already mentioned, Berry seemed to have a keen awareness that the modern world was profoundly changing. He saw it to be in crisis, "not working." Hence, his research and study of world religions were brought to bear on such questions as: How did people make their cultures work in the past? Is there anything in the other world traditions that is valuable in reinvigorating the Western Christian world? Thus, he attempted to bring together the modern existential questions and the insights of the ancient religious traditions.

In 1974, Berry addressed a group of psychologists at Fordham University on the subject of alienation. He began by noting that the problem of alienation is "in some sense, the oldest and most universal issue man has ever faced." It arose from "the profound ambiguity that lies at the center of all that man is and all that man does."[6] He related the modern intensity of this human experience to the loss of traditional religious symbolic structures, the ancient symbols and myths together with the spiritual disciplines by which they were appropriated. These were the means by which humans explained the human condition to themselves. The contemporary sense of existential angst so predominant in the West had its roots in the Western penchant to overemphasize the experience of time to the relative exclusion of spatial sensitivities.[7] Berry advocated paying attention to the relevant Asian religious notions. Finally, he noted, in a theme that later recurred in many contexts, that a new universal symbolism was needed. In another place he spoke of the need for an effective new myth of the future, the first indication of his later proposal of the "new story."[8]

In "Religious Traditions and the Global Community of Man," Berry drew attention to the convergence of cultures in the modern world. He decried the lack of "dominant religious or spiritual motivations" in what he saw as a predominantly scientific and technological phenomenon. The academic work in world religions to date was inadequate. Reminiscent of humanists Thomas More's and John Colet's attack on scholasticism, his complaint was that scholars did not purvey religious truths in a manner that related to the human lifeworld.[9] In his view, scholars did not amply associate the texts studied with the "profound realism" and "intimate life involvement" out of which these texts emerged and in which they functioned best. Here Berry contrasted the work of scientific textual analysis with the "subjective" appropriation and interpretation of the data. While he conceded that the former was necessary and significant, he concluded that the time had come for the hermeneutical task of interpreting the data for a larger cultural context. If this does not happen, he wrote, "then, it would seem, the study of man's religious and cultural traditions comes to an abortive conclusion."[10]

Calling on historical precedents for what he had in mind, Berry mentioned St. Paul, Augustine and Thomas Aquinas as religious personalities with the creative intuition and vision to bring about a synthesis of spiritual insights and to give direction to generations of scholars who filled in details within differing contexts and times. These references continued to be important for Berry in his call on Christianity and the other traditions to integrate scientific insights. The aim of religious scholarship was a truly "functional" religious vision.[11] The word "functional" later became the hallmark of his ecological proposal.

It is clearly obvious here and in other places that Berry's own work in world religions was an attempt not only to bring to his colleagues in the academy an awareness of the direction he considered necessary for the study of religion, but also to make some contribution to the task himself. This was the motivational framework in which his efforts at this period of his life are best understood. It is noteworthy that in his own teaching, primarily at Fordham University, he considered his work to be in the area of spirituality, which he defined as "a way of managing the human condition which leads to authentic human existence." Consequently, Berry's teachings on the religious traditions and the elements of the traditions were in the broader context of the cultural and anthropological study of humankind. The influence of thinkers such as Mircea Eliade, Carl Jung and Joseph Campbell is clear in his propensity to situate religious traditions within the nature of humankind as makers of symbols and myths, and, therefore, seekers of meaning.[12]

Finally, the nature of Berry's work in world religions recalls the historical humanist tradition. One of Berry's earliest essays was "Christian Humanism: Its New Universal Context." In this essay, he spoke of his desire to set his discussion within the "rich tradition of humanism to be found in the Fathers of the Church, in the Justinian Code, the Summa of Thomas, the Commedia of Dante, the School of Chartres; the humanism of Petrarch, Erasmus, More, Grotius, Newman, and so many others." His intent was to deal with the "cultural-historical order" rather than the "literary, scientific, socio-logical, or philosophical orders."[13] Hence, the essay enunciated a vision of Christianity within a universalist humanist context.

Responding primarily to Vatican II's pronouncements on the relationship of Catholicism to the non-Christian religions, Berry argued, "There is no non-Christian world. The People of God is mankind." Christians must move beyond "Christian tribalism," a sectarian view of Christianity that distorted and fragmented humankind. Together with the members of other religious traditions, they must learn to think of all the religious traditions not in a fragmented way, but as the common heritage of contemporary humans. Berry referred to this attitude as a "world-embracing humanism."[14]

Several characteristics of historical humanism are evident in Berry's work in world religions. These are significant to this project because, although they were pronounced with more clarity in this period of his work, they continued to set parameters within which he articulated his ecological vision.

First, there was the strong faith in the basic goodness of humankind and its ability to shape a future. History was primarily a human project. Although there were the archetypes of Jung, the dreams and the myths that consistently emerged in the unconscious, the human was being called upon to consciously shape and reshape these for the cultural project that the modern world presented. Berry linked spirituality with humanism, claiming that the basic supposition of both is that the human personality is not determined by external or prior forces, but rather is capable of "self-determination, self-formation, and self expression."[15]

Second, there was a preference for the humanities, aesthetics, creativity and life in the everyday world over the scientific, objective and analytic world of science. The true person of vision who would contribute to the world was the one who could bring the insights of history and research to the project of living, which in turn gives rise to human discovery. This was clearly a Vichian principle and an underlying assumption of the humanist tradition to which Vico contributed. Berry decried B.F. Skinner's position on human behaviour, which he saw as an "extreme application of the technological mentality." "What needs to be kept in mind," he argued, "is the capacity of the individual to so place himself within the realities of the present that he will be able to function in some true depth of his being."[16]

Third, there are the persistent existentialist themes of alienation, quest for authenticity, human responsibility both for the past and for the future, and the relationship of tension to creativity.[17]

Underlying Assumptions

Berry's Configuration of the Relationship among the World Religions

Berry's interest in the world religions was primarily cultural. He was concerned with the implications of an emerging world secularity for interreligious dialogue and religious self-understanding. In his articulation of this concern and particularly in his own response regarding what he saw to be the desired configuration of the relationships among the religions, Berry relied on two prominent Western traditions: the notion of plenitude and the organicist metaphor. "Plenitude" is Arthur O. Lovejoy's label for a conglomeration of related ideas that ensued from the Platonic idea of the one and the many. It is closely related to the organicist metaphor that has persisted as a significant world view within Western culture.[18]

While Berry saw each of the great religions as complete in itself, an integrated accumulation of ways of dealing with the existential questions of humankind in particular times and locations, he also held that the religions developed always in mutual influence and/or opposition. They had in many ways been important to each others' developments. Within their own cultures, the religions had been complete and full, but, in the increasingly global culture of the contemporary world, they were no longer merely Indian, Asian or Western religions. They were also world religions. He explained:

> Within this larger world of mankind the multiple spiritual and humanist traditions implicate each other, complete each other, and evoke from each other higher developments of which each is capable... Each is panhuman in its significance.[19]

A larger world culture was evolving, brought about by secular, scientific and technological developments. Within the global culture, the particularity of each religion (its microphase) would remain. Each would also have an impact on all other religions, however, and produce effects beyond its own native culture; that was the macrophase of each religion.

What would be the mutual relationships among religions in this context? As Berry said, they "evoke from each other higher developments" and "implicate each other."[20] While, on the one hand, he described here what may have already occurred to some degree in an emerging world culture, he also implied an "oughtness." These were the parameters of interreligious dialogue as Berry understood it.

It is obvious from the nature of Berry's interest in the world religions that he was concerned primarily with the spiritual practices and attitudes engendered by the religions. How might Yoga or Buddhist meditation techniques evoke from Western religions an increased awareness of their own mystical traditions? How might the social emphasis of the West evoke this-worldly concerns within Oriental traditions? How could the religions continue to be effective forces in human life within a rapidly changing secular and global milieu? [21]

Berry characterized religions as living processes integrally related, yet differentiated. The tension of difference within an overarching unity was the source of creativity.[22] In "The Catholic Church and the Religions of the World" and "The Cosmology of Religions,"[23] he dealt with the topic of difference among the religions as qualitative and not quantitative. In the traditional Christian view of this distinction, according to Berry, a qualitative difference meant that non-Christian traditions did not qualify as "revelation," but merely as "natural religions." A quantitative difference was usually stated in terms of the fullness of revelation. All religions were founded on revelation, but Christianity alone possessed that fullness.

Berry insisted that the use of the term "revelation" in this sense (as used by Vatican Council II, for example) referred precisely to Christian or biblical revelation. He used the term in a wider sense that understood all religions as the result of revelatory experience. Berry proposed "a qualitative difference within the authentic revelatory process itself." While he did not precisely define "revelation," his usage suggests the Eliadean sense of hierophany. All religions arise from experience/s of the manifestation of sacred reality (revelation, in Berry's sense); the so-called "qualitative" differences refer to the cultural and historical thematizations of these experiences. This kind of difference "cannot be resolved in terms of fullness or completeness, but only by mutual presence of highly differentiated traditions," he wrote. The attraction to uniformity at the expense of diversity impoverished the divine-human communication. More than any other "element of reality" the sacred required variety in its expression, a point Berry clarified as follows:

> For the biblical concept to be the universal concept of deity to the elimination of Shiva and Vishnu, of Kuan-ya and Amida, of Shang-ti and T'ien, or Orenda, Wakan-tanka and the Manitou, would be to impoverish the concept of deity. For the Bible to be the only Scripture to the elimination of the Vedic Hymns ... would constrict rather than expand divine-human communication. For any situation the ideal is the greatest tension that the situation can bear creatively. [24]

The tension between the different modes of expression was needed for the sake of creativity.

Thus, the traditional ideas (unity in the tension of diversity and culture as a living organic process), which continued to serve him well in the articulation of his ecological proposal, were first employed by Berry in his understanding of the relationships among the world religions. A brief survey of the origin and history of these notions will help clarify their particular usage by Berry during this time of his career as well as their expanded reference in his later work.

The Notion of Plenitude and Its Use by Berry

Lovejoy credited Plato with bequeathing to the Christian West a set of contradictory notions that have preoccupied philosophers ever since.[25] These notions were the explanation he gave of the one, the many and the relationship between the two. The one referred to the totally otherworldly good, or god, eternally separate, unmoved by any creature, self-sufficient unto god's self and beyond human comprehension. For Plato, then, the idea of the one necessarily implied self-sufficiency. The many referred to the creation in all its imperfection, the multifarious creatures, animate and inanimate, that exist, live, die and decay.

Plato's solution to the problem of how the one and the many are related gave rise to what Lovejoy called the notion of plenitude. Besides the question of the good, that otherworldly reality in which alone the human soul could find fulfilment, Plato was concerned with the intelligibility of the many. Was this world just totally capricious, without meaning or rational basis? Two questions arose from this pondering: (1) Why is there anything at all outside the eternal one? and (2) What accounts for the number and variety of things? Plato argued that perfection itself was the source of all imperfect beings.[26] In the *Timaeus*, he wrote:

> let us state the cause wherefor [sic] he who constructed it did construct Becoming and the universe. [The reason is that] he was good, and in one that is good no envy of anything else ever arises. Being devoid of envy, then, he desired that everything should be so far as possible like himself. This, then, we shall be wholly right in accepting from wise men as being above all the sovereign principle of Becoming and of the cosmos.[27]

There was material, sensible existence in various forms, then, because fecundity itself was inherent in the idea of perfection. The perfect could not be envious of any other being; hence, they must all exist. So, Lovejoy succinctly noted of Plato's argument,

> The concept of Self-Sufficing Perfection, by a bold logical inversion, was—without losing its original implication—converted into a concept of a Self-Transcending Fecundity.[28]

Implied in the answer to "why anything at all" was the answer to the question of "why so many kinds." Because the perfect one could not be envious of any being at all, *all* ideals (which from Socrates meant ideals of every conceivable being, event, etc.) must be embodied. The world, the sensible presentation of the ideal world, must be complete, beautiful and a perfect image of the whole. Hence, the world *as it is,* "the exhaustive replica of the World of Ideas," could not be otherwise; it was the only possible world. With this implication of necessity in the good, the West inherited a contradiction. Two gods were conjoined in one; a self-sufficient being at the same time inherently dependent on the existence of creation.

Lovejoy used the term "principle of plenitude" to refer not only to the idea of the universe as a *plenum formarum* as suggested in the reasoning of Plato, but to include also the deductions that could be, and later were, drawn from Plato's description of the one and the many. These ranged from the idea that all genuine potential must be fulfilled, and that to the extent of possibility inherent in a perfect and inexhaustible Source, to the further assumption that the greater variety in the world the better it is.

In all, the principle of plenitude as it originated with Plato implied that this world had value; the world of ideas could, in fact, not really exist without it. It also implied "a sort of absolute cosmical determinism" that would reach its highest expression in Spinoza and not be entirely overcome in the attempts of Leibniz to maintain some sense of freedom in the godhead.[29]

Another idea associated with the principle of plenitude that figured in Thomas Berry's thought and was often directly mentioned by him is that of the great chain of being.[30] Lovejoy credits Aristotle with originating this idea with his description of being as a continuum. Unlike Plato, Aristotle held that the universe was contingent in all its aspects; he recognized God, the unmoved mover, merely as the final cause of existence. For him, what existed potentially did not necessarily exist actually. Yet this important notion of Aristotle developed into a law of continuity, which was later interpreted in relation to the Platonic conception of the one and the many.

Aristotle defined a continuum as follows: "Things are said to be continuous whenever there is one and the same limit of both wherein they overlap and which they possess in common." He observed that quantities, notably time and space, did not exist discretely but rather in a continuum. Similarly, though not definitively (for Aristotle), species or classes of plants and animals, when compared according to a single characteristic, could be seen to differ only by minute grades, in some cases not even observable to the senses. In particular, organisms were observed that could not be discretely classified as either plants or animals. [31]

When the two ideas, continuum and plenitude, were wedded, the universe was described as a great chain of being extending from the lowliest and least perfect all the way up to God. Every grade of imperfection was represented, including all grades of evil. This implied a theodicy that saw evil as originating in God for the sake of the beauty, that is the perfection, of the whole. There were no gaps whatever in the universe. In practical spiritual terms, what this came to mean was that the ascent of the soul to God was a gradual passage up the ladder representing the grades of being; hence, the image of the ladder of ascent. This image, of course, as well as all the associated notions of the principle of plenitude, was understood within a static universe.

For Berry, Dante best incorporated the image of the ladder of ascent. He consistently referred to Dante's idea of the ordered connection of all things in relationship to the Divine as found in *The Divine Comedy*. It is something akin to this sense of things that Berry wished to recover, as he noted in such passages as:

> The human mind ascends to the contemplation of the divine by rising through the various grades of being, from the physical forms of existence in the earth, with its mountains and seas, to the various forms of living things, and so to the human mode of consciousness, then to the soul, and from the inner life of the soul to god... So,... the journey of Dante through the various spheres of reality up to the divine vision in itself. Initiation into the basic human and Christian values was initiation into this cosmology... The mysteries of Christianity were integral with this cosmology.[32]

Within the context of world religions, Berry had already associated the ascent of the chain of being as he found it in Dante with the spiritual journey, whether applied to the individual person, a society or the whole human race.[33]

Berry pointed out, however, that the ascent of the chain of being as conceived by Dante (and generally in his day) was within a static universe.[34] It was only in the eighteenth century with the emerging realization of evolution that philosophers, theologians, scientists and poets sought to recast the whole principle of plenitude in terms of temporality. The key then became whether or not one could understand plenitude as encompassing time. Could it be that the totality of the ideals became embodied only over the entire time span of evolution? As Lovejoy commented on this later development, "The Demiurgus is not in a hurry; and his goodness is sufficiently exhibited if, soon or late, every Idea finds its manifestation in the sensible order." [35]

Despite the imputation of necessity to God's action involved in the principle of plenitude from its origin, even orthodox Christian theologians, who maintained the freedom of God and the consequent contingency of the universe (on the basis of biblical revelation and Aristotelian philosophy), often referred to the principle as well. Thomas Aquinas was a notable example, and one of the most recurrent quotations in Berry's works is the following excerpt from Aquinas' use of the principle of plenitude:

> For He brought things into being in order that His goodness might be communicated to creatures, and be represented by them; and because His goodness could not be adequately represented by one creature alone, He produced many and diverse creatures, that what was wanting to one in the representation of the divine goodness might be supplied by another. For goodness, which in God is simple and uniform, in creatures is manifold and divided; and hence the whole universe together participates in the divine goodness more perfectly, and represents it better than any single creature whatever.[36]

Thus, Aquinas maintained that creation is related to the goodness of God, but ruled out the cosmic determinism of Plato. The whole universe in its diversity represents God "more perfectly" or "better" than "any single creature whatever," but this universe is not the perfect, nor the only possible, representation of God. This excerpt would imply, however, that the greatest diversity possible is desirable. In this sense, Berry applied Aquinas' idea to the diversity of expressions of the "revelatory experiences" from which the various religious traditions developed. In his words,

> This law of diversity holds not only for the other areas of being and of action but also for the religious life of the human community, for revelation, belief, spiritual disciplines, and sacramental forms. If there is revelation it will not be singular but differentiated... The greater the differentiation, the greater the perfection of the whole since perfection is in the interacting diversity; the extent of the diversity is the measure of the perfection.[37]

Hence, the Divine would be more fully revealed, according to Berry, in "the fabric of the whole," that is, in the totality of religious expressions.

With the romantics, another turn in the meaning and application of the principle of plenitude occurred. Throughout the classic, medieval and Enlightenment periods, the principle of plenitude was employed to undergird the intelligibility of the universe. As is the case with Aquinas, it was the whole, the unity of all things, that was emphasized. The abstract rational argument, which grounded becoming in being, was of paramount importance. With the romantics, just the opposite occurred. Particularity, individuality and diversity were the order of the day. Idiosyncrasies of culture were celebrated and encouraged as the interesting and in some sense divine features of the world. The romantics were against the Deists, proponents of natural religion, who flattened all features of particular religious expression into that which could be accepted by all.[38]

The romantics were not against all universalism, however. Rather, the brand of universalism they adhered to and promoted was different. Reminiscent of Vico, the romantics advocated a universalist mind, that is, one that had experienced, mostly in the academic sense of reading and discussion, as many diverse opinions, cultures, religious beliefs, artistic expression, etc. as possible. In other words, it was not the logical, rational unity—a sameness, essence, or commonality—that they sought, but a knowledge of things as they are and as many of them as is possible.

Berry's use of the romantic construal of the principle of plenitude appeared in his emphasis on the need to maintain diversity. As he expressed it, "The extent of the diversity is the measure of perfection," to which he added, "so long as the diversity is integral with the larger unity of the whole." The tying together of these two dimensions of the principle of plenitude in his application to world religions seemed to have laid part of the foundation for what Berry later articulated as the three principles (sometimes called tendencies) of the universe: differentiation, subjectivity and communion. He defined these principles as follows:

> [Differentiation] The universe by definition is a differentiating process. The universe is not an homogeneous smudge. It is composed of clearly articulated entities each of which is unique and irreplaceable.
> [Subjectivity] Secondly, each of the component members of the universe has its own interiority, its radiant intelligibility, its spontaneity, its subjectivity.
> [Communion] Thirdly, each member of the universe community is bonded inseparably with every other member of the community. The entire universe is genetically related. Every individual being is cousin to every other being in the universe since everything emerges by an unbroken sequence from the same physical-spiritual source... Each member of the universe is immediately present to and influencing every other being in the universe. [39]

While each creature of the universe is clearly and uniquely an articulated individual, each also becomes itself by the nature of its participation in the whole universe.

The three principles emerged primarily in Berry's presentation of his cosmology and will be treated more fully later. Yet it is worth noting that in Berry's view they held also for the pattern of relationship among the world religions. Each religion is differentiated, unique and irreplaceable in its expression. It has its own inner life or subjectivity. Its full self, however, depends for its completion on its "bonding" (communion) with the other traditions.[40]

Thus, Berry applied the principle of plenitude to the conception of cultures and religions as readily as he did later to an understanding of the physical universe. This is not surprising, since the idea of the one and the many was first formulated in relationship to nature. Neither is it novel that culture or religion should be understood on the basis of understandings of nature. This particular understanding of culture and its relationship to nature was informed by the traditional world view, philosophy or root metaphor known as organicism.[41]

The Organic World View

Traditional Meanings Influential in Berry's Thought

G.N.G. Orsini characterized organicism, applied to a work of art, as a double relationship among the parts of the work: (1) the parts of the work are in keeping with each other and with the whole and (2) alteration of a part will bring with it the alteration of the whole. Such a relationship is based on the assumption that the work of art can be compared to a living organism. Hence, the work will have an inner form or vitality (organic form) in contrast to an external form (mechanical form). The form of the work develops spontaneously from within. The outer form thus produced arises from the nature of the subject itself.[42]

The organic world view has been applied not only to works of art, but also to the society, the culture and the whole universe. The unifying factor in organicism is the metaphor of organism. Since organicism often functions as a world view, it has also been referred to as a root metaphor, that is a metaphor that, on the common sense level, provides the context for "relatively adequate" world theories or understandings of the world.[43]

While the concept of organic unity had many derivations and was conjoined with other notions throughout the centuries after Plato, it came into its full flowering in the eighteenth century with the romantics. In opposition to the increasing allegiance to a mechanistic view of the world, the romantics emphasized the view of nature (as well as art and society itself) as a living organism. The writings of many of the romantics are replete with references and analogies to plants and other living organisms supported by a turn in biological study at the time toward a greater interest in the organism as a whole.[44]

Besides the references to organisms, the overall philosophy of Goethe, Herder, Coleridge, Schelling and Wordsworth saw the whole universe as a kind of vital, creative, living organism, imbued with spirit. In viewing nature in this fashion, they defied the analytic scientific rationalism of the Enlightenment. Isaiah Berlin summarized this attitude of the romantics and particularly of Schelling as a kind of conspiracy between the human genius and nature. Only the imaginative capacities of artists and seers can enter into this mutual questioning process with nature and thence become "conscious of the contours of the future." This surpassed the mere calculating and analytical capacities of scientist or politician. The contrast between the analytic methods of the prevailing science and a more intuitive, imaginative knowing continued to hold sway with thinkers such as Fichte, Hegel, Wordsworth, Coleridge, Goethe, Carlyle, Schopenhauer, and, later, Bergson and the antipositivist schools.[45] Relevant to the discussion at hand is the fact that such knowing was considered possible because of the intimate (organic) bonding understood to exist between the human knower and the universe as a whole.

As in the case of the related notion of plenitude, the romanticist emphasis on variety and creativity changed the balance of the organicist metaphor. Traditionally, the one was emphasized; now it was the many. This allowed the adherents to move away from the rigidity of static rules and structures and to emphasize freedom of individual expression and diversity of culture. The unifying element is not enforced from without but grows from within; it is in the nature of the process itself and the end toward which it strives. While opposing forces and all types of variety appear, they will all be reconciled in the harmony of the whole. So, Arnold Bergstrasser wrote of Goethe's "certainty about the intention of God-in-Nature to grant the moment of reconciliation" as follows:

> The human universe as a whole, which through its polarities tends toward harmony and attains it when the time has come, is the theme of Goethe's *Märchen* or *Parable*. The old man with the lamp, its central figure, knows that the secret of the creative moment of reconciliation creates a whole out of the parts which could not achieve their full meaning while each was left to itself.[46]

It is within the communion of the whole that the full meaning of the part is achieved.

Pepper pointed out that for the organicist "every actual event in the world is a more or less concealed organic process." Under careful scrutiny such an organic structure of most world processes can be revealed, at least partially. Herder, for instance, relied heavily in his early works on the images of the growth of a person from childhood to adulthood, and of the growth of a tree from a seed.[47] As Pepper also observed, this belief that differences were only apparently irreconcilable related to the underlying idealist philosophy of the romantics and the consequent differentiation of appearance from reality.[48]

Berry showed familiarity with many of the strands of tradition that fed into or displayed aspects of the organic world view. These included alchemy, the mandalas, the psychocosmograms of India, hermeticism, neo-pythagorianism, gnosticism, stoicism, platonism, neoplatonism, kabbala, along with the thought of Aquinas, Augustine, Eckhart and Nicholas von Cusa. What he affirmed in these traditions was the awareness of the unity of all things, human and non-human, which he described as follows:

> The outer world and the inner world are reciprocal in their functioning and in their destiny. All is in all. As above so below. As within so without. Microcosmos and macrocosmos correspond. All things move in sympathetic relation to each other... Especially the human, in its deepest reality, is consubstantial with the entire range of the universe. The sequence of experiences leading to fulfilment of the human is shared by all the universe. Indeed this fulfilment is attained in a comprehensive communion experience of the cosmic, the divine, and the human.[49]

All of these traditions, he concluded, were a rich source of psychic and spiritual symbolism. Furthermore, their basic insights were needed in order to supply some of the psychic-spiritual symbols lost in the "deep cultural pathology" of the twentieth century, in which the functional relationship between humankind and the rest of the universe was essentially lost.

Worthy of note, also, are the facts that (1) Berry considered elements of this tradition to be kept alive in post Renaissance times in the works of such thinkers as Goethe and Coleridge and (2) he saw the necessity of combining the rational skills of science with the symbolic insights of the alchemical and other traditions, as Jung, for instance, had done.

Whitehead's "Organicism and Temporality" in Berry's Work

Throughout much of its Western tradition, the organic world view was a static one, connected to the hierarchical notions of society and family life. This is not a necessary connection, however, as witnessed by the fact that other cultures (Mesopotamia is one) associated the organic metaphor with constant flux and change.[50] Whatever its interpretation, a hallmark of the organicist view was that it kept alive the connection of human culture and society to cosmos and bios. The organic world view of the romantics, for instance, rested to a large extent on their insistence of the validity of their experience of space and time. This was an experience that went beyond the unilateral, calculated and rational premises of the Enlightenment to a rootedness in what they perceived to be the psycho-spiritual reality of nature.

Berry's use of the organicist metaphor included the notion of temporality. He spoke of Asian civilization as a "dynamic equilibrium of... many forces," which at each period of history "is something other than it was in the previous period," although it maintained a continuity. There are numerous other organic, developmental images in Berry's work on the world religions: "the Hindu tradition is a creative force of unique range and power," and "Indian civilization is rather a process than an accomplished reality. We can best describe the spontaneous forces of Indian civilization by analogy with the luxuriance of a tropical jungle... The spontaneous and luxuriant growth [of Buddhism] is likewise a sign of its tremendous vitality and its correspondence with the needs of the societies in which it was received." [51]

While the traditional metaphor did contain the notion of development (growth of trees, germination of seeds), Berry's usage included historical development, time itself, within the organic metaphor. In this he followed the philosophy of Alfred North Whitehead, who attempted to show how time was constitutive of the organic nature of the universe. Hence, he proposed that reality was composed of "occasions" or "limit-events," singularities of interacting and relatively enduring patterns of energy in time.[52] The occasions converge in memory as events.

Besides "memory," Whitehead used the terms "nexus" and "prehensive unity" to indicate the relatedness of events to each other. "Nexus" referred to shared aspects of occasions within an event. "Prehensive unity" was the quality of all events in the universe analogous to human anticipation.[53] As humans selected from memory aspects of their past to incorporate into the present in anticipation of desired outcomes, so in an analogous way did all the events of the universe. Hence, the entire universe, all of reality, was an interconnected, organic process.

Whitehead sought to integrate the modern awareness of time, the most recent discoveries of science and the notion of the imaginative experience of (or "feel for") nature, expressed by the romantics, into an organic philosophy. In *Science and the Modern World*, he focused on the clash between the scientific portrayal of nature as determined and mechanistic and the more holistic portrayal by artists, particularly the romantic poets.[54] Having illustrated William Wordsworth's "sense of the haunting presence of nature," Whitehead says:

> the point which I wish to make is that we forget how strained and paradoxical is the view of nature which modern science imposes on our thoughts. Wordsworth, to the height of his genius, expresses the concrete facts of our apprehension, facts which are distorted in the scientific analysis. Is it not possible that the standardized concepts of science are only valid within the narrow limitations, perhaps too narrow for science itself?[55]

This citation is significant not only because it connects the traditional organicist metaphor with Whitehead's philosophy, but also because it reveals the counter-scientific, counter-Enlightenment stance integral to the organicist view.

According to Whitehead, it was possible for humans to know nature in a way that included, though not exclusively, a knowing through "indirect inferences from aspects of shape and sense-objects" because humans were part of the process of nature, intricately bound up in its processes of becoming. Hence, there was a kind of human "feeling" for occasions or events as well as for the process as a whole. The mistake of materialism, he claimed, was to substitute abstract models for concrete experience. Hence, the machine model of the universe understood a static sum of parts to be "all there is" to the universe.[56]

Whitehead pointed out that the materialists in their attempt to explain human knowing in exclusively materialist terms were, in fact, professing belief in the continuity of humans with the rest of the universe and attempting to overcome duality. He claimed that establishing the existence of "consciousness" throughout the entire universe was a more accurate way to overcome the duality and better accounted for the full dimensions of the human experience of nature.[57]

Whitehead's organic philosophy grounded Berry's contention that the analytic, scientific study of religions alone did not capture the living actualizations of the religious archetypes and symbols. The same applied to his view of religions as different processes, all interconnected in one overarching dynamic process. In speaking of changes in religious language, he said:

> neither history nor culture nor language knows the type of permanence or the type of constancy that is sought by those who would isolate language or thought from the stream of time, from the temporal conditionings to which all things are subject; nor can we accept the attitude that thought systems or religious traditions or spiritual disciplines are incommunicable with each other.[58]

Referring to the holism of the East, especially of Chinese civilization, he commended the participatory, mutually present and organic relationship that it engendered among humans, society and the cosmos. He found echoes of the Chinese "expression of relatedness, wholeness, inner cultivation, spontaneity, authenticity, universal reverence, communion with all of the living and non-living components of the universe community" in Western notions, such as "the organicism of Whitehead... biological integrity of the planet presented by Lewis Thomas... hologram metaphor of David Bohm, the synchronicity of C.G. Jung..."[59]

While Whitehead's process-oriented organicism was clearly recognizable in Berry's own adoption of that world view, Berry criticized Whitehead's sense of time as not fully adequate. Whitehead's universe was organically interconnected, but, in Berry's words, it was "not going anywhere"; the sense of real, phenomenal, historical time was missing.[60] Berry found the latter primarily in Teilhard de Chardin, whose influence will be considered below.

Key Influential Ideas from the Content of the World Religions

The Religions of China and India

In constructing his proposal to meet the ecological crisis, Berry relied on key concepts of Chinese and Indian religions. In speaking of the relation of the classical civilizations to the natural world, for example, he highlighted Hindu, Buddhist and Chinese conceptions of that relationship. He noted the Hindu's "pervasive sense of compassion" for all living beings, of a similar sense evident in the Buddhist legends and thought (Shanti Devi of the fifth century C.E. offered to take upon himself the sufferings of all beings) and Mencius teaching in the *Book of Ritual* that "all things are complete within us." According to this teaching of Mencius, the completely authentic human was established as a Third (or mean) bringing into being all things and carrying them to completion.[61] Another idea commonly mentioned by Berry was the relationship of macrocosm and microcosm as it showed up within Chinese cosmology.[62] This was the idea that individuals incorporated the whole universe in some sense and must exhibit the order of the cosmos in their lives. It is related in Confucianism to the idea of authenticity treated further below.

Berry realized that while these teachings existed, the practices of the religious believers themselves were not always benign, although it may be significant that in those cultures the extent and power of human devastation on the natural world was not so great as it was in the West. Christian teachings provided a favourable climate for the emergence of modern science and technology, which in turn are responsible for the degree of ecological damage associated with Western-style development.[63]

The ideas from the religions of China and India that were most consistently mentioned by Berry and that contributed most to an understanding of his ecological proposal were the Chinese ideas of authenticity and communion with all reality, and the Indian belief in the numinous quality of the whole universe.

By authenticity the Chinese meant a process whereby human identity is established in a threefold manner: with oneself, with the total human community and with the cosmic and divine orders. This understanding of authenticity was based on the belief that nature, including human nature, was directed toward its own best development. As humans developed from naive self-identity into a dialectical period of self-awareness, they lost what Mencius variously called the "original mind," "the mind of the child" or the integrity of "the heavenly endowed nature." A process of interior spiritual development was necessary in order to regain the lost mind. This process headed toward a fulfilment of the human vocation to perfect one's nature. The perfection of nature was true authenticity. When humans acquired it, they could then act spontaneously with the assurance that they were doing the right thing. It was only through authentic persons that correct order in human affairs and in the cosmos would be maintained. The human constituted the "mean" between heaven and earth.[64]

In Chinese thought, then, spontaneity was integrally connected to the communion of humans with the cosmos. For Berry also, to live in communion with the earth was part of what it meant to be human. Using modern scientific knowledge of genes, he reinterpreted this ancient Chinese notion; the true guidance for living in communion was attained when humans acquired the capacity to understand and act out of the genetic coding by which they are bonded to the rest of creation. As in the Chinese teaching, this rediscovery of an individual's identity involves a re-establishment of one's rootedness in the universe.[65]

Berry commented on the special communion (*Jen*) that the Chinese sought to establish with all of reality, as follows:

> This special way of feeling [*Jen*], of sympathetic communication, this mode of presence, is an experience in which all the world is

expressed in its human meaning and man discovers the wonders of himself in all the world.[66]

The *Book of Ritual* is the expression of the ritualization of this integration of the human and the universe. The similarity of language used here, "sympathetic communion," and that of Whitehead is worth noting. This is indicative both of the common organic world view and of Berry's gradual synthesis of his sources.

Summarizing these learnings from Chinese cosmology, Berry wrote of the holistic view that also entered into his discussion of the ecological crisis:

So in the History, the Ritual, and the Cosmology of the Chinese, there is constant reference to the full development of the microphase mode of the human in terms of its ability to understand and commune with the larger dimensions of reality that constitute the macrophase of one's own personal existence.[67]

In describing what he considered a correct sense of the human role in the universe, Berry often referred to the Chinese cosmology, in which the human was seen as the *hsin*, mind and heart of the universe.[68]

In the introduction to the new edition of *Religions of India*, Berry said of the relevance of Indian thought to the ecological crisis:

The relevance of this book is enhanced rather than diminished by the years since its original publication... What strikes us immediately is the extent to which the experience of the divine is inseparable in India from the experience of the natural forms that surround us throughout the universe... We read in the Upanishads that the divine is the numinous presence within every visible form... One of the most profound doctrines of India is the doctrine of Ahimsa (non-injury) a term that can be understood as a negative way of expressing a positive all-embracing love or affection for every being in the universe.[69]

The numinous quality of the universe and all its components continued to be a theme in Berry's ecological writings. In his thought, as in the Indian perception, the idea of extending "love and affection" to all beings in the universe was based on a belief that the universe was more than a mere material reality.[70] The experience of human presence to the universe was not adequately embodied in the mechanistic and instrumentalist metaphors of post-Enlightenment development in the West.

North American Native Religions

Berry's expressed interest in the North American native peoples began in the 1940's with his desire to "get beyond the classical civilizations, back into the early Shamanic period of the human community."[71] He found that this primal religious culture exhibited clearly the archetypal forms that exemplified human bondedness to the earth.

As mentioned above, Thomas Berry's own declared interest in the religions of the world was in the area of spirituality. In confronting the challenges of the future, whether that meant interreligious dialogue or religious-scientific integration or the ecological crisis, he felt that a spiritual transformation was needed. The first succinct presentation of what would be involved in such a transformation was contained in his course description of a fourteen-session seminar in contemporary spirituality given in 1973.[72] In the introduction, Berry described the purpose and context of the course. He observed that contemporary American society, in its expressed desire for authenticity, was showing an increased interest in spirituality. Such authenticity required the re-appropriation of traditional religious myths and symbols in a process of self-transformation. He attributed the ideas for the basic outlines of the seminar to Carlos Castaneda, Carl Jung and Mircea Eliade.

Each session of the seminar established the basic meaning of various religious images and symbols that focused on self-transformation. These included Castaneda's image of "Stopping the World" (a confrontation with the world as presently constructed),[73] the mythic spiritual journey with its confrontation of demonic forces, the Jungian archetypes, death-rebirth symbols and rites, and others. In a session entitled "Cosmic Communion," Berry spoke of the earlier civilizations as experiencing "a communion with the cosmic order." This provided a context for spirituality that is no longer available to contemporary humans. The communion has been shattered by "the plundering economy of a scientific technological secularistic age," which is "totally devoid" of such a mystical sense of the cosmos. The last manifestation of this sense in the West was in romanticism of the early nineteenth century. In Berry's view, a new surge of that feeling was beginning to awaken in the present time.[74]

This seminar gave very little direct reference to American native religions. (Most of the sources suggest Berry was referring to earlier stages of the classical civilizations.) Yet it was precisely in this area of self-transformation that he later referred to the native American contribution. In "Spirituality of the Earth," he wrote of Crazy Horse, the Sioux Indian, calling "upon these depths [where man discovered himself in the universe and the universe discovered itself in man] of his own being when he invoked the cosmic forces to support himself in battle." This was signified through the use of cosmic insignia. A similar meaning was expressed in the cosmic insignia of the Sun Dance Ceremony: "So the spiritual personality should feel that he is constantly in communion with those numinous forces out of which he was born."[75]

Berry referred to this type of spirituality of the native peoples as "land mysticism," admitting that it was unique and difficult to designate. In delineating the ways in which the native peoples could contribute to the present culture, he listed as one of their great strengths "their interior communion with the archetypal world of the collective unconscious." In the context of the familiar refrain, that Western humankind has so developed its "rational processes [and] phenomenal ego" that it has lost an earlier communion with the archetypal world of the unconscious, Berry claimed that the "American Indian... is the living exemplification of recent understandings of the collective unconscious." He mentioned, often giving examples, "the journey symbol, the heroic personality, the symbolism of the center, the mandala symbolism of the self, the various transformation symbols," as well as "the Earth Mother archetype and the heroic ideal."[76]

Berry held that the present addiction of Western society to the technological-industrial way of life is based on a release of psychic energy, empowered by a mythic conception of the whole enterprise. He associated the myth of progress with the secularization of the religio-mythic paradisal vision of a new earth. This kind of energy could only be counteracted by an intense psychic energy committed to a more integral presence of the human to the earth community. It was in this context that he brought to the fore his knowledge of the archetypal religious symbols and myths, and hence the role of the American native peoples. Having indicated the relationship between "the new story of the earth" and the archetypal symbols of the Great Mother, the Great Journey, the mandala, self-transformation and the Cosmic Tree, he concluded that these archetypal symbols provide the means necessary for evoking the psychic energy required to confront the devastating course of human presence on the earth and to establish new patterns of human behaviour.[77]

Berry also spoke of this aspect of the native peoples' religions when pointing up inadequacies in Christian spiritual beliefs and practices. An example is his reference to the Omaha initiation of a child ceremony to point out the Christian baptismal failure to introduce the child to the whole earth community. Community, in the Christian context, included only the human-human, and human-divine relationships. The Omaha, on the other hand, called on the entire universe to welcome and make smooth the pathways for a new life. Behind this comparison was the idea that the North American natives, like other primal peoples, possessed a cosmic consciousness that in the Christian tradition was replaced in modern times by historical consciousness. Berry held that both were necessary.[78]

Although modern Western culture may view the mystical communion of native Americans with the earth as difficult to accept and even to recover if tried, Berry contended that the dominant culture must relearn this "art of communion" from the Indian.[79] This contention arose from his critique of mainstream contemporary culture, a critique that constituted a hermeneutics of suspicion on the religious and scientific tradition. Obviously, it is a question whether anything like the native American's sense of the natural world could be recovered in modern times. Berry, however, made the notion that it could and must be recaptured as an integral part of his hermeneutics of recovery or retrieval, his "new story." He did not mean this statement naively, however, but in the sense of a "second naivete" or post-critical return, which will be treated more extensively within the full discussion of his ecological proposal below.

From the initial interest in North American native peoples as a primal group, Berry's involvement with many of the native groups increased over the years. He saw their survival to be important for themselves as well as for the North American continent. While there is an inherent danger of instrumentalization in the tendency of the ecology movement to look to native spirituality for guidance and resources, Berry's sensitivity toward the history of suffering of the native peoples and recognition of their integrity would seem to mitigate such effects of his own thought. The mutual respect that is indicated in his relationship with the native peoples seems to have its basis in his appreciation of their own strengths and traditional resources, rather than in a socio-political stance. The latter was presumed as a starting point for any further cultural development in statements such as:

> Our first duty is to see that the Indians dwelling here have the land, the resources and the independence they need to be themselves... We have won our battles with the Indian in the military-political order, in the possession of property, in the power to control the exterior destinies of the native peoples, but we have lost in the moral sphere...[80]

Berry's position was that the native peoples must be permitted to choose their own course of development rather than be actively assimilated into the dominant culture. It is only then that they can be expected to make an optimum contribution to the future of the North American continent.

Summary

Berry's writings in world religions were motivated by his own desire to understand the cultural constructs whereby humans across time and geography dealt with issues of meaning. The impetus for that project originated in his own disillusionment with post-Enlightenment Western development and the perceived failure of modern Christianity to provide adequate meaning for the challenges of the twentieth century. Just as Vico and the counter-Enlightenment tradition suggested alternative ways of understanding, and hence constructing, society, so, too, did the non-Christian religions. In fact, it was always with an alternative in mind that Berry culled the religio-cultural history he studied. Underlying all his efforts was an unquestioned conviction that real change originated and was effected by cultural movements. Change occurred when visionary and comprehensive ideas or images, such as plenitude and organicism (or on the other hand, mechanicism and materialism), interacted with archetypal psychic sensibilities. As already evidenced, especially in his writings to and about the North American native peoples, that conviction and emphasis remained consistent as his efforts focused more exclusively on the ecological crisis. His motivation, assumptions and knowledge were brought to bear on what he saw to be the most devastating outcome of the kind of myths and images that empowered modern Western development. With the further influence of Teilhard de Chardin, his own positions deepened and became more clearly articulated.

Notes

1.   Cf. Anne Lonergan, "Introduction: The Challenge of Thomas Berry," in *Thomas Berry and the New Cosmology*, ed. by Anne Lonergan and Caroline Richards (Mystic, CT: Twenty-Third Publications, 1990), 3.

2.   Berry, *Befriending the Earth*, 143.

3.   Huston Smith, *The Religions of Man* (New York: Harper and Brothers, 1958), 12.

4.   Berry, *Buddhism* (New York: Hawthorn Books, 1967), 183.

5.   Berry, "Introduction to the First Edition," *Religions of India: Hinduism, Yoga, Buddhism*, 2nd ed. (Chambersburg, PA: Anima Publications, 1992), no pagination.

6.   Berry, "Alienation," *Riverdale Papers II*.

7.   For a similar critique, cf. Edward Said, *Culture and Imperialism* (New York: Alfred A. Knopf, 1993), 35, 123, 280-281 and passim.

8.   Berry, "Contemporary Spirituality: Seminar Guide," 26.

9.   Cf. *New Catholic Encyclopedia*, 2nd ed., s.v. "Humanism," by W.J. Ong.

10.   Berry, "Religious Studies and the Global Community of Man," paper presented at the Faculty Seminar of Oriental Thought and Religion, Columbia University, 1972, and at the Cross Centre Conference, Zurich, Switzerland, 1973, *Riverdale Papers III*, 1-2, 11.

11.   Ibid., 16-17.

12.   Berry, "Seminar," 24; also 7, 9, 14.

13.   Berry, "Christian Humanism," *Riverdale Papers II*, 1-2.

14.   Ibid., 13.

15.   Berry, "Seminar," 24. See also "Dynamics of the Future," *Riverdale Papers I*, 14-15.

16.   Ibid., 24-25.

17.   Cf. Berry, "Traditional Religions in the Modern World," *Cross Currents* (Spring 1972): 134; "Seminar," 17; and "The Christian Process," *Riverdale Papers IV*, 1968, 12.

18.   Lovejoy, *The Great Chain*, 52.

19.   Berry, *Religions of India*, 193-194.

20.   Ibid.

21.   Berry, "The Catholic Church and the Religions of the World," *Teilhard Perspectives* 18,1 (Aug. 1985): 4.

22.   Berry, "Oriental Philosophy and World Humanism," in *International Philosophical Quarterly* 1,1 (Feb. 1961): esp. 32-33.

23.   Berry, "The Cosmology of Religions," *Pluralism and Oppression, The Annual Publication of the College Theology Society* 34, (1988): 100-113.

24.   Berry, "The Catholic Church and the Religions of the World," 4.

25.   Lovejoy, *The Great Chain*, 25. The following explication of Plato's concept of the one and the many relies on Lovejoy, 25ff.

26.   There is a discussion concerning Plato's works about whether the actual creator was the First Soul or Demiurgos. This is not relevant to the discussion here. See Lovejoy, *The Great Chain*, 46ff.

27.   *Timaeus*, 29, 30, in Lovejoy, *The Great Chain*, 47.

28.   Lovejoy, *The Great Chain*, 49. Obviously, the phrase "without losing its original implications" means apparently so. Later philosophers will challenge this assertion, as Lovejoy himself pointed out.

29.   Ibid., 52-54, and 145-182.

30.   Cf. Berry, *The Dream of the Earth*, 129; "Perspectives on Creativity," 12; *Befriending the Earth*, 11.

31.   Lovejoy, *The Great Chain*, 55.

32.   Berry, *The Dream of the Earth*, 129. See also "Dante: The Age in Which He Lived," commentary presented on Channel 5 TV, New York, 1965, on the occasion of the seventh centennial of the birth of Dante, *Riverdale Papers IV*.

33.   Berry, "Global Community of Man," 20.

34.   Berry, *The Dream of the Earth*, 129.

35.   Lovejoy, *The Great Chain*, 244.

36.   *Summa Theologica I, 47, 1*, quoted in Thomas Berry, "The Earth: A New Context for Religious Unity," *Thomas Berry and the New Cosmology*, 30. See also Berry, "Cosmology of Religions," 109; and *The Dream of the Earth*, 79.

37.   Berry, "The Earth: A New Context for Religious Unity," *Thomas Berry and the New Cosmology*, 30-31.

38.   Lovejoy, *The Great Chain*, 288ff, and Berry, *Management: The Managerial Ethos and the Future of Planet Earth*, 5.

39.   Berry, "Cosmology of Religions," 109.

40.   Ibid. See also Charlene Spretnak's book, *States of Grace* (San Francisco: Harper, 1991), esp. 28-29.

41.   See Edgar B. Schick, *Metaphorical Organicism in Herder's Early Works* (The Hague, Netherlands: Mouton and Co., 1971), 104-105. See also Anna Bramwell, *Ecology in the 20th Century: A History* (New Haven and London: Yale University Press, 1989), esp. 39-63.

42.   G.N.G. Orsini, "The Organic Concepts in Aesthetics," in *Comparative Literature* 21,1 (Winter 1969): 3, 16-17.

43.   Stephen C. Pepper, *World Hypotheses: A Study in Evidence* (Berkeley and Los Angeles: University of California Press, 1961), 91-92.

44.   Schick, *Metaphorical Organicism*, 108-109.

45.   Berlin, *Against the Current*, 17.

46.   Arnold Bergstrasser, *Goethe's Image of Man and Society* (Freiburg: Herder, 1962), 228. See also, Schick, *Metaphorical Organicism*, 121.

47.   Schick, *Metaphorical Organicism*, 105, 116-127, citing Stephen C. Pepper, *World Hypothesis*, 281.

48.   Pepper, *World Hypotheses*, 292-304.

49.   Berry, "Alchemy and Spiritual Transformation in C.G. Jung," *Riverdale Papers IX* (1982), 10-11.

50.   Gibson Winter, *Liberating Creation* (New York: Crossroad Publishing, 1981), 128. See also Jef van Gerwen, "Root Metaphors of Society: Linking Sociological and Moral-Theological Analysis," in *Louvain Studies* (Spring 1986): 41-59.

51.   Berry, "The Spiritual Form of the Oriental Civilizations," in *Approaches to Asian Civilization*, edited by T. deBary (New York and London: Columbia University Press, 1964), 85, 76 and passim.

52.   Alfred North Whitehead, *Process and Reality: An Essay in Cosmology*, ed. David Ray Griffin and Donald W. Sherburne (New York: Macmillan Publishing Co., 1978), 22-28.

53.   Ibid. See also 43.

54.   Alfred North Whitehead, *Science and the Modern World* (New York, Toronto, London: Macmillan and Company, 1925), 72-90.

55.   Ibid., 80.

56.   Ibid., 137. See also Whitehead, *Process and Reality*, 20-23.

57.   Ibid., 157-167. Whitehead's whole program is an effort to support this contention; cf. 214.

58.   Berry, "Religious Studies and the Global Community of Man," 16.

59.   Berry, "Individualism and Holism in the Chinese Tradition," paper presented at the conference, "Individualism and Wholism: The Confucian and Taoist Philosophical Perspective," Breckinridge Center for Public Affairs, York, Maine, June 24-29, 1981, *Riverdale Papers IX*, 2, 23-24. See also "Authenticity in Confucian Spirituality," in *Monastic Studies* 8 (Spring 1972): 53-158.

60.   Berry, "The Divine and Our Present Revelatory Moment," *Befriending the Earth*, 28.

61.   Brian Swimme and Thomas Berry, *The Universe Story* (San Francisco: Harper Collins Publishers, 1992), 183-205.

62.   Cf. Berry, "Individualism and Wholism in Chinese Tradition." Other references include *The Dream of the Earth*, 17; and *Befriending the Earth*, 22, 77.

63.   Swimme and Berry, *The Universe Story*, 199.

64.   Berry, "Authenticity in Confucian Spirituality," *Monastic Studies* 8 (Spring 1972): 154, 156. Reference to *Doctrine of the Mean*, 32,1.

65.   For different sources, including Chinese cosmology, for this idea in Berry, cf. Berry, "Authenticity in Confucian Spirituality," 156-157; "Cosmology of Religions," 107-108. "Religious Studies and the Global Community of Man," 8.

66.   Berry, "Affectivity in Classical Confucianism," Paper presented at the Annual Meeting of the Association for Asian Studies (1973), *Riverdale Papers III*, 22.

67.   Berry, "Individualism and Wholism," 11.

68.   Berry, *Befriending the Earth*, 21; *The New Cosmology*, 31; *The Dream of the Earth*, 20; "The Spirituality of the Earth," *Liberating Life: Contemporary Approaches to Ecological Theology*, ed. by William Birch, William Eakin and Jay B. McDaniel (Mary Knell, NY: Orbis Books, 1990), p. 153.

69.   Berry, Foreword to *Religions of India*, [i, iii].

70.   Berry, *The Dream of the Earth*, 20, 168.

71.   Reported in "Introduction," *Thomas Berry and the New Cosmology*, 3.

72.   Berry, "Seminar: Contemporary Spirituality," *Riverdale Papers IV*.

73.   Carlos Castaneda, "Stopping the World,"*Journey to Ixtlan* (New York: Simon and Schuster, 1972); Part I, 17-255.

74.   Berry, "Seminar," 17-18.

75.   Berry, "The Spirituality of the Earth," 152.

76.   Berry, *The Dream of the Earth*, 184, 187, 190 and passim.

77.   Berry, *The Dream of the Earth*, 28, 34, 54-55 and 75-77.

78.   Berry, *Befriending the Earth*, 48, 71.

79.   Berry, *The Dream of the Earth*, 186-187.

80.   Berry, *The Dream of the Earth*, 182-183. See also Berry's essay, "The Indian Future," *Cross Currents* (1976), which was presented at a conference "The Good Red Road," with Philip Deere, Cree Indian, sponsored by International Grail. Many Indian nations have recognized his support and respect for their culture with invitations to speak and with awards. In 1994, he was awarded a plaque by the Haskell Indian Nations University in the name of all the Indian Tribes of North America.

CHAPTER THREE

INTERACTION WITH THE THOUGHT OF TEILHARD DE CHARDIN

Introduction

Two early essays of Thomas Berry, "Creative Evolution" and "The Christian Process," suggest a reason for his initial interest in Teilhard. Berry, like Teilhard, raised questions about the increasing split he perceived between religion (Christianity, in particular) and the world of the twentieth century. They both attributed the increase in secularization and the growing sense of human alienation from religion to a ghettoized Christianity, whose efforts to meet the needs of the modern world had, to date, been minimal.[1]

In these two essays, Berry dealt primarily with the radical change that he saw occurring in culture and society, change in which the wider society was leaving behind traditional Christianity. The fault, he thought, lay within Christianity itself and its failure to be cognizant of its own biblical mission of revolutionary change in history. To that effect, he wrote:

> The more carefully we study the modern revolutions the more clear it becomes that they are all in the direct line of descent from the spiritual revolution of Christianity and this in turn goes back to the prophetic and apocalyptic visions of the Old Testament.[2]

In Berry's thought, it was Christianity that claimed the relevance of the "death-rebirth" symbolism to the historical process itself. The "saving revolution" would be achieved not by accepting the world or society or the human as is, but through a "mounting historical sequence" of death and rebirth. A second exodus was needed, Berry declared, in which Christianity would leave its own isolated space and enter the new "Holy Land," the modern, historically conscious world.[3] Teilhard was also concerned with the split between the two worlds in which he lived—the secular, scientific world that brought him in contact with many people for whom Christianity was no longer a vital force, and the Christian world, which, he felt, failed to communicate with a modern humanity. His lifelong pursuit was to bring together these two worlds that he loved. In the preface to *The Divine Milieu*, Teilhard spoke of the problem of the gap between the two worlds as follows:

> As a result of changes which, over the last century, have modified our empirically based pictures of the world and hence the moral value of many of its elements, the "human religious ideal" inclines to stress certain tendencies and to express itself in terms which seem, at first sight, no longer to coincide with the "Christian religious ideal."[4]

One of Teilhard's goals in writing this essay was to show that the two worlds were indeed related.

Despite similar starting points, there was a much more sustained effort by Teilhard than by Berry to enunciate new meanings for the major Christian doctrines. While Berry continued to see the necessity of this task, it was not a significant focus of his own work.[5] He claimed to focus more on the larger society. This difference, however, occurred *not* because Teilhard wished to address Christians as such and Berry didn't; both thinkers were interested in a religiously disenchanted group. Teilhard's primary audience was the secular scientific community to which he belonged;[6] Berry's was the more general public secular society. The difference lay mainly in the source of their religious ideas; Berry drew many of his religious ideas from non-Christian religions, while Teilhard was specifically concerned with reinterpreting Christianity. This became obvious as Berry declared his departures from Teilhardian thought.

Berry distanced himself from Teilhard's thinking about the role of the past and of non-Western civilizations in human evolution. This led to a broader thematization by Berry of how human psychic energy empowered further evolution. He also critiqued Teilhard's notion of Western progress. Berry's critique was directly related to his sensitivity to the ecological crisis.

Berry's Development of Teilhard's Thought—Role of Classical Civilizations and Non-Christian Religions

Berry's essays, "Threshold of the Modern World" and "Building the Earth," faulted Teilhard for underestimating the role of the great civilizations in the future evolution of humanity.[7] For the most part, Teilhard considered the classical civilizations to be mere extensions of the Neolithic period. Berry quoted Teilhard on this point:

> The better we get the past into perspective, the more clearly we see that the periods called "historic" (right down to and *including* the beginning of "modern" times) are nothing else than direct prolongations of the Neolithic age. Of course, as we shall point out, there was increasing complexity and differentiation, but essentially following the same lines and on the same *plane*.[8]

Berry took a more positive view of the contributions of the classical civilizations and saw in them the seeds of present changes. "The very words we use," he said, "with all the spiritual and cultural values they contain come from these traditional cultures." Human ideals, deepest thoughts, emotional responses, work, worship, music and songs are all products of the cultures in which they live.[9]

Teilhard's fascination with Western development and the scientific enterprise that took hold there led him to downplay the contribution of other civilizations, referring in one place to China as "encrusted in its soil" and India as "lost" in its metaphysics. Whereas Berry agreed that the West presented the best resources for evolution into the future, he called attention to the contributions of the Chinese and Indian cultures.[10] A significant example of their different perspectives on the relative importance of diverse cultures was how Teilhard and Berry dealt with the "how" of crossing what they both called "thresholds."[11] At the time of the essays under discussion, Berry accepted Teilhard's vision of the modern threshold. He later understood it more in terms of the ecological crisis.

Both Teilhard and Berry were supremely aware of modern humankind's sense of history. They saw the human community as poised to control its destiny. Despite the overwhelming continuity between the rest of the animal kingdom and the human species, the emergence of the human species introduced a new state, that of self-reflective thought. Edward O. Dodson commented on Teilhard's definition of humankind in terms that clearly revealed Teilhard's reliance on the modern notion of the human construction of history. Teilhard, he said, saw the individual as a *"center* about which he mentally organizes the world and puts it in perspective." Such a center is *"a person* capable of free choice and responsible for his acts, capable of good and evil."[12]

The present with its increased global interconnectedness and rapid advancement in technological power indicated to Teilhard an emerging new threshold, which he described as "a harmonized collectivity of consciousnesses equivalent to a sort of superconsciousness... the plurality of individual reflections grouping themselves... and reinforcing one another in the act of a single unanimous reflection."[13] The collectivity was becoming as one person while at the same time expanding to encompass all of humanity. Teilhard designated the final result of this personalization process as Omega, which operated in his thought as a variable awaiting his solution within Christianity. For Teilhard, Omega ultimately was Christ.

Crossing this threshold was, first of all, a profoundly human effort; in this regard Berry followed Teilhard as indicated by such statements as: "We must take up our work as men and enter into this next phase of the human adventure" and "The human community itself must build the new dimensions of the earth." "[It] cannot be said," he concluded, "that the modern scientific developments destroyed the spiritual life of man. The evidence is all to the contrary... It is clear that the modern world has renewed rather than destroyed the inner vitality of man's life."[14] As noted above, this assertion of the predominant role of the West was associated with the historical consciousness that developed in the West as well as the scientific research and discovery that occurred there.

While both Teilhard and Berry talked about the courage and sacrifice involved in willing the future, they also agreed that an act of the will alone would not sustain the effort; a psychic energy was needed. Different emphases emerge, however, in their thematizations of the meaning of psychic energy.

In *Phenomenon of Man*, Teilhard maintained that the intimate unity that existed between the human and the rest of the universe was not merely physical, sharing the same matter or a large percentage of DNA. On the basis of his principle that whatever new emerges really reveals what was there all along, Teilhard held that matter in whatever form it took had an inner and an outer reality. Besides the physical that one sensed, there was a psychic aspect to the whole universe; this was the aspect that came to self-reflective consciousness in the human species. The human psyche, then, shared in the energy that activated the whole evolutionary process. That is what empowered the will to act. Teilhard referred to that energy in humans as a passion for the world and as a "zest for living."[15]

The passion for the world was evidenced by the quasi-religious sense of involvement in the world that Teilhard claimed to observe among his contemporaries, many of whom had deserted Christianity. By Teilhard's interpretation, such a passion for the world was, potentially at least, a mystical experience of the Christic centre of the evolving universe. The psychic attraction toward unity exhibited in an increasingly unified world was none other than the person of Christ. Reflecting on his own experience, which brought him to this conclusion, Teilhard wrote:

> On one side there was a flux, at once physical and psychic, which made the Totality of the Stuff of Things fold in on itself, by giving it complexity: carrying this to the point where that Stuff is made to co-reflect itself.
>
> And on the other side, under the species of an incarnate divine being, a Presence so intimate that it could not satisfy me, without being by nature universal.
>
> This was the double perception, intellectual and emotional, of a *Cosmic Convergence* and a *Christic Emergence* which, each in its own way, filled my whole horizon.[16]

Having described the process within himself by which he realized that "the double perception" was really single, that the convergence of the universe was none other than the emergent Christ, he proclaimed, "Energy, then, becomes Presence."[17]

Teilhard also spoke of faith, a religious faith, as the source of psychic energy for the evolutionary task. In this association of psychic energy with faith, he left no doubt that the source of the energy needed to transform the world was, in traditional terms, a transcendent, divine one. What is needed is "a great faith,"

> a faith which assures us that we are not prisoners... that there is a way out, that there is air and light and love, somewhere beyond the reach of all death... that it is neither an illusion nor a fairy story."[18]

This was clearly not the faith of a secular humanist. It came about through religion, even if religion might have to be recast. The God of the above became, in Teilhard's system, the God of the "ahead"; humankind strove not upward but into the future. Yet Teilhard was undoubtedly speaking of a transcendence in the sense that this "future" extended beyond the end of time. Furthermore, relevant to the discussion at hand, this magnetic, ahead God acted upon the present and empowered the zest for life through revelation, grace and love. For Teilhard, the "vital charge of the world" and the source of all energy for further human (and hence universal) evolution was ultimately God. He reflected:

> [Through] the tradition of the great human mystical systems, along the road of contemplation and prayer, we succeed in entering directly into receptive communication with the very source of all interior life.[19]

Thus, his own experience of the mystical union of the converging universe and the emerging Christ became for him the paradigm within which the activation of human energy for the evolutionary process was understood.

Relying on his knowledge of world religions and the history of cultures, Berry gave a different thematization to the psychic process by which humans were empowered to cross the new threshold. Berry saw in the religious symbols, myths and archetypes, especially as expressed by primal peoples, an expression of bondedness with the natural world. He considered this quality of primal peoples to be a potential source of spiritual and psychic energy for the empowerment of the vision he shared with Teilhard. In "Dynamics of the Future," he spoke of Vico's "age of the gods" as a time of intimacy between the earth and humans. He added:

> Despite all the changes that have taken place in identifying the human quality of life this age still keeps its basic normative value... If much of the past was inadequate to the reality of things, much of the heritage from the past is irreplaceable by other modes of knowing.[20]

Later, he wrote:

> This inner compact mode of consciousness is such that the inner archetypal world of later times derives from the psychic imprint of the entire cosmic order as this was received inwardly at that time and which was later experienced in more differentiated fashion.[21]

While Teilhard emphasized the continuity between the psychic-physical energies of the universe and the cosmic Christ, Berry emphasized the continuity between the same energies of the universe and the many expressions of the archetypal unconscious, as cosmic person, across various cultures. Here he relied on the work of Carl Jung as well as on his own knowledge of cultural history.

Berry interpreted Teilhard's cosmic Christ to be one instance of the archetypal "cosmic person." The archetypal cosmic person, Berry explained, referred to the macrophase of the individual human person; that is, "the human aspect of all reality." Various expressions of this concept arose across time and culture, as Berry indicated in the following passage:

> This mode of awareness [human aspect of all reality] is found in the Great Man, the One Man, the Sage Personality of China; in India's Mahapurusha or the Cakravartin; in the Tathagata reality of Buddhism; in the Anthropos of the West; in the Cosmic Christ of St. Paul. It is the background of St. Augustine's sense of history. It is related to the unity of the Active Intellect in Averrhoes and Siger de Brabant... the Anthropos concept of Gnosticism and in the Alchemist traditions of the later medieval period.[22]

The list continued to include the modern period.

The point Berry made in this development of Teilhard's notion of the cosmic person was that it was confined to the Western process and hence earned for him the criticism of particularization and entrancement with the Western idea of progress. In the meantime, he commended Teilhard's historicization of the cosmic archetype. The personalized element is for Teilhard, Berry commented, within the "entire converging process of the real and the final goal toward which the earth process is striving." He saw special value in Teilhard's expression of the cosmic person as Christ because it included more than any of the other expressions the concept of time or history.[23]

Berry himself considered the difference between his own thought and that of Teilhard relative to psychic energy and the personalization of history as merely a shift from an exclusively Christian expression to a broader religious focus. He later recognized different implications in this concept than Teilhard did. While for Teilhard the re-establishment of the compact state of unity was a spiritualized process culminating in the divinization of humankind and the cosmos outside real time, Berry was more concerned with the implications within concrete space and time. The bondedness of the human psyche with cosmic energy and the personalization of that energy in the archetypal cosmic person grounded the integral relationship of human and earth, this concrete planet Earth in the here and now. Furthermore, the archetypal cosmic person represented for Berry a memory of an actual human bondedness with the earth in historical primal times, an observation for which he also found support from Vico and from the native peoples.[24]

It was also in conversation with Teilhard's work, in the essay "Creative Energy," that Berry laid the foundation for his idea of the connectedness of "the story of the universe" to the human psyche. Besides the historicization of the cosmic person symbol, Berry saw in Teilhard's account of evolution a historicized creation myth. Berry had already associated the ancient religious myths with the existential needs of humankind for meaning and order in life. Drawing on the insights of Vico, Jung and Eliade about the formation of the primal myths, he understood the myths to be extrapolations from the archetypal images, which were themselves expressions of human intimacy with the earth. In Teilhardian terms, he now saw the primal myth as a communicator of the creative energy of the universe. Furthermore, Teilhard's *Phenomenon of Man* suggested that the whole universe was sharing in the archetypal sacred journey, hitherto understood as applying only to individuals or to human communities.

Berry argued that the myth out of which modern humans found the energy for the rational scientific enterprise was the paradisal myth. In the modern period, humans strove to create the heavenly paradise on earth through increasingly rational and manipulative processes. They were no longer in touch with the "deeper realms of the unconscious" and so lost the intimate communion with the earth. Humans no longer experienced the "all-pervasive numinous presence" and so lost also the psychic energy "which formerly was experienced with this presence of the sacred." For Berry, this contributed largely to the existentialist experience of "modern angst and alienation." [25]

What was needed in this modern condition, Berry argued, was "a functional relationship" between the rationalized paradisal myth and a new creation myth. This was a need he saw fulfilled in large part by the work of Teilhard de Chardin. Commenting further on the story of the universe that was based on the latest scientific investigations and theories, he said:

> The important thing to realize is that it is a journey story as well as a creation story. The spiritual journey is no longer simply the interior journey of the individual or of the hero savior personality, or the journey of the individual sacred communities or of the comprehensive human community, it is the journey of the earth itself through its various transformations.[26]

Berry added that the story was "the pan-human journey of man as a cosmic person" and as "our basic psychic support." Thus, the idea of the integral relationship between the story of the universe and human psychic energy formed the basis of Berry's ecological proposal.

Berry's integration of Teilhardian notions was not merely an elaboration or addition. It was rather a genetic development. Teilhard's ideas were integrated into a new synthesis and refocused in a new direction. While Teilhard focused on the historical task of the human to create history based on humankind's (especially the West's) ingenuity in conquering nature, Berry refocused Teilhard's synthesis of science and religion toward retarding this kind of so-called progress. For Berry, the historical task of the human involved looking backward to what was lost and reclaiming it in some sense for a future life more integral with natural processes. The psychic energy, which for Teilhard pushed the human quest for progress forward, established for Berry a bondedness with the earth that could redirect human effort toward recovery of earth relatedness, healing technologies and a new understanding of the scientific project. The new horizon of ecological responsibility was certainly the primary influence in Berry's refocusing of Teilhard's contribution. Those early conversations with

Teilhard's work also affirmed that the influence of Vico, other cultures and Berry's particular kind of interest in the existential and archetypal aspects of the world religions laid the groundwork for departures from significant aspects of Teilhard's vision.

Berry's Critique of Teilhard in the Light of the Ecological Crisis

The second major fault Berry found with Teilhard's vision was the latter's uncritical association of the evolution of humanity with Western scientific-technological progress. Berry's critique of the notion of progress began to temper his own optimistic view as he became more aware of the ecological crisis. Concurrent with this growing awareness was his change of focus from the human community to the earth community.

One of the consequences of Teilhard's optimism about science and technology was his failure to take seriously or even to notice, perhaps, the post-Enlightenment fall-out, including ecological devastation, that was already evident to others. Many of the evils (threat of world destruction by nuclear bombs, intense poverty of large segments of the world, suffering caused by war) accompanying so-called Western progress did not capture his attention. Even on the poignant occasions when he came face to face with these realities, he was caught up in the vision of the onward march of humanity despite the suffering and sacrifice that might entail.[27] Although there was a growing consciousness of ecological problems during Teilhard's lifetime, he remained either unaware or unconcerned with that effect of Western progress. This was despite the fact, as Berry pointed out, that nature writers such as Aldo Leopold and Edward Hyams were already drawing attention to ecological problems.[28]

Berry brought his awareness of the ecological crisis into a discussion of Teilhardian themes in "Dynamics of the Future." Here he did not comment on Teilhard's neglect of this consequence of Western progress as he did later, but he did interpret the human responsibility for the future as including care for the earth. Speaking of the existential burden of fear and hopelessness often accompanying modern historical consciousness, Berry said:

> But while this peril [existential anxiety] is a cause of concern it is also a cause for advancing consciousness since the powers that man has recently assumed have brought about a state of profound reflection on the mystery of the earth. Responsible men no longer think of the world simply as a collection of "natural resources."

They realize that the earth is an awesome mystery, ultimately as fragile as man himself is fragile... But man's responsibility is not simply that of preserving the earth and establishing an equilibrium of forces upon the earth, it is the task of leading the earth on through its next series of transformations...[29]

The overall message of this essay was still the transformation of history and of the earth by humans. In this sense, it was clearly Teilhardian.

In later writings, Berry placed much less emphasis on this theme. He began to see a negative impact in the human drive to transform the earth and gradually departed from Teilhardian rhetoric. In "Cosmic Person and the Human Future," he wrote much more assertively of earth-centredness than he had previously. He proposed that "we turn from consideration of man to consideration of the earth, that we view the entire problem of human energy and man's future in terms of earth energy and earth future."[30] "Creative Energy" and "Dynamics of the Future" also contained references to the human treatment of the environment, but "Teilhard in the Ecological Age" was Berry's clearest and most comprehensive critique of Teilhard on this issue. By this time Berry had clearly moved to a primary concern with the ecological crisis and had his own response in place. His essays "The New Story" (1977) and "The Ecological Age" (1978) had already been composed.

In the essay "Teilhard in the Ecological Age," Berry articulated clearly his own position in relationship to Teilhard's. Toward the end, he presented his evaluation of Teilhard's contribution to the ecological movement as well as his perceptions of how the ecological movement must go beyond Teilhard's thought.[31] This presentation provided a good overview of how Berry integrated but, at the same time, developed Teilhard's thought in producing his own synthesis.

Berry mentioned five concerns of Teilhard that needed further development if they were to be integrated within an ecological vision:

(1) Interpretation of the evolutionary process: Teilhard saw the entire evolutionary process as converging in the human community. Berry suggested that the human community was unintelligible without the entire earth community. Therefore, the evolutionary process converged in the earth community of which the human was a unique component, but still only one component. As support for this idea, he cited the principle of plenitude discussed above, the research of scientists on the complex interrelationships within and between ecosystems of the earth and the "functional unity of the universe" in the thought of Alfred North Whitehead. Teilhard's references to the

"living earth" could easily be extended to include these notions that Teilhard himself neglected.

(2) The dimension of consciousness within the universe from the beginning: Teilhard held that the human revealed the latent powers of the universe and of the earth in particular, so that consciousness, an interior, was part of the evolutionary process from the beginning. Yet, he did not work out the implications of this integral relationship of the human to the planet; "Teilhard establishes the human as the exclusive norm of values." On this basis, he justified the intrusion without any limits into the natural workings of the planet and reduced nature to the level of the artificial. Teilhard had written: "All organisms are the result of invention; if there is any difference, the advantage is on the side of the artificial."[32]

On the contrary, Berry maintained, "the proper role of human intelligence would be not to exploit but to enhance the natural world and its functioning." Here Berry relied not only on the increased awareness of the ecological fallout of modern industrial-technologies, but also on the thought of Lewis Thomas (who described the earth as a living cell), René Dubos (who used the metaphor "wooing of earth" to describe how humans enhance aspects of the earth), Rachel Carson (who condemned the use of pesticides and other artificially produced chemicals) and others who wrote on the modern ecological problem.[33]

(3) The turn of Western religious thought from its dominant redemption orientation to a dominant creation orientation: In an essay entitled "The Sense of Man," Teilhard wrote, "What must mark the Christian in the future is 'an unparalleled zeal for creation.'"[34] Teilhard was not only concerned that Christianity deal with creation, but he proposed major reinterpretations of traditional doctrines to fit the evolutionary perspective. While appreciating Teilhard's effort in this regard, Berry pointed out that Teilhard turned the attention of Christians not so much to the created world itself as to science, technology and research. His mission did not include the nurturing of the biosphere and geosphere. His principles could be extended, however, to foster these values. Berry noted:

> The absence in Teilhard of any reconciliation between his general affirmations of the sublimity of the natural world and his support for activities destructive of the natural world can be remedied by developing within the context of his thought a religious concern for the natural world.[35]

In contrast with Teilhard, Berry held that human affective, intellectual and religious life suffered from the impoverishment of the earth.

Echoing the principle of plenitude, he asserted that with the loss of species, humans also lost modes of divine presence.

(4) Activation of human energy at a new level of intensity: Teilhard was extremely aware of the existential angst that accompanied the phenomenal changes occurring in the twentieth century. He saw the existentialist fears as counter-evolutionary. On reflection, he said, modern humankind should see the evolutionary process as supportive, as converging to an ultimate intimacy and as a personal process. Once this awareness happened, modern humankind would achieve an incredible freedom in the realization that "the world has a heart."[36]

Berry pointed out that the affective relationship that Teilhard held to exist between humans and the rest of creation was not a human intimacy with actual creatures. Despite Teilhard's mystical sense of creation, he considered the created forms in themselves to be of little importance. His enthusiasm was for the conquest of creation in the concrete, its re-creation in the human quest for knowledge and mastery. Berry suggested that the voices of natural historians such as Alexander von Humboldt, Henry Thoreau, John Muir, Aldo Leopold, Rachel Carson or Wendell Berry must supplement that of Teilhard, although in Teilhard's own mind these voices would certainly be seen as "retarding forces in the evolutionary process."[37]

Berry also insisted that the existential angst and the decline in religious sensibilities noted by Teilhard was in fact partially a result of the separation of modern humans from the natural world in its particular living forms. Thus he proposed that Teilhard's thought be extended to include this notion of the potential spiritual riches of the actual plants, animals and other forms and processes of the natural world.

(5) Concern for scientific endeavour: Berry contended that Teilhard saw the scientific endeavour almost exclusively in terms of conquest, conflict and confrontation. Berry, on the other hand, advocated a nurturing role for science.[38] The knowledge, power and technical skill celebrated by Teilhard required an added wisdom whereby scientists would extend their responsibilities to include protection of species, care in the application of genetic technologies, purification of the environment and education of the public toward a greater knowledge and appreciation of the natural world.

Summary

As Berry acknowledged in his critique, Teilhard's thought can be developed to include a way of thinking more congenial to ecologists.

Certainly, as has been shown above, Berry's own position owed much to the work of Teilhard. On the other hand, Berry brought to the reading of Teilhard a cultural historical background and a counter-Enlightenment stance in the tradition engendered by Vico. This enabled Berry to maintain a certain skepticism toward Teilhard's optimistic notion of Western progress and the role of the human within it. Berry was predisposed to a more ready awareness of the fallout of the Enlightenment, and that fact, along with his personal interest in the natural world from childhood, gave him an openness toward and concern about the ecological crisis.

Teilhard offered an appealing narrative of evolution that combined science and spirituality and presented the human as an integral part of the evolutionary process. While Teilhard's narrative tended to swallow creation into human history and real history into idealism, it was a story that could be refocused on a renewal of the spiritual and historical dimensions of nature and a recontextualizing of the human within, rather than above, the natural world.

Finally, Berry acquired from Teilhard's work a sense of the mythic power of science on which Berry grounded his ecological vision. In this regard, he wrote of Teilhard:

> Teilhard is carrying out a unique role in guiding human affairs to their fulfillment in the twentieth century. He provides a comprehensive vision of the universe in its evolutionary sequence with a powerful sense of the emergent consciousness manifested by this sequence. His overview of the way into the future is strengthened by the scientific research on which he bases his thought and by the entire religious and humanistic heritage of western tradition which is present throughout his work.[39]

While Berry distanced himself from Teilhard's optimism over scientific-technological progress, he remained committed to an optimism about the power of science itself to ground a vision for the future. Like religion, however, science would also have to be recast. Primarily, its status as something independent from culture would have to be challenged. To those who took up the challenge, Berry was a willing listener and supporter. Science would provide an answer for the ecological crisis, not primarily through the technical know-how it produced, but in the cultural artifact, the story, it engendered.

Notes

1.   Berry, "Christian Process," *Riverdale Papers IV*, 5-7. See also Teilhard de Chardin, "The Road of the West," in *Toward the Future*, trans. by René Hague (New York and London: Harcourt, Brace, Jovanovich, 1975), 52-53; and "Note on the Presentation

of the Gospel," in *The Heart of the Matter*, trans. by René Hague (New York and London: Harcourt, Brace, Jovanovich, 1978), 213.

2.   Berry, "Creative Revolution," *Riverdale Papers V*, 11.

3.   Berry, "Christian Process," 20-21. Berry adapts the "second exodus" metaphor from Eric Voegelin, *Order and History*, vol. 1, *Israel and Revelation* (Louisiana State University Press, 1956). Cf. "The Ecozoic Era," *E.F. Schumacher Society Lecture*, (Oct. 19, 1991), 22.

4.   Pierre Teilhard de Chardin, *The Divine Milieu* (New York: Harper and Row, Publishers, Inc., 1965), 43.

5.   Cf. Teilhard, *Science and Christ*, trans. by René Hague (New York and Evanston: Harper and Row, Publishers, Inc., 1968); Claude Tresmontant, *Pierre Teilhard de Chardin—His Thought*, trans. by Salvator Attanasio (Baltimore: Helicon Press, 1959), 70-77; Berry, *Befriending the Earth*, 10, 53-55.

6.   Pierre Teilhard de Chardin, *The Phenomenon of Man*, trans. by Bernard Wall (New York: Harper Torchbooks, 1965), 35-36.

7.   Berry, "Threshold of the Modern World," paper presented at the Teilhard Conference of the Human Energetics Research Institute, Fordham University, NY, 1964, *Riverdale Papers II*; and, "Building the Earth," paper presented to American Teilhard Association for the Future of Man, Pace University, NY, 1969, *Riverdale Papers I*.

8.   Teilhard, *Phenomenon of Man*, 207.

9.   Berry, "Threshold of the Modern World," 6-7.

10.   See Teilhard, *Phenomenon of Man*, 211. Cf. Berry, "Threshold of the Modern World," 9; and "Alienation," 9.

11.   Cf. Teilhard, "Threshold of Reflection," in *Phenomenon of Man*, 164; "A Mental Threshold across Our Path: From Cosmos to Cosmogenesis," in *Activation of Energy*, trans. by René Hague (New York and London: Harcourt, Brace, Jovanovich, 1970), 251.

12.   Edward O. Dodson, *The Phenomenon of Man Revisited: A Biological Viewpoint on Teilhard de Chardin* (New York: Columbia University Press, 1984), 167.

13.   Teilhard, *Phenomenon of Man*, 251. Cited in Dodson, *Phenomenon Revisited*, 191.

14.   Berry, "Building the Earth," 2, 10.

15.   Teilhard, *Phenomenon of Man*, 54, 56, 163-190; *The Heart of the Matter*, 214, and "Zest for Living," *Activation of Energy*, 231-243.

16.   Teilhard, *The Heart of the Matter*, 82.

17.   Ibid., 99. See also "Zest for Living," 242.

18.   Teilhard, "Zest for Living," 238.

19 .   Ibid., 242.

20.   Berry, "Dynamics of the Future," paper presented at the Annual Meeting of the American Teilhard Foundation, Trinity Church, New York, 1974, *Riverdale Papers I*, 6-8.

21.   Berry, "Cosmic Person and the Human Future," *Anima* 3,1 (1975): 25. Originally a presentation to the Symposium for the American Teilhard Association for the Future of Man and the C.G. Jung Foundation of New York, International House, New York, 1975.

22.   Ibid., 26-27.

23.   Ibid. Cf. Teilhard, *Science and Christ*, trans. by René Hague (New York and Evanston: Harper and Row, Publishers, Inc., 1968) esp. 14-20, 53-56, 151-173; and *Phenomenon of Man*, 257-272.

24.   Swimme and Berry, *The Universe Story*, 245; Berry, *The Dream of the Earth*, 117, 196-198.

25.   Berry, "Creative Energy," paper presented at the Conference on the Future of India, SUNY, 1976, *Riverdale Papers I*. A revised edition of this essay is published in *The Dream of the Earth*, 6-10, 24-35.

26.   Ibid., 10.

27.   Cf. Teilhard, "Nostalgia for the Front," and "The Great Monad," in *The Heart of the Matter*, 167-195; and "On Looking at a Cyclotron," in *Activation of Energy*, 349-357. For a discussion of Teilhard's liberal orthodoxy with regard to solving economic problems, cf. Joseph A. Grau, *Morality and the Human Future in the Thought of Teilhard de Chardin* (London: Associated University Presses, 1976), 288-292.

28.   According to Berry, Aldo Leopold, "A Land Ethic" (1948) and Edward Hyams, *Soil and Civilization* (1954) were two significant publications written during Teilhard's later years that drew attention to ecological problems. See Berry, *Teilhard in the Ecological Age. Teilhard Studies No. 7* (Chambersburg, PA: Anima Books, Fall 1982), 16, 32; and Bramwell, *Ecology in the 20th Century: A History*, 18-19; 82-85.

29.   Berry, "The Dynamics of the Future," 15.

30.   Berry, "Cosmic Person and the Human Future," 6.

31.   Berry, *Teilhard in the Ecological Age*, 23-31. The following synthesis of Berry's overview, including citations, is taken from these last pages of this essay.

32.   Teilhard de Chardin, *Activation of Energy*, 159.

33.   Lewis Thomas, *The Lives of a Cell* (New York: Penguin Books, 1974); René Dubos, *The Wooing of Earth* (New York: Scribner Books, 1980); Rachel Carson, *Silent Spring* (Cambridge: Riverside Press, 1962).

34.   Teilhard, "The Sense of Man," in *Toward the Future*, 32.

35.   Berry, *Teilhard in the Ecological Age*, 28.

36.   Teilhard, "The Phenomenon of Counter-Evolution in Human Biology: Or the Existential Fear," in *Activation of Energy*, 183-195.

37.   See works of these authors in the bibliography.

38.   See also Berry, *The Dream of the Earth*, 50-69.

39.   Berry, *Teilhard in the Ecological Age*, 31.

CHAPTER FOUR

THE INFLUENCE
OF MODERN SCIENCE

Introduction

Given the nature of the genetic development of Berry's thought, it is
no surprise that Berry's interest in science was primarily in scientific
critiques of mainstream post-Enlightenment scientific methodology.
While he always maintained a respect for many of the contributions
of Western science, he relied especially in his own work on scientists
who tested new waters and were often only tentatively accepted by
the established scientific community. He considered these scientists
to give credibility to the counter-Enlightenment traditions that he
upheld. His overriding interest remained cultural; therefore, his questions for science were concerned with the cultural assumptions and
effects of the new scientific developments. On the other hand, however, Berry's conversation with contemporary scientific movements
influenced the development of his own thought by giving a concreteness and a practical edge to his vision.

There are three aspects of contemporary science that are identifiable supports for Berry's own proposal to meet the ecological crisis:
(1) the changing conception of scientific epistemology; (2) new discoveries and theories in scientific cosmology; and (3) the rising profile
and significance of ecology and ecologists.

Changing Conception of Scientific Epistemology

The Cultural Context of Science in Berry's Thought

As indicated above, Berry belonged to a tradition that was critical of the narrow confines inflicted on culture by the notion of pure reason. Realizing the impact that a Cartesian epistemology would have on the humanities, Vico had proposed that humans concentrate on their own creation, namely history as opposed to nature, which could be known only to God. While modern scientists, in particular, did not heed this injunction, Vico's perception of the split between nature and human history, or science and the humanities, was prophetic.

Today some scientists themselves are engaged in a critique of the long-standing assumptions underlying scientific epistemology. Berry's conversations with their insights have influenced the elaboration of his proposal. While Berry would have clearly seen the significance of the scientific revolution in the history of the Christian West, his interest in science clearly came to the fore in his writings related to the works of Teilhard de Chardin. As indicated in the previous chapter, he saw in Teilhard's integration of science and religion a very significant basis for a response to the ecological crisis, despite Teilhard's own disregard for the problem. In Berry's continued involvement with Teilhard's work and with the Teilhardian associations, he was aware of the controversy over whether or not *The Phenomenon of Man* constituted real science. Scientists sympathetic to Teilhard's program were generally considered by Berry to support his own vision as well. Those considered supportive by Berry were those willing to cast doubt, at least, on the accepted premises governing the modern understanding of the nature of science.

Berry's relativizing of scientific epistemology was implied in his essay "Science and Technology for Development: The Cultural Context." His argument was that the cultural context within which Western science evolved and operated was a major influence in bringing about the deleterious effects of science that were now evident. Such themes as the ambiguity of the biblical contribution to Western civilization and the secularization of religious notions by modern culture occurred frequently in Berry's writings. One effect of interpreting the scientific enterprise as driven by mythic visions was that it undermined the idea of science as an objective activity unaffected by cultural, social or psychological factors. Furthermore, he indicated that he was familiar with changing perceptions of science within the scientific community itself. With particular reference to the scientific account of evolution, he commented that both religious and scientific personalities were beginning to see more profound meaning in the scientific enterprise.[1]

Besides highlighting the cultural context in which science developed, Berry also criticized the scientific method as it had generally been understood since the seventeenth century. The emphasis on quantitative measurement and analytical reduction of wholes to their component parts skewed the notion of reality to a mechanistic one, which virtually excluded any consideration of the design of the whole. The new perception of scientific epistemology, on the other hand, recognized the subjective nature of all knowledge. The human relationship with nature would be that of a communion of subjects rather than a subject-object dichotomy.[2]

Two scientists who began their critique from a cultural perspective were Ilya Prigogine and Isabel Stengers.[3] They (Prigogine, more frequently) were often cited by Berry as support for his sense of a changing self-perception within the scientific community.

Prigogine and Stengers' Critique of Western Science

Prigogine and Stengers identified a fundamental conviction about the world underlying classical science, namely "the *world is simple* and is governed by time-reversible fundamental laws." They further contended that "the quest of classical science" was really an "illustration of a dichotomy that runs throughout the history of Western thought."[4] In Platonic thought, only the immutable world of ideas was considered intelligible, whereas the messy affairs of humankind were merely illusion. The incorporation of this Platonic notion into the modern scientific project led to a marginalization of people, disciplines and segments of culture who saw "life, destiny, freedom and spontaneity" as central to the experience of humanity, and often to the experience of nature. In the views of some, this marginalization resulted in distortions and irrational turns in otherwise legitimate counter-movements.[5]

Referring to religious associations, Prigogine and Stengers relied on Joseph Needham's analysis that Western thought has "always oscillated between the world as an automaton and a theology in which God governs the universe." Needham called this "characteristic European schizophrenia." Prigogine and Stengers contended that these perceptions go hand in hand. "An automaton needs an external god."[6]

No doubt, such broad strokes missed many of the subtleties and nuances of Western development and of the Christian theology of

God. The point being made, however, was that a split was apparent in Western culture; and whether that split originated in the biblical tradition or in Greek philosophy or later with the scientific revolution, it was clearly recognizable in the consequent separation of science from other cultural activities. Prigogine and Stengers referred to this separation as "The Two Cultures."[7] The two cultures are obvious in the various attempts by philosophers, such as Kant, Diderot and Bergson, to reconcile them.

Classical scientists no longer recognized God as the rational ground for a connection between science and nature. Furthermore, the association of time with human history only and not with nature opened the way for a significant rift between humans and nature. Prigogine and Stengers maintained that Kant attempted to settle the division by proposing two levels of reality: the phenomenal and the noumenal. How one gained knowledge of each of these levels differed. A phenomenon taken as the object of knowledge was assumed *a priori* to obey a set of transcendental principles. "Insofar as it is perceived as a possible object of knowledge, it is the product of our mind's synthetic activity." Hence, the "scientist himself is... the source of the universal laws he discovers in nature." Knowledge of noumenal reality, however, had a transcendent or spiritual ground. This kind of knowledge supported practical moral life.[8]

From an admittedly brief and broad-stroked presentation of Kantian epistemology, Prigogine and Stengers concluded that the division between the two levels of reality and the sets of disciplines associated with these levels consolidated and perpetuated the rift between the "two cultures." Furthermore, they contended that Kantian philosophy removed science from the whole realm of questions (ethical and aesthetic) considered significant in human life and set the human subject on a course considered alien to nature. There was nothing in nature that could provide meaning or claim normativity in the human construction of history.

Similarly, Henri Bergson would accept the idea that there were two distinct kinds of knowledge: the rational knowledge of the sciences, and intuition. For Bergson, rational knowledge was incapable of understanding duration. It dealt only with the reversible, eternal laws in which time was merely "a sequence of instantaneous states." It was intuition that captured the changing circumstances that constituted real time, hence, human life.[9]

Prigogine and Stengers pointed out that a new science was emerging in which time was a significant variable. Recent discoveries in cosmology, quantum physics and the life sciences forced the notion that change was an undeniable quality of nature. Time was now a dimension to be reckoned with in the physical as well as the social sciences, notably as the microscopic and cosmological levels. The entire universe as a whole was seen to have a history. For Berry, the acceptance of time as a datum by science made a scientific story possible.

One consequence of the change in perceptions of how one does science, or knows anything at all, according to Prigogine and Stengers, was a change also in assumptions about the nature of the universe. Classical science assumed the universe to be transparent, totally available to explanation, whereas contemporary science saw it as more opaque, and hence considerably beyond human capacity to explain. Experiments based on deterministic causality have given way to a growing recognition that stochastic description is the best one can do and indeed all one can do. Hence, they asked, "Is this a defeat for the human mind?" They saw the answer to this difficult question to be related to recent discoveries about the human mind, especially the role of the unconscious.[10] Their reflections are significant, however, in that they indicated changes in the underlying assumptions of scientific epistemology. These are the changes that have opened the way for a unification of nature and human experience, and of science and the rest of culture. Berry saw this unification as necessary if the contemporary human community was to respond adequately to the ecological crisis.

Supportive Theories in Scientific Cosmology

Other contemporary scientific theories that seem to give credible if not definitive support to Berry's vision include the theory of self-organization, the anthropic principle and the Gaia theory.[11] Berry's own dialogue with these theories certainly postdates the original formulation of his proposal of a new story of the universe, but he did call upon them in more recent presentations of his proposal noting their affinities to his own thinking and setting them in the context of his own ideas.

Self-Organization Theory

Erich Jantsch's Account of Self-Organizing Systems

Traditional Western science considered states of equilibrium to be the permanent states toward which all matter and processes in the universe tended. Any activity or force was seen as intermediary between states of equilibrium. Within such a view, the task of the evolutionist was to explain the passage from one state to another by identifying the operative forces. Based on Ilya Prigogine's work on dissipative structures, however, Jantsch maintained that such a view was explanatory of a mere fraction of the evolutionary process. At best it applied to closed systems that lost energy in their transitions between states (subject to the second law of thermodynamics). For living systems, in particular, the traditional view was no longer adequate. Living systems are characterized by openness. They are embedded in complexes of other systems, where interchange of energy, matter and information is part of their nature. A living system that reaches equilibrium does not maintain an exchange with its environment and, hence, is dead.[12]

Jantsch described three systems operating at three different levels of scientific inquiry. On the first level, Newtonian (classical) dynamics holds for "ideal" movement of single particles, all else being equal; the movement is reversible, the starting force external and (as in a machine) there is no self-organization. The second level is that of thermodynamics. Here irreversibility is introduced; only average effects of movements can be estimated. This applies to isolated systems, such as formation of snowflakes, crystals and biological membranes, all of which are highly entropic structures. The third level is that of self-organization: dissipative structures and far from equilibrium conditions. This latter level includes evolving systems.

Dissipative structures arise in open systems. They are characterized by a state of fluctuation followed by the emergence of order at a critical threshold in the fluctuation factor. A simple illustration used by Jantsch was the change that occurs in water flow as one opens a water tap. In the laminar flow of water, molecules move at random. As the pressure increases when the tap is opened further, an apparently turbulent but stronger flow emerges after a certain point. The latter is the more organized state. Molecules group in powerful streams to enable an increase in flow-through. The so-called "limits of growth" are surpassed as a new and dynamic system evolves. Often what develops is one of many structures available or for which a potential for development exists.[13]

With the capacity available in large and sophisticated computer technology, Ilya Prigogine was able to describe mathematically the processes that occur when structures in open systems fluctuate, even when the variables involved are complex and numerous, as is the case for living systems. Non-linear development included phenomena such as *autopoiesis*, symmetry breaks and co-evolution.[14]

Autopoiesis (Greek: self-production) refers to the tendency of an organism or a system to act in its own interests, i.e., for its own self-preservation. Its function is first and foremost to renew itself. Its function is intrinsic to its being as in a living cell, which over time consists of totally different molecules, unlike a machine the function of which is forever determined from the outside. The chemical-biological systems or elements within autopoietic systems act to preserve themselves even in the face of major fluctuations in their environment. Sometimes this involves radical new processes, change for the sake of continuity of the metasystem, in which both the organism or system and the environment itself are changed. An example in cosmogenesis is that of the introduction of oxygen. While most of the then hydrogen-consuming organisms died, some mutated to cyanobacteria capable of using oxygen for their own benefit.

Autopoiesis considered within one organism or one system at a particular level is the confirming aspect of the universe; the organism or system ensures the continuation of its own survival. *Autopoiesis* considered at different levels and between different systems and organisms on the same level produces co-evolution; organisms or systems co-operate in their mutual survival, even if in a new form.

Symmetry breaks are thresholds. Different spatial realities are identifiable on each side of the break, and past and future enter into the composition of order. Thus, temporality is seen as constitutive of the physical universe. Prior to work by Prigogine and others in describing the order of non-equilibrium states, scientists thought of such states as temporary, totally random and chaotic disruptions in equilibrium. What was evident to Jantsch (through the work of Prigogine) was that breaks in time and space symmetry that non-equilibrium states represent are highly probable sources of "spontaneous structuration." The resulting "new ordering principle," called "order through fluctuation," describes the "evolution of a system to a totally new dynamic regime."[15]

The notion of symmetry breaks is used in the formulation of the most accepted present theories of evolution. For example, a symmetry break between the number of matter and anti-matter particles near the origin of the expanding universe is believed to have unfurled the evolutionary processes. Others include breaks between the strong nuclear and the gravitational forces, and the weak nuclear and electromagnetic forces. In a co-evolutionary system, Jantsch explained, there is an interdependence between microscopic and macroscopic structures; a change in one effects a change in the other.

The mechanism of co-evolution is the feedback link between the two sides (system and environment) as indicated in the chemico-biological research of Prigogine. It holds not just for systems at the same level, such as the predator-prey relationship, but for the "entire complex system plus environment." The universe evolves as a whole. The corollary to that is a warning sounded by Jantsch: the environments cannot be "one-sidedly adapted to a powerful system," as we have learned from human use of technology to subdue natural systems.[16]

Berry's Use of Self-Organization Theory

The incorporation of ideas such as those of Jantsch is evident in Berry's later work. As suggested above, he associated the new scientific research with elements of his proposal and of the counter-Enlightenment tradition on which he consistently drew, thereby giving more credibility to his overall vision.

In "The Cosmology of Peace," Berry spoke of the role of tension and conflict in creativity from the beginning of the universe (distinguishing it from the excess associated with possible catastrophic human-caused violence today). He wrote:

> From Heraclitus to Augustine, to Nicholas of Cusa, Hegel, and Marx, to Jung, Teilhard, and Prigogine, creativity has been associated with a disequilibrium, a tension of forces, whether this be in a physical, biological, or consciousness context.[17]

Similarly, in discussing the visionary power of dreams as the experience of "the depths of our own being and of the cosmic order," he made the following associations:

> There we discover the Platonic forms, the dreams of Brahman, the Hermetic mysteries, the divine ideas of Thomas Aquinas, the infinite worlds of Giordano Bruno, the world soul of the Cambridge Platonists, the self-organizing universe of Ilya Prigogine, the archetypal world of C. G. Jung.[18]

Berry's interpretation of cosmogenesis and of the human relationship to the natural world was primarily a mythic and/or metaphoric extension of scientific concepts and theories. He claimed that science was inherently mythic. Even terms such as energy, life, matter, universe and gravitation have metaphoric and mysterious connotations.

That the opposite, namely, the use of scientific terminology to concretize more mythic interpretations, was also the case is clear in how Berry developed the meaning of subjectivity as he applied the term to the universe. In "The Ecological Age," Berry designated the three principles on which the universe functions as differentiation, subjectivity and communion. Here he described subjectivity largely in terms of complexification as Teilhard had. Subjectivity operated along the line of development that led to the human. Berry explained:

> From the shaping of the hydrogen atom to the formation of the human brain, interior psychic unity has consistently increased along with a greater complexification of being. This capacity for interiority involves increased unity of function through ever more complex organic structures... With the nervous system and the brain comes greater freedom of control over the activity of the organism. In this manner Earth becomes ever more subject to the free interplay of self-determining forces. With subjectivity is associated the numinous quality that has traditionally been associated with every reality of the universe.[19]

In another place, he included in the articulation of the principle of subjectivity the capacity of each "articulation of the real" (each component of the universe) for "interior depth, a special quality, a mystery that expresses not only a phenomenal mode, but also an archetypal mode."[20] Similarly, he stated:

> Each particle has its own interiority. Every particle has its identifying inner structure, its inner being. In a sense, everything participates in "person," as it were, everything has its voice.[21]

In *The Universe Story*, however, the primary emphasis in the articulation of the notion of subjectivity as a principle in the evolution of the universe was on *autopoiesis* and self-organizing dynamics as found in Jantsch. In fact here the three principles were listed as characteristics of the one cosmogenetic principle, which stated that the evolution of the universe is characterized by *differentiation, autopoiesis and communion. Autopoiesis* replaced subjectivity, but it maintained a continuity with the meanings given above. Having given a definition and examples of *autopoiesis* that closely follow Jantsch, Berry and co-author Brian Swimme tie together Berry's concept of subjectivity with that of *autopoiesis* in the statement: *"Autopoiesis* points to the interior dimensions of things."[22] The explanation of *autopoiesis* here is nuanced in a slightly different direction than that given by Jantsch, however. Jantsch's definition was primarily in terms of self-preservation; Swimme and Berry's in terms of "cosmos-creating endeavour." The latter does not imply that "each thing" is intentionally creating the cosmos, but the word "endeavour" does imply that there is an intentionality at work. This is more than Jantsch actually says, but the possibility is not excluded by Jantsch.

Berry (or Berry and Swimme in the case of *The Universe Story*) was not speaking as if the mechanisms of *autopoiesis* as Prigogine and Jantsch used them were proofs that a Soul of the World existed, or that there was a vitalism operative in the universe, or that consciousness as it exists at a human level had some analogue throughout the rest of the non-human world. The suggestion was that recent scientific research indicated that some such reality is likely. Jantsch made a similar suggestion when he wrote:

> An *autopoietic* system is characterized by a certain autonomy *vis-à-vis* the environment which may be understood as a primitive form of consciousness corresponding to the level of existence of the system.[23]

Speaking of the evolution of more and more complex systems, he further observed that fluctuations in systems often produce novelty when the self-organizing dynamics of the system itself break through environmental influences. Then the "urge toward higher autonomy" can be seen and interpreted as "an urge toward higher consciousness."[24] This interpretation seemed as compelling to Jantsch as it did to Berry.

Berry insisted that the earth is "the primary self-nourishing, self-governing and self-fulfilling community."[25] This also suggests the self-organizing dynamics of the earth. Berry concluded that the most significant interpretation of modern science was that the evolutionary process was self-shaping, containing in itself its own directions and fulfilment.

Similarly, some aspects of Berry's notion of communion within the universe gained scientific support from Jantsch's notion of co-evolution. While the notion did not imply the full sense of mutual presence as Berry's sense of communion did, co-evolution did highlight the mutual nature of evolution. Organisms and systems alter each other's composition and functions as they respond to change. Living organisms on the earth adapt to atmospheric change and in turn reconstitute the atmosphere over time. Likewise, symbiotic and other co-dependent relationships in plants and animals indicate co-evolution between organisms. So in *The Universe Story*, communion was described as a web of evolving relationships.[26]

Berry's first conception of the idea of communion was as a primarily psychic, mythic sense of the presence of the human to the natural world. It is reminiscent of Vico's age of the gods, reinforced by Berry's familiarity with the spirituality of the North American Indians. He spoke of the Indians' "mystical sense" of presence to the North American continent and of their "communion with the natural world, understood with a certain distinctive awareness by tribal peoples."[27] Philosophically, the notion of communion was captured in the Platonic idea of the one and the many, that each component somehow contained the whole. Teilhard de Chardin also used the idea.[28]

In characteristic fashion, Berry combined the philosophic and religious ideas with scientific. Besides the idea of co-evolution, others such as gravitation, genetic relatedness, energetics, quantum physics[29] and ecology were all evidence of communion in the universe. Berry spoke of the law of gravitation as the "most elementary expression" of communion, much as Teilhard does in *Phenomenon of Man*. In another place, he called the universe "a single, if multiform energy event." In the following passage, he tied together the various influences:

> The unity of the entire complex of galactic systems is among the most basic experience of contemporary physics. Although this comprehensive unity of the universe was perceived by primitive peoples, affirmed by the great civilizations, explained in creation myths the world over, outlined by Plato in his *Timaeus*, and given extensive presentation by Newton in his *Principia*. Nowhere was the full genetic relatedness of the universe presented with such clarity as by the scientists of the twentieth century.[30]

Thus, modern scientific theories were interpreted within Berry's reading of the history of relevant ideas.

In the actual telling of the "new story," it was the co-evolutionary aspects of communion that were emphasized. The addition of the concept of temporality to an understanding of the physical universe was what distinguished the new cosmology and made a story possible at all. Notions of co-evolution and self-organization, which also had continuity with Berry's religio-philosophical understandings, provided scientific "how's" within the organizing framework of the story.

The Anthropic Principle

The anthropic principle deals with the relationship of the human to the evolution of the universe. It is based on scientific observations of the so-called *finely tuned* universe. This latter designation of the universe refers to the fact that according to mathematical calculations using present theories of cosmology, the universe is finely tuned to life and even to self-conscious reflective life (i.e., the human). This means that there were highly improbable occurrences in the evolution of the universe, occurrences that were necessary for the emergence of life.

One example of such improbable occurrences was the evolution of the universe against the odds of either its collapse or too rapid expansion. Scientists calculate that the probability of obtaining the required balance of the forces of expansion and contraction so that the present universe could emerge had to be a mere one part in 10^{60} in the first second of the universe. Another crucial condition for the eventual appearance of life on earth was the distance between stars; if it had been smaller by a factor of ten there would have been extremely high probability that some star would either have collided with our sun or come close enough to set up an eccentric orbit making the earth too hot or too cold to sustain life.[31] Such precise tuning for life seems to indicate an internal goal-directedness in the universe such that self-conscious life would be the appropriate outcome.

The Weak Version of the Anthropic Principle and Its Relationship to Berry's Thought

The anthropic principle has two versions, namely, the strong and the weak versions. The weak version states that the universe is observed to be finely tuned to the existence of human life because humans are doing the observing. On the widely held assumption that the evolution of carbon made the emergence of life possible, John Barrow and Frank Tipler stated this version as follows:

> The observed values of all physical and cosmological quantities are not equally probable but they take on values restricted by the requirement that there exist sites where carbon-based life can evolve and by the requirement that the Universe be old enough for it to have done so.[32]

Hence, the universe appears to be as it does because "carbon-based life" has evolved and in one form, at least, is doing the observation. Stated this way, the anthropic principle is an epistemological statement; we *know* the universe to be as it is because we are here.

Because this statement implies that human presence selects what we know of the past, it is opposed to the prevalent scientific perception that initial conditions in the universe are starting points from which subsequent developments can be predicted. It establishes an integral connection between not only the organic and non-organic world, as Barrow and Tipler indicated, but also the self-reflective knowing of humans and the non-human world. There is no known universe apart from human presence. In fact, as Barrow and Tipler say, "The universe is observing itself."[33] The weak version of the anthropic principle resembles Berry's understanding of human relationship to the rest of the universe. He described the human as the "most elaborate expression and manifestation" of the universe itself. In the human, the universe reflects on itself.[34] Thus, in Berry's thought, the universe knows itself only through a dimension of itself, namely the human. There could be no purely spectator knowledge of cosmological processes.

Berry explicitly linked his perception of human/universe intimacy with the anthropic principle. This identity of the human in relation to the universe, he said, is "expressed by physicists in terms of the anthropic principle." He further maintained that the re-establishment of this sense of human/universe intimacy was crucial in overcoming the estrangement of the whole human development from the natural processes of the universe. By such a principle, as the anthropic principle, science provided not just "a new revelatory experience," but a new sense of "intimacy with the earth."[35] The following passage, which occurs in *The Universe Story*, could be considered a reformulation of the weak anthropic principle:

> Scientific knowledge in a developmental universe is no longer understood as information about an objective world out there... The mathematically formulated designs of the scientists are not the unrestrained fantasies of humans; they refer to something real. On the other hand, the designs do not and could not exist in their mathematical formulations except for consciousness. The human is not simply noting an objective external design, but is rather intrinsically participating in the creation of these designs.[36]

This quotation followed on a previous section in which the point was made that to understand any component of the universe—carbon, for instance—one had to understand not just its past (i.e., the components from which it emerged), but its future. Carbon cannot be fully understood apart from the living beings in which it "lives and thinks."[37] Thus, in this context, we can also say with the weak anthropic principle that the design of carbon that we attempt to explain is already operative in the explainer.

An extreme interpretation of the weak anthropic principle is a relativist position that assumes that human knowledge (in this case, of the evolution of the universe) has no referent beyond human perception. This was not Berry's position. While the quotation above acknowledges the role of the observer as participant, it clearly means a participant in a process that is not merely a human construction.

The Strong Version of the Anthropic Principle and Its Relationship to Berry's Thought

Ernan McMullin pointed to the difference between the weak and strong versions of the anthropic principle when he claimed that whereas the weak version merely states that we find certain features of the universe because we expect them to be there, the stronger version would have to show that the anthropic features are explainable in terms of their connection to human presence in the universe.[38] That is precisely what the strong version attempted to do.

According to Barrow and Tipler, this version states, "The Universe must have those properties which allow life to develop within it at some stage of its history." The implications are highly speculative from a scientific viewpoint, but belong to a tradition of perennial philosophical/cosmological questions with respect to the nature of the universe. The interpretations and related traditions include:[39]

> A. There exists one possible Universe "designed" with the goal of generating and sustaining "observers."

This evokes the design arguments of the natural theologians. There are, however, twentieth-century scientists who feel that there is a natural or physical basis for this consideration.

> B. Observers are necessary in order to bring the Universe into being.
> C. An ensemble of other different universes is necessary for the existence of our Universe.

Interpretations B and C enter into scientific discussions of a "satisfactory explanation" of quantum mechanics. Since these interpretations are only remotely related to Berry's positions, they will not be discussed here. The first interpretation is, however, relevant.

A "designed" universe means that there is some metaprinciple operating in such a way that the whole of evolution must have the properties necessary for the eventual evolution of life. Thus, scientists who hold this view opt for a teleological view of evolution. The evolution of the universe from the beginning acted toward a goal, namely, self-conscious life. Freeman Dyson, for example, felt compelled toward the view that some kind of "mind" is operative in the pre-human universe. He made the following statement on the basis of contemporary observations of quantum reality:

> I think our consciousness is not just a passive epiphenomenon carried along by the chemical events in our brains, but is an active agent forcing the molecular complexes to make choices between one quantum state and another. In other words, mind is already inherent in every electron, and the processes of human consciousness differ only in degree but not in kind from the processes of choice between quantum states which we call "chance" when they are made by electrons.[40]

Hence, the strong version of the anthropic principle became the focus of a confluence of questions regarding directionality and purpose in the universe. In this version, the observed direction does not originate with the observer, but is judged to inhere in the observed itself. Here we strike on epistemological questions surrounding the relationship of subject and object and the nature of knowing itself. It is further intensified by the deconstructionist rejection of all wholistic constructions as inherent denials of freedom. These challenges face

Berry's proposal as a whole and will be considered in a later chapter. For the moment, we will deal only with the apparent coherence between his thought and the strong version of the anthropic principle.

Did Berry hold the strong version of the anthropic principle? Berry's motivation was to contribute to a solution to the ecological crisis. To that end, he attempted to inspire a comprehensive change in how humans relate to the universe and in particular to the earth. Consequently, he wanted to redirect spirituality away from an excessive and extensive preoccupation with otherworldly or totally humanistic concerns, and toward a comprehensive vision of the universe. This is the context in which he attributed characteristics such as agency, subjectivity, mind or soul to the universe (the earth in particular). He indicated the need for an understanding, such as that represented by Dyson and others, in which the universe itself has an intrinsic spiritual aspect. He saw a need for a "functional cosmology" that would provide a "mystique," "a sense of reverence" that recognized the universe as a psychic-spiritual as well as a physical reality.[41] What Berry called "extrinsic spiritual interpretations," no doubt referring to the Christian understanding that the goodness of creation inheres from the fact of a transcendent creator, were no longer adequate for grounding the kind of human-earth relationship that could meet the ecological crisis.[42] The scientists he listed allowed the possibility, at least, of a psychic-spiritual dimension inherent to the universe.

In another place, Berry spoke of the anthropic principle (obviously in its "design" interpretation) as recent scientific support for Teilhard in "identify[ing] the human story with the universe story." He noted:

> Freeman Dyson says that the more he studies the structure of the universe, the clearer it is to him that the universe must have known from the beginning that we were coming. That is in accord with all the elements of chance and natural selection that go into shaping the universe as it now is. Ultimately there is in the universe, a direction toward "complexity-centration," as Teilhard says.[43]

Following this passage, Berry briefly addressed the question of whether or not scientific theories about the self-directedness of the universe inherently excluded the idea of a divine creator. He began, "This self-organizing dimension of the universe does not mean that there is not a deeper mystery in the origin of this power within the universe." Having observed that humans cannot really "know" the universe in "any adequate way because we have nothing to compare it to," or there is no context, he then asserted that this does not necessarily exclude the notion of a divine creator, but "God is not constantly running the show... It is not a puppet show." The universe functions out of its own integrity.[44]

With respect to the strong version of the anthropic principle, then, Berry would seem to be exercising a caution. Scientific mechanisms or theories could give possible explanations of the operation of the universe. Some scientists themselves saw these as pointing to a numinous quality about the whole process. Berry's overall position, however, requires a belief or assumption that there is some numinous reality. The prior divine-self realm offers a vantage point from which to understand the contingency of the story of the universe.

The most faithful interpretation of Berry's stand with regard to the strong version of the anthropic principle, however, would seem to be that he articulated no definite position. He did not indicate clearly whether this particular expression of a psychic dimension to the universe was or was not the answer or the best expression. It belonged among the theories of other contemporary scientists, such as David Bohm, Theodosius Dobzhansky and Barbara McClintock,[45] as adding credibility and concrete scientific language to past philosophical/theological arguments. In fact, this position was explored by some of the scientists themselves.[46]

Rupert Sheldrake suggested relationships between traditional archetypal figures and scientific theories. These included (1) Darwin's personification of nature as the Great Mother, "prodigiously fertile" and "spontaneously creative," and as the Great Hindu Goddess, Kali, the "devourer of her young"; (2) Jacques Monod's principles of Chance and Necessity as unconscious emergence of the European mythic figures called Fate (Three Spinning Women), who "allot and cut the thread of life," and Lady Luck, the blindfolded goddess of Roman sculpture—Monod holds that only "Chance has a well deep enough to provide the prodigious source of creativity on which the whole of Life draws"; and (3) the unified field of what is called the superstring theory (the universe began with a primal unified field that split by symmetry breaks into the presently existing fields) and the world soul of Plotinus, as the "primal organising structure of nature."[47]

Berry's use of the strong version of the anthropic principle would be consistent with Sheldrake's synthesis. It was one more instalment, as it were, in a tradition (counter-Enlightenment) that is multi-dimensional and long-standing. As this use of the anthropic principle shows, Berry was tentative in his commitment to some of the elements of that tradition, but he nevertheless upheld its overall counter-Enlightenment vision of the nature of the universe.

The Gaia Theory

The Scientific Formulation of the Gaia Theory

The Gaia theory was largely the work of James E. Lovelock. However, some of his articles and books on the subject were written with others, notably Lynn Margulis, who collaborated on the initial research with Lovelock.[48]

Having studied the nature of the earth's atmosphere in comparison to that of neighbouring planets Venus and Mars, Lovelock concluded that life itself accounted for the difference in the earth's atmosphere. In other words, the living organisms on the planet Earth contributed to the production of an atmosphere favourable to the support of life. In an article written with Sidney Epton, he explained:

> It appeared to us that the Earth's biosphere is able to control at least the temperature of the Earth's surface and the composition of the atmosphere. Prima facie, the atmosphere looked like a contrivance put together co-operatively by the totality of living systems to carry out certain necessary control functions. This led to the formulation of the proposition that living matter, the air, the oceans, the land surface were parts of a giant system which was able to control temperature, the composition of the air and sea, the pH of the soil and so on as to be optimum for survival of the biosphere. The systems seemed to exhibit the behaviour of a single organism, even a living creature. One having such formidable powers deserved a name to match it; William Golding, the novelist, suggested Gaia— the name given by the ancient Greeks to their Earth goddess.[49]

Lovelock and those scientists who support him did not argue that the earth was a living organism in the sense that living organisms came forth from their own kind and reproduced other individuals of their species. Nor did they contend that something like "mind" or a "world soul" was operating in the observed behaviour of the earth's biosphere. They did hold, however, that the whole was more than the sum of the parts.

> The Gaia Theory explained the interaction of systems on the planet in terms of feedback and adaptive mechanisms. Using a simple model of black and white daisies (Lovelock calls the model, "Daisyworld"), Lovelock illustrated how reflection of light by white daisies and absorption by black ones worked together to control temperature for the benefit of both. It was not that species, or living systems, "thought" of each other's welfare, in some sense. Rather, what worked for one had altruistic-looking consequences for others.[50]

On interaction with scientific colleagues, Lovelock refined the theory over fifteen years. His latest formulation is as follows:

[The Gaia Theory] can now be more clearly stated as a theory that
views the evolution of the biota and of their material environment
as a single tight-coupled process, with the self-regulation of climate
and chemistry as an emergent property.[51]

Lovelock saw his own proposal as giving scientific credence to an
idea (the whole is more than the sum of the parts when it came to
explaining the universe) that others had previously put forward. He
mentioned James Hutton and Vladimir Vernadsky, adding that they
could not describe the precise mechanism involved because the computer technology needed was not available to them.

Berry's Use of the Gaia Theory

As he did with other theories, Berry also placed the Gaia theory in a
broad historical tradition. While Margulis and Lovelock first gave
scientific evidence that the earth is a living organism, the idea was
not new, he said. It belonged in the tradition that included "the soul
of the world," hermetic teachings, Cambridge Platonists, vitalists,
Bergson, Vernadsky and Teilhard, as well as the scientific work of
Edward Seuss and Eduard LeRoy, both of whom influenced Teilhard
de Chardin. Of the twofold source of the "sense of the earth as a
living planet," the scientific study was more needed today, however,
"for the planet is severely affected" and "precisely as a living planet...
needs attention."[52]

On the other hand, Berry also claimed that the biological notions of Gaia must be understood within a visionary, cosmological
and mythic perspective. In a manner consistent throughout his work,
he insisted, "We need to think of the planet as a single, unique,
articulated subject to be understood in a story both scientific and
mythic."[53] He explained what he himself meant by speaking of the
earth as a living planet in terms that included, but went beyond,
Lovelock's theory:

> This term, in my own understanding, is used, neither literally nor
> simply metaphorically, but as analogy, somewhat similar in its
> structure to the analogy expressed when we say that we "see," an
> expression used primarily of physical sight but also used of intellec-
> tual understanding. A proportional relationship is expressed... The
> common quality is that of subjective presence of one form to
> another as other. In this experience, the identity of each is en-
> hanced, not diminished.[54]

The use of metaphor and analogy in speaking of the earth is not "a
diminishment," Berry explained, but an enhancement; "the more
primordial realities can be spoken of only in some symbolic manner."

He linked the notion to that of the "Earth as Universal Mother," "giving birth to all living forms upon the Earth."[55]

In elaborating on the significance of the Gaia theory, Berry summarized the way in which recent scientific theories and discoveries entered into his own vision. The benefit of the Gaia theory was the effort it represented to achieve a larger pattern of interpretation than is the common focus of scientists. He insists, however, that biological and chemical studies alone are not adequate to an understanding of the "superb achievement" of the emergence of the earth. The remainder of his discussion delineated in succession elements of the larger context to which he was referring: physics and cosmology, the psychic mode of human being and the mystical implications of what science does and discovers. Scientific inquiry has as its purpose "mystical communion," he said, despite the fact that scientists might well object to this understanding of their endeavours.[56]

The discussion of the Gaia theory provided an occasion for Berry to summarize very succinctly the role that science in general played in his own program. He did not propose to work within established and acceptable (to scientists generally) scientific norms. Science was for him a cultural and spiritual activity. It revealed what humans had in a sense known all along in the primal expressions and the archetypal spiritual images that survived in the unconscious. Scientific knowledge may not have been based on the same kind of experience as that of the ancients, but the interpretations bore a similarity. In his words:

> [O]ur scientific inquiry... establishes a basis for a new type of religious experience differentiated from, but profoundly related to, the religious-spiritual experience of the early shamanic period of human history.[57]

With obvious reference to Paul Ricoeur's "second naiveté," he clarified further: "We experience the universe with the delight of our post-critical naiveté."[58] Thus, Berry saw contemporary scientific activity to be the creation of a new mythic structure that could help redirect human attitudes and actions toward a more congenial human-earth relationship.

Ecology and Natural History

Berry preferred to speak of an ecological crisis rather than an environmental crisis. This reflects a particular philosophical stance. The science of ecology is the study of the interrelationships of living systems. Thinking of the human as a component within those systems allows one to focus on preserving an integral biosphere, all members of which have intrinsic value. Environmentalism, on the other hand, is fundamentally based on the same assumptions that were responsible for the ecological crisis, namely, a subject-object relationship between humans and the earth and the consequent instrumentalization of the earth. "The environmentalists," Berry said, "are basically anthropocentric; the ecologist is clearly biocentric in his/her approach." Berry also added, however: "I myself avoid somewhat the word 'ecology' because it is kind of a hard word and it does not have the proper warmth or proper resonance that a person might wish. I frequently use the term, the life community, for what a person might at times call ecology, or the environmental issue."[59]

The phrase "proper warmth or proper resonance" is indicative of Berry's own role as communicator and motivator, for whom it was important to appeal to the affect of his audience. In terms of influence on his thought, however, it may also have arisen from the natural history tradition and the naturalist literary genre. In his own words, the role of the poet and the natural history essayist was "the evocation of a mystique."[60]

The Influence of the Natural History Tradition

Berry frequently referred to a whole repertoire of nature writers, both past and contemporary. Those he frequently mentioned included John Muir, Henry Thoreau, Loren Eiseley, Wendell Berry, Gilbert White, Aldo Leopold, Lewis Thomas, Edwin May Teale, Rachel Carson, Annie Dillard, Leo Marx and E.O. Wilson. While some of these, such as Wilson, Teale and Carson, were professional scientists, they produced works designed for a wider audience and followed a certain literary style that was designated as literary naturalist; scientific facts and figures pepper their more aesthetic descriptions of nature.

Berry considered the naturalists of the late eighteenth and the nineteenth centuries as constituting (like the romantics, as some of the naturalists themselves were) a counterforce to the capitalist-industrial development and what he also called, "a managerial ethos." Their role, however, was slightly different as Berry indicated:

> These were men with scientific capacity for observation, but who also saw the total dynamics of the natural world and the manner in which the earth functioned as a single interacting organism... That they were creating a new religious mood can be seen particularly in John Muir whose writings reflect far less studied emotion or romantic aesthetics than the writings of Emerson but a more thorough science and a more deeply religious feeling.[61]

In another essay, he commented:

> Natural History is more observational and more intimate with natural forms, their spontaneous activities and their interrelations, than philosophical and cosmological studies...[62]

The difference Berry observed between the natural historians and the romantics is significant in understanding certain aspects of Berry's work. While the natural historians of recent centuries maintain a kind of alternative tradition to mainline exploitative attitudes, they can also be seen as a continuance of a classical biological method, which preceded efforts to explain biological realities primarily in terms of chemistry or physics.[63] A recent example was the change in genetics from the study of heredity in whole organisms to the focus on the chemistry of chromosomes and genes in themselves. Berry indicated his appreciation for the classical approach in his praise of the work of Barbara McClintock. What was needed, he said, was more of her "feeling for the organism"; a religious and imaginative sensitivity to other creatures.[64] His own writing reflected this sensitivity in passages such as the following in which he spoke of the American continent at the time of its discovery by Europeans:

> Never was the region more brilliant in its color, in the exuberance of its life expression, in the grandeur of its tall white pines, in its beaver population, in the abundance of its oysters and clams, in its shad and tomcod and striped bass. Never were the woodlands more resonant with their songbirds, never were the skies more often witness to the peregrine falcon, the red-tailed hawks, and the bald eagles.[65]

The natural historians, Berry said, brought to their subject "the literary skill and interpretative depth" that expressed appropriately "our full entrancement with various natural phenomena."[66] Berry himself preferred the natural history essay style, indicating his desire to contribute to this tradition as well as to learn from it. All of Berry's works are essays with the exception of *The Universe Story*.[67]

The Influence of Ecologists

Ecologists influenced Berry's work in two obvious ways: (1) their scientific investigations of particular instances of the ecological crisis, such as extinction of species, rain-forest destruction, soil depletion and various forms of pollution, offered support to Berry's ideas, and (2) their experimentation with alternative technologies, processes and lifestyles offered strategies for the implementation of Berry's vision. Berry includes under the term "ecologists" both professional scientists and those who work and write on behalf of ecological responsibility. Among those most frequently mentioned are Rachel Carson, Paul Erlich, Jay Forrester, Edward Hyams, Amory Lovins and Norman Myers.[68]

Supportive Evidence for Berry's Ideas

The first written evidence of Berry's concern for the ecological problem is found in his essay "Building the Earth," written in 1969. While the ecological crisis was not the primary focus of his writing at that time, he included the issue as part of the "human breakup" that was occurring in the modern world.[69] Berry attributed a large role in the general awakening of society to the ecological crisis to Rachel Carson's publication of *Silent Spring*. He wrote of her influence:

> Not until Rachel Carson shocked the world, in the 1960's with her presentation of the disasters impending in the immediate future was there any thorough alarm at the consequences of this entrancement [with technological progress].

and

> Suddenly we awaken to the devastation that has resulted from the entire modern process. A thousand pages would be needed to recount what has happened. It can best be summarized by the title of Rachel Carson's book, *Silent Spring*...[70]

He also called her an "archetypal figure," and the "matriarch" of the ecological movement.[71]

As noted above, Berry's primary interest turned to ecology at the end of the 1960's. Gradually from within a vision of the future, one that encompassed a critique of modern culture and spoke of the present as an emerging new age, Berry refocused his entire intellectual expertise on the ecological crisis. The ecologists of the 1960's, especially Rachel Carson, and the widespread reaction to the publication of *Silent Spring*, seem to have provided the stimulus. Likewise, the continual accumulation of evidence by ecologists since that time supported the sense of urgency that motivated Berry's program. Behind Berry's statements regarding the extent of the crisis is the evidence gleaned from such publications as *Worldwatch Papers*, monthly reports on ecological issues and the *Red Data Books* providing information on animals and plants on the brink of extinction.[72]

Strategies for Implementation of Berry's Vision

Berry's primary response to the ecological crisis was the enunciation of a vision, which will be further explicated below. Within that vision, however, he did indicate strategies for its implementation. He found these strategies, notably bioregionalism, among contemporary experiments with alternative lifestyles and methods of dealing with the natural world (organic farming, solar technologies). He saw in such contributions antidotes to the pathology of a culture that badly distorted human-earth relations. They were steps on the road to recovery.

Berry identified three approaches taken by people and groups within the ecological or environmental movement: "the confrontational approach, the transformational approach, and the creative approach, the marginal creative." He listed Earth-first and Greenpeace among confrontational groups. Transformational referred to those who tried to work for change within the existing political and social structures. The creative people were "creating the new language, bringing the story into its effective expression... people like John and Nancy Todd, Wes Jackson in agriculture, Rodale in the field of food and medicine... Hazel Henderson."[73]

While he advocated "a certain tolerance across the board," Berry generally referred to those whom he would designate creative when he gave practical examples of how his own program could be integrated. The effort to which he gave the most attention was the bioregional movement. Berry wrote two complete essays on this movement, thus giving an indication of how he viewed the implementation of his own proposal. He does not identify the bioregional movement alone with that implementation, however.[74]

The contemporary notion of bioregionalism was developed by Kirkpatrick Sale and depended largely on Edward Schumacher's work on appropriate technologies. Sale defined bioregionalism as follows:

> It [the word "bioregional"] comes from *bio*, the Greek word for forms of life... and *regio*, Latin for territory to be ruled. Together they mean a life-territory, a place defined by its life forms, its topography and its biota, rather than by human dictates; a region governed by nature, not by legislature.[75]

Bioregionalism attempted to define natural borders on planet Earth. This was in contrast to political borders that separate towns, cities, counties, states, countries. Hence, a bioregion referred to a desert, wetland, marsh, valley or mountain. The idea was to teach people to live consciously within their own bioregion. That meant developing a sustainable agriculture, using the appropriate technologies and becoming as self-sufficient as possible.

Sale listed four basic ideas behind the bioregional movement: knowing the land and its resources, learning both the human and natural history of the region, development within ecological restraints and developing individual potential within the community. The focus was to unite people locally or to save the earth one place at a time. The key notion was also referred to as "reinhabiting," a concept that rested on the notion that the present human habitation of the earth was dysfunctional and must be reconstituted. In support of bioregions, Berry wrote:

> The solution is simply for us as humans to join the earth community as participating members, to foster the progress and prosperity of the bioregional communities to which we belong.[76]

This idea resonated with another of Berry's, that of "reinventing the human at the species level." By this he meant the reconstitution of "a viable mode of human functioning within the context of a viable planetary process." Such a reconstitution, he maintained, required a renovation of all human systems: law, education, economics, medicine and even gender and language. Reconstitution was necessary because of the "deep pathology" by which the present human culture and society related to the earth.[77] In movements like bioregionalism, Berry saw an effort to overcome this pathology. He continued to define his own role as setting the context for the understanding and activity involved in such ecological efforts. Berry set a context for bioregionalism within the self-organizing dynamics of the universe. As is the case for the earth in total, so each bioregion is "self-propagating, self-nourishing, self-educating, self-governing, self-healing, and self-fulfilling." These functions require corresponding human awareness and activity. Self-propagation "requires that we recognize the rights of each species to its habitat," for example.[78]

Bioregionalism sought to establish the norm that humans, insofar as possible, ought to live on the food produced in their own bioregion. Berry agreed and set the discussion within the context of the self-nourishing capability of the earth, or the earth's economy. Humans ought to be constrained by that economy, which operates with a minimum of entropy, no sterile or toxic waste and no non-decomposing litter, he maintained.[79]

Self-education, in Berry's terms, requires humans to learn from the earth how to survive. "The earth, and each of its bioregions, has performed unnumbered billions of experiments in designing the existing life systems," Berry wrote.[80] Through the experiences of evolution, the earth learned which patterns work and which don't. This was the instruction available to humans. This particular way of speaking of bioregions was Berry's own. It was based on the work of scientists, such as Rupert Sheldrake, who contended that laws of nature evolved with the universe and were more akin to habits than determinative eternal principles.[81]

Self-governance referred to an interior bonding, or "integral functional order" within each bioregion. The community was such that its members were enabled to achieve the "fullness of life expression proper to each." Rituals, for example, were seen as celebrations of the entire community (non-human and human). Furthermore, governments ought to represent the needs and rights of all members, as well. Berry advocated biocracy over democracy, indicating this change of emphasis from the human community to the whole life community.[82]

Self-fulfilling activities meant the unique expression that each member of a bioregion brought to the community. "Flowering fields... great oak trees... flight of the sparrow... surfacing whales" are expressions, he said, of the "numinous mystery of the universe." Human expression is self-conscious and embodied in ritual and art. This latter contextual comment on bioregions reflected Berry's idea that the quality of human culture was largely dependent on the richness and variety of the earth.

As indicated above, concrete attempts at alternative lifestyles, such as bioregionalism, give some indication of the kind of change that, in Berry's own view, would embody his vision. In his interpretation of bioregionalism, he called for a radical refocusing of many social and political institutions as he did elsewhere. However, even in these instances, his penchant was for defining the cultural context in which change must take place. It is noteworthy that after calling for change in many institutions, he asserted that education and religion have the crucial responsibility in bringing about change. He explained:

> These professions present themselves as guiding our sense of reality and value at its ultimate level of significance. They provide our life interpretation. Education and religion, especially, should awaken in the young an awareness of the world in which we live, how it functions, how the human fits into the larger community of life, the role which the human fulfills in the story of the universe... Education and religion should communicate some guidance concerning the future.[83]

Thus, all Berry's suggestions for dealing with the ecological crisis returned to the cultural level. For he continued, "Education and religion need to ground themselves in the story of the universe." This was the overall sustaining context for all efforts by ecologists. The challenge that had to be met by Berry's assertion of the power of his cultural solution was that of effecting change in socio-economic institutions and activities. Since he saw the roots of the crisis to be cultural, then an intervention that would overturn the roots of the crisis would also effect the necessary reform in all other aspects of modern life.

Notes

1.   Berry, "Science and Technology for Development: The Cultural Context," paper presented at UN Conference, Vienna, Austria, 1979, *Riverdale Papers on the Earth Community*, 11. See also "The American College in the Ecological Age," *Religion and Intellectual Life*, 11.

2.   Berry, "The Gaia Theory: Its Religious Implications," *ARC: The Journal of the Faculty of Religious Studies, McGill University* 22 (1994): 10. Previous version presented at the conference, "Earth Alive: The Gaia View of Earth, Nature and Humanities," The Isthmus Institute, Dallas, TX, April 1990.

3.   Ilya Prigogine and Isabel Stengers, *Order Out of Chaos: Man's New Dialogue with Nature* (Toronto, New York, London, Sydney: Bantam Books, 1984).

4.   Ibid., 7. Italics theirs.

5.   P. Forman, "Weimar Culture, Causality and Quantum Theory, 1918-1927; Adaptation by German Physicists and Mathematicians to a Hostile Intellectual Environment," Historical Studies in the Physical Sciences, vol. 3 (1971), 1-115. Cited by Prigogine and Stengers, *Order Out of Chaos*, 6.

6.   Prigogine and Stengers, *Order Out of Chaos*, 7. Reference to Joseph Needham and C.A. Ronan, *A Shorter Science and Civilization in China*, vol. 1 (Cambridge: Cambridge University Press, 1978), 170.

7.   Ibid., 79-86. Cf. C.P. Snow, *The Two Cultures and the Scientific Revolution*. The Rede Lecture, 1959 (New York: Cambridge University Press, 1959), and Wilhelm Dilthey's *Pattern and Meaning in History: Thoughts on History and Society*, ed. and intro. by H.P. Rickman (New York: Harper and Row, Publishers, Inc., 1962), 1st ed., 68-74.

8.   Ibid., 86-87, referring to Kant, *Critique of Pure Reason* [trans. Norman Kemp Smith (New York: St. Martin's Press, 1965)].

9.   Ibid., 89-93, referring to Bergson, *La pensée et le mouvant en œuvre* (Paris: Éditions du Centenaire, PUF, 1970); trans. *The Creative Mind*, trans. by Mabelle L. Andison (Totowa, NJ: Littlefield, Adams, 1975).

10.   Ibid., 311-312.

11.   Cf. Erich Jantsch, *The Self-Organizing Universe* (Oxford, New York, Toronto, Sydney, Paris, Frankfurt: Pergamon Press, 1980); John D. Barrow and Frank J. Tipler, *The Anthropic Cosmological Principle* (New York: Oxford University Press, 1986; J.E. Lovelock, *Gaia: A New Look at Life on Earth* (New York: Oxford University Press, 1979).

12.   Jantsch, *Self-Organizing Universe*, 5-7, 33.

13.   Ibid., 21-35.

14.   Ibid., 14, 33, 41, 83, 110-115.

15.   Ibid., 28.

16.   Ibid., 81-85.

17.   Berry, *The Dream of the Earth*, 217.

18.   Ibid., 197.

19.   Ibid., 45.

20.   Ibid., 107.

21.   Berry, *Befriending the Earth*, 15.

22.   Swimme and Berry, *The Universe Story*, 71-75.

23.   Jantsch, *Self-Organizing Universe*, 10.

24.   Ibid., 142.

25.   Berry, *The Dream of the Earth*, 88, 107.

26.   Swimme and Berry, *The Universe Story*, 77-78.

27.   Berry, *The Dream of the Earth*, 189.

28.   Cf. Donald Gray, *The One and the Many* (New York: Herder and Herder, 1969).

29.   See Swimme and Berry, *The Universe Story*, 77. "Alienation for a particle is a theoretical impossibility."

30.   Berry, *The Dream of the Earth*, 46-47, 106-107.

31.   Cf. Christopher Mooney, "The Anthropic Principle in Cosmology and Theology," in *Horizons* 21,1 (Spring 1994), 105-129.

32.   Barrow and Tipler, *The Anthropic Cosmological Principle* (Oxford, UK: Clarendon Press and Toronto: Oxford University Press, 1986), 16.

33.   Ibid., 4. Cf. Mooney, "The Anthropic Principle."

34.   Berry, "The Viable Human," *Revision* (Jan. 1987): 5.

35.   Berry, *The Dream of the Earth*, 16-18.

36.   Swimme and Berry, *The Universe Story*, 40.

37.   Ibid., 16-17.

38.   Ernan McMullin, "How Should Cosmology Relate to Theology?" in *The Sciences and Theology in the Twentieth Century*, ed. by Arthur Peacocke (Notre Dame, IN: University of Notre Dame Press, 1981), 43-44.

39.   Barrow and Tipler, *The Anthropic Cosmological Principle*, 21-23.

40.   Freeman Dyson, *Disturbing the Universe* (New York: Harper and Row, Publishers, Inc., 1979), 249.

41.   Berry, *The Dream of the Earth*, 67.

42.   Cf. Berry, *Befriending the Earth*, 24. Cf. Vine Deloria, *God Is Red* (New York: Delta Publishing, 1973), 91-107.

43.   Ibid.

44.   Ibid., 24-25.

45.   Berry, "Individualism and Wholism in the Chinese Tradition," 24; *The Dream of the Earth*, 199; and *Befriending the Earth*, 98. Works by or about the scientists mentioned are listed in the bibliography. (See Evelyn Fox Keller's book about McClintock, *A Feeling for the Organism*.)

46.   Barrow and Tipler, *The Anthropic Cosmological Principle*, ch. 2 and 3; Paul Davies, *The Mind of God* (New York: Simon and Schuster, 1992), esp. ch. 2 and 7; Dyson, *Disturbing the Universe*, 245-253 and passim; Rupert Sheldrake, "Is the Universe Alive?" in *The Teilhard Review* 25,1 (Spring 1990).

47.   Sheldrake, "Is the Universe Alive?" 20-22.

48.   J.E. Lovelock, "Gaia," in *Gaia 2: Emergence*, ed. by William Irwin Thompson (Hudson, New York: Lindisfarne Press, 1991), 30. Reference is to L. Margulis and J.E. Lovelock, "Biological Modulation of the Earth's Atmosphere," *Icarus* 21 (1974): 471-489.

49.   J.E. Lovelock and Sidney Epton, "The Quest for Gaia," *New Science* 65 (1975): 304.

50.   Lovelock, "Gaia," 33-35. The model is more complex than what is simply stated here. Time and several generations of daisies are required to produce the desired

effect. See J.E. Lovelock, *The Ages of Gaia* (New York and London: W.W. Norton & Co., 1988), 34-39.

51.   Lovelock, "Gaia," 30.

52.   Berry, "Human Presence," *The Dream of the Earth*, 22.

53.   Berry, "The Gaia Theory," 18-19.

54.   Ibid., 14-15.

55.   Ibid., 15.

56.   Ibid., 17, 19. See also Berry, *The Dream of the Earth*, 18.

57.   Berry, "The Gaia Theory," 18.

58.   See original version of the paper, "The Gaia Theory," 20. While the phrase "post-critical naivete" is omitted from the published version, the meaning is clearly the same.

59.   Berry, speaking at the Holy Cross Centre Colloquium, Port Burwell, Ontario. Audiotape 2, Earth Communications, Laurel, MD.

60.   Berry, *The Dream of the Earth*, 33.

61.   Berry, *Management: The Managerial Ethos and the Future of Planet Earth*, 5-6.

62.   Berry, *Teilhard in the Ecological Age*, 9.

63.   Cf. Berry, 10-11. Those mentioned include John Ray, *Methodus Plantarum Nova*, 1682) and Georges Louis LeClerc de Buffon (*Natural History*, 44 vols., 1749-1804) and Carolus Linnaeus (*The Oeconomy of Nature*, 1749).

64.   Berry, *Befriending the Earth*, 98. Reference to Evelyn Fox Keller, *A Feeling for the Organism: The Life and Work of Barbara McClintock*, esp. 188-189.

65.   Berry, *The Dream of the Earth*, 173.

66.   Berry, "Introduction," in Martha Heyneman, *The Breathing Cathedral: Feeling Our Way into a Living Cosmos*, 1.

67.   Cf. *Management*, 6. On several occasions, in conversation with the author, Berry expressed his desire to continue this tradition.

68.   Cf. Berry, *The Dream of the Earth*, 73, 106, 204 and 207; "The Elderly," 1980, 7; "Teilhard in the Ecological Age," 29; "Perspectives on Creativity," 17; "Contemporary Spirituality: Seminar Guide," 19; "Wonderworld as Wasteworld: The Earth in Deficit," in *Cross Currents* 35 (Winter 1985-1986), 418.

69.   Berry, "Building the Earth," *Riverdale Papers I*, 4.

70.   Berry, *The Dream of the Earth*, 38, 205.

71.   Berry, "Holy Cross Centre Colloquium," 1986, Audiotape 1.

72.   Cf. Berry, "Bibliographies," Riverdale Center, unpublished.

73.   Berry, " Holy Cross Centre Colloquium," 1986, Audiotape 1. See also *Thomas Berry and the New Cosmology*, 18, 20-21.

74.   Ibid.; Berry, *The Dream of the Earth*, 163-170.

75.   Kirkpatrick Sale, *Dwellers in the Land: The Bioregional Vision* (San Francisco: Sierra Club Books, 1985), 336. For the purpose of the discussion here, see Sale, "Bioregionalism—A Sense of Place," in *The Nation* 241 (Oct. 12, 1985): 326-33; adapted from *Dwellers in the Land*. For reference to previous bioregional movements, see Anna Bramwell, *Ecology in the 20th Century*, 89.

76.   Berry, *The Dream of the Earth*, 164, 166.

74.   Berry, *Reinventing the Human*, produced by Friends of Creation Spirituality, 45 min., videocassette. See also Berry, "The Viable Human," 10.

78.   Berry, "The Viable Human," 7, and *The Dream of the Earth*, 165-166.

79.   Cf. Sale, "How to Bioregion," *The Nation* 252 (Sept. 27, 1986): 269.

80.   Berry, *The Dream of the Earth*, 167.

81.   Sheldrake, "Is the Universe Alive?" 15-24.

82.   Berry, *The Dream of the Earth*, 167-168.

83.   Ibid., 101.

CHAPTER FIVE

BERRY'S PROPOSAL FOR THE ECOLOGICAL CRISIS

Introduction

While most of the relevant categories of Bernard Lonergan's thought will be employed in more detail below, some comments about his distinction between two language categories (description and explanation) shed initial light on the nature of Berry's proposal. Succinctly stated, description deals with things as they relate to us; explanation with things as they relate to each other.[1] So, for instance, to speak of a wheel as round is to *describe* the wheel as we see or feel it; that is how the wheel relates to us. On the other hand, to speak of wheels in terms of the relationship of radius to circumference in a mathematical formula is to *explain* the roundness of wheels. Generally, accounts of human experience, whether UFO sightings, love at first sight, witnessing a crime or simply tasting good food, are descriptive. Explanation, when required, may sound quite unlike the description of any of these experiences. All the mystery, fear or excitement associated with the UFO may dissipate in the scientific language explaining something like a meteor shower. An account of the chemistry of taste is not going to sell cookbooks; rather it functions for the curious or more technical-minded chef to explain the relationship between the taste buds and the composition of the food. The two kinds of languages and their functions are quite different.

Description and explanation are related to each other, however, in both genetic and complementary fashion. Explanation grows out of description, but description does not dissolve. On the one hand, the descriptive accounts of witnesses to a crime give way to the explanation of what actually happened; on the other, the descriptive accounts remain not only as integral elements of the explanation, but also as independent and vitally important controls or checks on the explanatory accounts put forward. A story is a descriptive account; it may often be given a theoretic explanation. Theology is a case in which theoretic language arises from the stories of the Bible. The explanation, however, is very unlikely to accomplish what the story accomplishes in terms of motivation, inspiration or even changing lives. Conversely, a descriptive language may be employed to teach or communicate abstract concepts that appear initially in explanatory language. Thus, the different languages maintain an integrity of their own. To paraphrase Lonergan, explanation abstracts from data, which describes experience. Description also mediates explanation into the ordinary, common-sense world.

Another way of understanding the relationship of description and experience is to think in terms of questions. I may describe an experience of a celestial event in terms of lights, shapes, duration and effect on me. I say what I saw, heard and felt. I then ask what exactly it was I saw and why it appeared in that way. The answers are explanation.

Berry's "new story," his proposal for dealing with the ecological crisis, is primarily descriptive. It is a story of the experience of the universe itself, of our new scientific knowledge of the universe and of how the phenomenal facts of the evolution of the universe relate to us, particularly within the horizon of the ecological crisis. The task we are attempting is to *explain* Berry's descriptive account. Since Lonergan derived categories for the explanation of experience, his categories will be used in that task. For the present, however, we will examine Berry's proposal seeking the meaning he intended by his terms and statements. A sentence of Lonergan, in which he related description to explanation, is especially pertinent here. He wrote:

> The two [description and explanation] are not independent, for they deal with the same things and, as we have seen, description supplies, as it were, the tweezers by which we hold together things while explanations are being discovered or verified, applied or revised.[2]

Thus, we will expect Berry's descriptive account to give rise to questions for explanation. We will not expect that Berry usually addressed them in explanatory categories. Such was not his intention. He did, however, call on the academic disciplines to do the theoretical work needed to explain and appropriate his proposal.[3] Such explanations are not meant to replace the language and effect of Berry's "new story" itself; rather, they assist in its appropriation by academic disciplines, especially by theology.

As is the case with Lonergan's own account of description and explanation, the significance of these designations will develop and deepen as we proceed to ask further and further questions of Berry's "new story." The chapters following will return to the notions of description and explanation as the nature of Berry's work is further examined.

Berry's proposal can be summarized by his assertion that everything is a question of story and his further query, how is this so. His own exploration took him through (1) his critique of the modern age and (2) his proposal for recovery.[4] In his exploration he frequently employed the terms "myth," "story" and "cosmology"; an examination of what he actually meant by these is informative in seeking to understand his critique and proposal.

"Myth," "Story" and "Cosmology" in Berry's Work

"Myth" is an ambiguous term in contemporary culture, often having negative connotations. While Berry did see how myth functioned negatively in society, his view was that myth in its integral and original forms played an essentially positive role. He did not explicitly define myth, but his use of the term relied on the understanding of Carl Jung and Mircea Eliade.[5] Thus, myth was a carrier of the archetypal symbols identified by Jung. It was also a paradigmatic model in the Eliadean sense.

According to these understandings, myth and symbol are the means by which the unconscious comes to expression. Myths function in life by providing intelligibility and value to human affairs. They model life in the sacred realm, the realm of being. Humans participate in that realm of being through ritual enactment of mythic narratives. For the religious or primal person (sometimes connected to Vico's age of the gods),[6] every human activity was ritualized by imitation of sacred actions or words and thus consecrated and given meaning. Myth is a forceful ensurer of a system of meanings and values; in the Eliadean sense it conveys apodictic truth.

In Berry's usage, then, myth was distinguished by its origin in the numinous dimension of the universe, its apprehension in the human psyche and its function as existential meaning-giver and model for human activity. Myths had a fixed or stationary quality. They expressed an organic bondedness to place, to sacred reality or to the universe in general.[7] Traditionally they functioned in a universe in a spatial mode of consciousness. Even myths that embodied archetypal journeys referred to an interior journey into the depths of consciousness or an external pilgrimage within a fixed universe.

It was the timeless quality of myth that distinguished it from "story." While stories might have mythic aspects, they belonged to the historical mode of consciousness. They referred to the narrative quality of human existence.[8] Thus, the biblical Christian tradition presented a story, which admittedly also carried mythic themes, such as journey, paradise and hero-saviour. Furthermore, a story might function as a myth in terms of providing meanings and values for living.

In Berry's sense, however, it was the mythic aspects of the story that gave the meanings and values it carried power, depth and even truth and normativity. The whole scientific venture was seen to have mythic roots. The power by which it was driven was associated with the same sense of communion that primal peoples experienced in relationship to the universe.[9] It was necessary, Berry maintained, that we see the "numinous quality" and the "deeper psychic powers" associated with the empirical account of the universe. The construal of the events that made up the story of the universe relied on the recognition of these mythic dimensions.[10] What differentiated story from myth, then, was the introduction of a sense of historical realism, whereby the narrative was constituted by concrete events originating in time. This was in contrast to the myth that originated with and elaborated on invariant and recurring archetypal structures.

The story that interested Berry was the story that carried a cosmology. He used the term "cosmology" to refer to an understanding of the structure of the universe. Inherent in that understanding was a set of meanings and values especially with regard to the place of the human in the universe. Hence, *The Universe Story* contends, "Traditionally, the cosmological enterprise aimed at an understanding of the universe and the role of the human in the universe."[11] Since different cosmologies have engendered different ways of relating human society to the physical cosmos, the actual cosmology one held was crucial. Particular cosmologies supported particular sets of meanings and values.[12]

The modern scientific account of cosmology, understood as a process or sequence of transformations of the physical universe, was seen as an extension of human history. Human history was just one phase in the sequence that began with what scientists called the Big Bang. Humans carried a unique role; they were that species in whom the universe came to self-consciousness. What the human species did mattered in terms of whether or not the universe would continue, especially as it included the biosphere on planet Earth. Wonder, awe, contingency, fragility, beauty and a certain quality of self-determination characterized this cosmology and carried implications for the present and future construction of human society. Hence, the cosmology functioned as meaning-giver and driver of action. More precisely, Berry argued that this cosmology *ought* to function in this way. Hence, his warning that "all human professions, institutions and activities must be integral with the earth as primary self-nourishing, self-governing and self-fulfilling community."[13]

Myth, story and cosmology, then, were interrelated. While the story of the universe was the history of the universe in that it was the relating of concrete events in real historical time, it was also an expression of that same numinous quality of the universe that was present to the psyche of humankind for ages and expressed in the traditional myths. The process (scientific, rational) by which the present story was discovered was very different from the process to which the ancients referred in symbol and myth. Yet, Berry said, at least for those scientists who recognized the full significance of what they were doing, there was an experience akin to what the ancients expressed. Furthermore, as the ancient myths carried a cosmology by which peoples understood and worked out their role in the universe, so the "new story" carried a cosmology that could and should do the same. It was a *new* cosmology, however, because precisely what differentiated the story from the ancient myths, namely history, was now understood as integral to cosmology.

According to Berry, the ecological crisis resulted from the breakdown in this relationship between myth, story and cosmology. Cosmology became the domain of science and lost its sense of meaningfulness for human life. The story by which Western humans attempted to live, namely the Christian story, lost its relevance and contributed to a false sense of relationship to the natural world. Myth revealed itself only in the distorted activities and beliefs of the industrial-consumer society of the West with its commitment to "progress" and a secularized eschatological vision of history.

Critique of the Modern Age

While Berry conceded that humans have always had an ambiguous relationship with the natural world and have caused environmental havoc from very early times, he maintained that no peoples devastated the earth to such critical dimensions as has the West in the modern era. What was it about Western culture in particular that caused the increasing rift in the human-earth relationship? This was the question that moved Berry's hermeneutic of Western traditions.

Berry's critique was the now familiar uncovering of the innocence of modernity, but within the horizon of the ecological crisis. It must be emphasized from the beginning that his particular critique of modernity was a cultural one. While he did deal with the economic and political realm, even there he concentrated on the underlying myths and attitudes that accounted for the concrete way in which economic and political institutions evolved and operated. While economic structures may be an immediate problem, the source of all economic activity is the "religious cultural context," he said.[14] From that perspective, he critiqued the modern age on three fronts: (1) the mythic distortions at the base of modern society; (2) the cosmological story that informed Western society in the pre-modern period; and (3) the inherent nature of the human species as cultural.

Mythic Distortions

Despite modernity's priding itself on a sense of realism, Berry maintained that it derived its energy from implicit mythic instincts present in the psyche of Western humanity. Thus, modern advertising launched its "seductive appeal to the deepest and most sacred archetypal forces of the individual"; the corporate enterprise created a "mystique," "absorbing all the mythic and cultural language and even the attitudes and emotions formerly associated with our religious and humanist traditions"; and the whole technological-industrial society was "entranced with the progress myth."

According to Berry, this mythic dimension of the modern world created a kind of blindness to the deterioration of the natural systems of the planet and a deep resistance to any substantial change. The myth of progress was "so entrancing for the modern world that no doubt of its validity is permitted." In Berry's estimation, the subversion of myth from its religious context to a secular one was a powerful influence in the alienation of the human from the rest of the natural world. The roots of this distortion were to be found in the pre-modern cosmological story, that is, in the Christian story within which the West was formed.[15]

Cosmological Story of the Pre-Modern Period

In Western civilization, Berry observed, the reigning cosmology up until about the fifteenth century was a combination of Greek speculation and observation regarding the nature of the universe and Christian beliefs about creation, God and salvation.[16] The cosmology was carried in a story.

The traditional story came about as a result of the overriding influence of Christianity, with its sense of irreversible historical time, over the Ptolemaic cosmology. Berry noted how this traditional story successfully functioned in history. Augustine used it to confront the sense of disaster at the evil inherent in the breakup of the Roman Empire. Christianity reacted "with horror" against the situation and offered "a sense of the role of the poor... a discipline, a lifestyle... companionship... community... thinking people and literary writers." The Christian story, particularly as formulated in Augustine's *City of God,* brought about individual and social healing by infusing the culture with "an overwhelming psychic energy."[17] In fact, this traditionally perceived accomplishment of Augustine had a significant influence on Berry in suggesting "story" as a paradigm for the facing of crises. Likewise such watershed contributions as Dante's *Divine Comedy* and Aquinas' integration of the Christian story with Aristotelian science were indicative to Berry of the adaptability of Christianity to change. This adaptability was not brought to bear on the scientific revolution, however, and in Berry's mind this failure was one major cause of the disintegration of the traditional Western cosmological story.

Berry cited two major factors that contributed to the disintegration of the Western traditional story: social conditions of the fourteenth and fifteenth centuries, especially the experience of the Black Death and the changing understanding of the natural world.[18] These historical occurrences were exacerbated by tendencies within the biblical-Christian tradition from the beginning. These tendencies or "orientations," as Berry labeled them, included the location of all sense of the sacred in a transcendent deity, belief in a redemption *out of* the present world, the transcendence of the human over the rest of the natural world and the eschatological hope of a "new heaven and a new earth."[19]

The Black Death, which killed about one third of Europe's population by 1349 and continued to recur into the seventeenth century, had a traumatic psychological and social effect on the survivors. Nature seemed ever more terrifying in its power to control human destiny, and the benevolence of God was in serious question. Largely

due to the Black Death, two major directions could be identified—
"one toward a religious redemption out of a tragic world, the other
toward greater control of the physical world." These responses contributed to a growing rift between the believing religious community
and the secular, scientific community. The Christian religious community concentrated its energy on the notions of redemption, the
personal Saviour and the supernatural world.[20] In the context of a
natural world that could not be trusted and that was frightening and
deadly, the impulse to gain greater control of nature heightened scientific efforts in that direction. There were great successes in this
area and a sense of "absolute progress" invaded all human activities.

At the same time that social forces were eroding the faith of the
Western world in its traditional story, scientific discoveries were
changing the picture of the universe. Gradually over a few centuries,
an accumulation of findings that countered the medieval synthesis
began to hold sway. The most challenging change came in the discovery of the historical nature of the universe itself especially because of
the general failure of humans to make the transition from a spatial
mode of consciousness to a historical one when it came to understanding the natural world. Hence, there was also a failure to integrate human technologies with the natural technologies of the physical universe. To accommodate this change of consciousness, a much
greater adaptation than ever before of the Christian story had to take
place. This, however, did not happen. Religion and science parted
ways.[21]

Of all the easily distorted Christian notions that entered into
the Western process of civilization, Berry saw the idea of progress to
have had the most devastating influence. "It would be difficult to
exaggerate its importance," he said. The myth of progress and the
consequent instrumentalization of nature were related to how the
Christian cultures came to appropriate the sense of history, which
Berry recalled was a contribution of Israelite Yahwist religion.[22] The
Divine was revealed primarily in the events of human history, rather
than in a cosmology as most other religions of the time held. Furthermore, the idea, first, of messianism and, then, of final fulfilment gave
history a forward dynamism in which human moral behaviour was
associated with the building of a supra-historical kingdom.

With the discrediting of the traditional world picture, the growing sense of historical realism in Western thought held full sway. The
natural world dropped out of religious consciousness and became a
mere resource for the human production of history. Berry contended
that the Western sense of history as it developed had the effect of iso-
lating the human as a historical being from the natural environment.

The latter became a stage and a resource for human history. The growing realization of the evolutionary nature of the universe did not necessarily solve the problem, however. As Berry observed about Teilhard's *Phenomenon of Man*, cosmogenesis can serve to enhance modernity's sense of unlimited progress if it is overridden with the human (or human-divine) role in bringing about a fulfilment in a spiritualized world. Hegel and Whitehead's thought were also inadequate under the ecological horizon because the evolutionary process became disembodied; it was an abstract process out of touch with the concrete events of cosmology and history. There was need for a cosmological story in which the natural world mattered for its own sake.

Ambiguity of the Human Capacity for Culture

On another level, Berry spoke about the ecological crisis as resulting from the ambiguous presence of humans within the ecosystems of the earth. Humans, unlike other animals, were both genetically and culturally coded. The latter accounted for the ambiguity.

Genetic coding obviously referred to the DNA inheritance of the human species, approximately ninety-nine percent of which is shared with the next closest mammalian species, the chimpanzee. The one-percent difference, however, included genes for the creation of culture. Humans were genetically coded to use language, for example, but the specific type of language was not determined. Which language was spoken was an element of cultural coding.

The idea of coding when applied to culture connoted the forceful influence of culture as it was handed on to the next generation from the previous one. The question of the viability of the human species within the natural systems of the earth had to do with cultural coding; other species were not so obviously coded for culture, and they did not pose a real threat to the existence of the biosphere. Berry still maintained, however, that the human belonged intimately to the rest of the earth process. "There is no earth without the human; no human without the earth," he wrote. "Any other earth or any other human is a pure abstraction." Furthermore, it was the earth itself in its evolutionary process which genetically coded the human for a "transgenetic cultural coding."[23] The problem was that the human production of culture had ignored its true place within the overall evolution of the universe. In other words, human history was threatening to become not the culmination of evolution, but the eclipse of all other evolutionary processes in the universe.

Berry set his notion of genetic and cultural coding within the context of the historical-cultural eras. Like Vico, he understood the transition between eras to be accompanied by a change in consciousness. This change, he said, was analogous to a genetic mutation. With each era, something new entered the picture. Within each era, as a certain mode of consciousness was established, the educational processes maintained relative stability; between eras these processes must negotiate a transition. As something new was gained, something else was lost in the transition. Berry was concerned mostly with what was lost.

In the transitions that occurred since primal times, a valuable sense of the human's place in the universe was lost. Primal humans acted spontaneously from their genetic coding. Their myths and rituals expressed a sense of bonding with the rest of the universe. Berry's sense was that the primal cultures were cosmologically based and that their awareness of the cosmology was intuitive and psychic. Following some of Jung's work, Berry associated dream experience, myth and symbol with archetypes; hence, his notion of genetic coding seemed to give a material basis to an idea he had already found in Jung and in his own understanding of the primal peoples.[24]

Within the classical cultures, some of this primal, intuitive and genetically based awareness was carried on and integrated into more elaborate cultural cosmologies, as indicated above for the Western Christian world. In the transition from classical to scientific-technological culture, the results of these intuitions and even belief that such experiences were real, in any sense, were dropped from mainline culture as cultural coding of this later period became established.

In continuity with his insistence on the importance of spirituality, Berry concluded that this distortion (also called a supreme pathology) resulted not from too much introspection, but from a neglect of "the contemplative and imaginative capacities for dealing with the numinous presence or aesthetic insight into the inner structure of reality."[25] Hence, scientific exploration of the "outer world" became largely disconnected from any sense of spiritual meaning or value. "The scientific venture," he said, "has been unable to understand the significance of its own achievements."[26] Following Vico, Berry noted that cultural accretions have a tendency to decay, and then society needs "a new descent" into "a more primitive state" and to "the natural forces out of which our cultural achievements came about originally."[27]

Before leaving this discussion of Berry's notion of genetic and cultural coding, it must be acknowledged that this is a problematic area in Berry's thought. Separation of cultural and genetic coding in anything other than the most abstract way would seem to be impossible for human individuals and society. Berry's presentation raises certain questions: Was he suggesting some return to the romantic concept of a kind of primitive, paradisal existence? Or was he expressing a new kind of Platonic idealism in which genes played the role of the Platonic forms? On the other hand, is this a materialist interpretation of human behaviour? While there is room for these interpretations in various elements of his work, Berry clearly denied that he intended these meanings. Moreover, these interpretations would blatantly contradict other important contentions within his work, such as his arguments for proper scale and appropriate technologies and economics that respect the ecosystems of the earth.[28]

The idea of the two "codings" first arose in Berry's essay "Individualism and Wholism in Chinese Tradition: The Religious Cultural Context." Here he pointed out that within the organic world view of Confucianism, the society was not formed around social contract, but was grounded in the origin, structure and functioning of the physical universe. Berry associated with genetic coding the spontaneity of thought and action, which was the goal of human life for Confucius. Hence, the whole disciplinary process of Confucianism, that is, the cultural coding, was directed toward an authenticity or integration within the *T'ien*, the Supreme Ultimate or Mother of Things. The relationship between the ultimate order of the universe and the human was an organic one, available to the human through genetic coding. He observed:

> If the Greeks in their generally objective way of knowing discovered in the subjective order of the psyche the source of order in the universe, the Chinese discovered a more profound, more integral and more intimate presence of the universe and the individual to each other with the discipline that would provide the functional efficacy needed by the individual.[29]

Thus, what Berry called genetic coding can be understood as that integral organic bond of the individual to the larger universe. The discipline whereby the individual makes universal processes, such as the reciprocity of giving and receiving, present and efficacious within human activity must be an integral part of human culture, that is, of cultural coding. Viewed from the other direction, human culture ought to incorporate the forms of discipline, ritual and other activities that enable humans to function efficaciously within an integral and viable relationship with the universe.

The idea of cultural and genetic coding enforced the notion that human culture ought to intentionally incorporate a reverence for nature and the humble recognition that humans are bound to a greater universe. Ultimately the human species cannot totally escape cosmic and biotic rhythms. The ecological crisis of the modern era is testimony to the foolhardiness of denying or trivializing human interconnectedness with nature. Berry's injunction "to pay attention to the gene" or, as alternately expressed, "to reinvent the human at the species level" was a plea to refocus on the inescapable union of culture to its organic base and the foolhardiness of attempting to cut the ties. His own proposal can be seen as an attempt to re-establish the relationship between cultural and genetic coding.[30]

Berry's Proposal—A "New Story"

In an essay called "The Ecozoic Era," Berry stated that an account of the past was necessary in order to provide an adequate response to the present and guidance for the future. As Berry's account of the past was a critique of Western Christian culture, so, too, his solution was a cultural one—implant a new set of meanings and values in the global community by means of a story available to the entire community.

The term "Ecozoic Era" (replacement for his former designation, "Ecological Age") represented a change in consciousness occurring in the present, a change comparable to the transitions between the scientifically designated ages of the earth, Paleozoic (up to 220 million years ago), Mesozoic (220 to 65 million years ago) and Cenozoic (65 million years ago to the present). The Ecozoic Era would be a time characterized by a consciousness of human bondedness to the earth and a consequent change of lifestyle and behaviour to face the ecological crisis. While he saw evidence in present environmental movements and sensitivities that the Ecozoic Era had begun, there was an implicit "should" or even "must" in this assertion of the emergence of a new age; that is, the Ecozoic Era ought to be initiated and lived. On the one hand, the "new story" was already part of the Ecozoic Era; on the other hand, it claimed to initiate a different future.

Why a "New Story"?

Even before he had made the ecological crisis the prime focus of his attention, Berry believed that what was needed in the modern world was a "new story," first referred to as a myth of the future. While he did not argue his point in terms of contemporary scholarship on the role of narrative, his observations with regard to the power of myth, his interest in the existential dimensions of religious stories and myths and his esteem for Augustine's *City of God* and Dante's *Divine Comedy* were all likely influences on his conviction regarding the role of story in culture.[31]

In the past, Berry said, cultures were informed by a unifying story or cosmology, which supplied answers to existential problems and values to guide decisions. While he recognized that these were not always the best answers nor the most desirable values, nonetheless the power of the story was illustrated. In this regard, he wrote:

> Our traditional story of the universe sustained us for a long period of time. It shaped our emotional attitudes, provided us with life purposes and energized action. It consecrated suffering and integrated knowledge... It did not necessarily make people good, nor did it take away the pains and stupidities of life or make for unfailing warmth in human association. It did provide a context in which life could function in a meaningful manner.[32]

Berry's major cultural critique was that the culture no longer had an integrating story, a functional cosmology. The religious stories that did remain were no longer adequate to provide answers and values for dealing with the ecological crisis. The Christian story, for instance, overemphasized human redemption themes to the virtual exclusion of creation themes. Hence, a "new story" with the power of the old story was needed. Only such a story could adequately inform the culture with the meanings, values and inspiration necessary to "[shape] emotional attitudes, [provide] us with life purposes and [energize] action" toward the solution of the ecological crisis. Other problems must be set within this context, since the ecological crisis is the most urgent concern of the present.

Since rationalism was itself subject to distorted myths, Berry had no faith that rationalistic answers to the present crisis would work. The scientific-technological age was powerfully driven by such distorted myths. The "new story" would have to appeal to the emotional, aesthetic and psychic-spiritual dimensions of the human. Only then would it be powerful enough to overturn the distortions of modernity and to dislocate it from its hold on modern consciousness.

Berry believed that modern science provided the basis for a story with this power. Teilhard de Chardin had already illustrated the potential for a spiritual interpretation of the scientific account of evolution. His effort was inadequate, however, within the horizon of the ecological crisis. *The Universe Story*, as related by Berry and Swimme, was inspired by Berry's desire to provide a "new story."

What Is the "New Story"?

Can this story of the universe provide a context for a Christian theology of ecology? This is the question that is under investigation. The immediate task, however, is to identify how this story responds to the ecological crisis, first as a story and second in the specific meanings and values it intended. To these ends, it is necessary, first of all, to explore how this story arose from the scientific account of evolution, in what sense it is a history and in what sense a religious history. At each of these levels of construction (scientific narrative, history and religious history) the horizon of the ecological crisis was operative. Second, it is necessary to inquire about the meaning of what Swimme and Berry called the cosmogenetic principle, which included Berry's now familiar characteristics of the universe: differentiation, subjectivity and communion. This principle was the stated and intentional configurational element of the "new story," although there were other configurational elements (such as the ending of the story). Here, too, Berry's primary interest was to engender meanings and values needed to confront the ecological crisis. As will become clear, questions relative to other horizons or an extended horizon also legitimately arise.

Nature of the "New Story"

As Scientific Narrative

The "new story" was, first of all, an account of the new cosmology, the result of the latest and most accepted theories of cosmologists regarding the origin and evolution of the universe. Berry did not take up the academic debate regarding the status of narrativity as socially constructed or inherent in events.[33] He assumed that the universe emerged in a linked and orderly succession of events revealing a direction and a meaning and hence constituting a story. In more poetic fashion, he referred to this quality of the emerging universe as the universe itself telling the story.[34]

The term "new story" then has a double meaning. It refers to the ongoing unfolding of cosmic events as discovered by scientists, as well as to a human relating of the story, as Berry and Swimme did in *The Universe Story*. This implies that there was a reality prior to the observations of scientists and the construction of stories of the universe to which the story referred and which was more or less approximated by each telling. In other words, the claim is that the referent of the story was the universe as it truly is, at least insofar as we (and especially scientists) could presently judge. The telling of the story is open to revision, especially as the work of science continues. The story is new not because of this constant revision, however, but because the understanding of the universe as a story is new. It also carries a new intentional and normative dimension; it attempts to overturn and replace the present hegemonic attitudes of humans toward the natural world.

The story began with the "flaring forth" of the fireball and the stages of early cosmic evolution, as they are presently understood and accepted by most scientists. It proceeded with the formation of the planets and then focused on developments on planet Earth. A path was traced from the pre-life forms, through the emergence of life up to and including human life. The story continued through human history. The discovery of the story (the pursuit and accomplishment of science) was seen as an event in the story, as was its telling.

The human was "mandated" to tell the story and live out the Ecozoic Era with whatever changes of attitude and behaviour that entailed. Primarily, this meant acceptance of the "conditions determined by the larger course of earthly events, not by the subject brought into existence."[35] In other words, the universe was a self-propelled process that set its own conditions for survival, maximum diversity and quality of life. These conditions must be met by all beings within the universe, including humans, if the process was to continue in a viable fashion. It was this requirement and its grounding in the dynamics of interrelatedness of the whole universe process that established the functionality of the story as a cosmology in confronting the ecological crisis.

As History

The "new story" was also a history. The events in the evolution of the universe constituted real time. Nature itself was seen to display historicity and was no longer a mere backdrop to human society.

Historicity, of course, means more than chronology. The application of the term "historicity" to the physical universe rests on an intricate relationship of chance happenings and cause-and-effect links that gave rise to successive stages of the universe over time. So, we read of the formation of the stars from a galactic cloud of dust:

> The cloud that has drifted undisturbed for eons suddenly undergoes a profound transformation that destroys its basic form but gives birth to a cluster of ten thousand diamond lights in a sea of dark night.[36]

And because of this chance occurrence, hydrogen and helium atoms were brought into close proximity and were "drawn together by their mutual attraction." Thus, dynamics of chance and necessity interacted in the emerging, increasingly complex beings and dynamics that comprise the present universe.[37]

Historicity also implies contingency. The events themselves were unique. They were not merely the illustration of some pre-existent principle or archetype. They were the real constituents of time. Speaking of the ordering features of the universe, Swimme and Berry stated:

> These three features [differentiation, subjectivity and communion] are not "logical" or "axiomatic" in that they are not deductions within some larger theoretical framework. They come from a post hoc evaluation of cosmic evolution...[38]

Historical accounts of the same events differ, since history, like all story, is configured. A story results from a balancing of an episodic and a configurational dimension. Paul Ricoeur called this process "emplotment." Events are emplotted within a meaning. This meaning inheres, first of all, from the ending or conclusion. History is always constructed with a backward glance; it ends, for now, in the present even as it opens to the future.[39]

The ending from which the events of the new story were emplotted is the present ecological crisis. Humans are poised at a crucial point. Tragedy is a real possibility. The complex and intricate nature of the events by which the universe evolved evoke a deeper appreciation and a certain poignancy or pathos. An analogy to hearing the "new story" is the significance of learning the value, time and artistic genius involved in the production of a famous van Gogh, just at the point when one was about to destroy it in ignorance.[40] Can the laborious step-by-tiny-step, near-miraculous outcomes of errors and struggles for survival be all for naught, destroyed by the folly of human arrogance (or neglect or ignorance)? In the light of the ending, this question lurked beneath the surface of the "new story" and each of the events it comprised. The hope (or claim) of this history was to evoke a negative answer to the question it constantly raised.

As Religious History

Besides the ending, additional configurational elements include interpretations or descriptions that add meaning to the flow of events or to individual events. Some of these additional configurational elements in the "new story" suggest religious history, a religious interpretation of historical events, in this case the historical events that comprised cosmic evolution. "There is a special need in this transitional phase," Berry insisted, "...to awaken a consciousness to the sacred dimension of the earth. What is at stake... is the meaning of existence itself."[41]

According to Berry, an experience (or set of experiences) of the universe confirmed modern scientific discoveries. "Our new sense of the universe is itself a type of revelatory experience." He referred to this experience by such terms as "revelatory vision," "a deeper understanding," a sense of the numinosity of the universe, a change in consciousness, a sensitivity to the deep mystery of things.[42] The contemporary experiences (of some scientists, for instance) confirmed previous experiences witnessed in history by such groups as North American natives, other aboriginal peoples, the primal peoples of history, Platonists, neo-Platonists, hermetics, alchemists, romantics and transcendentalists. What was common to most of these was a perception of the universe as having a psychic-spiritual dimension and the general insistence or assumption that this perception was based on an intuitive experience of the universe. The designation of this experience as revelatory, however, would seem to be Berry's own, in all probability inspired by the Christian designation of nature as one of the Books of Revelation.[43]

For Berry, however, the meaning of nature as a Book of Revelation was different from what it was in previous times. It was not only the static components of the cosmos that revealed the Divine, but more prominently the events of cosmogenesis. Like the scriptural account of divine action in human history, nature was a story of divine action in the history of the universe. History in this larger sense (including nature) was also revelatory. "I consider this [events in the evolution of the cosmos] revelatory in a magnificent way, because it tells us something about the powers that brought the universe into being at the beginning," Berry wrote.[44]

Berry considered the story of the universe to be revelatory and religious. His sense of revelation, however, included not only the Christian or biblical sense of revealing an external creator or source, but also ideas associated with the land mystique of the North American native peoples, the Chinese Tao, the personal archetypal dimension of the earth as expressed by Teilhard, the Mother Earth Goddess and all such designations of the numinous and psycho-spiritual dimensions of the earth. In one place he wrote of "the ultimate form of human wisdom" that was encompassed in the "ancient sense of Logos in the Greek world, of *rita* in Hinduism, of *dharma* in Buddhism, of *tao, ch'eng* and *jen* in the Chinese world."[45] These were spiritual ordering principles believed to be cosmological as well as social. In the Asian world, he added, even the terms *jen, ch'eng, bhakti* and *karuna*, which designated affections, were considered to refer to cosmic powers. For Berry, then, to speak of the revelatory or religious nature of the universe was to open the possibilities for any of these interpretations. Minimally, his references to the religious or revelatory dimension of the universe were his way of saying that the universe was more than a material or mechanical reality.

In Berry's view, the "new story" was in continuity with the historical sense that the biblical tradition of the West applied to human society, with the pre-Enlightenment sense of cosmology and with the more cosmological frameworks of other religious traditions. Berry went beyond them all, however, in creating a history that also functioned as a cosmology. The rift between history and nature, endemic to the modern world, was overcome and nature was restored to that world of meaning and value, which since the Enlightenment, was largely reserved for human history.

There is also another precursor in pre-Enlightenment Christian tradition to the idea, at least, of this story. There is ample evidence of the struggle of Christian thinkers to keep the creation account of Genesis, in the sequence of its events (the six days), within history. While there are, perhaps, even more examples (even in the works of the same thinkers) of the usurpation of a Hebraic sense of the concreteness of the historical nature of creation to allegory and other forms of symbolism and to Platonic interpretations, some Christian thinkers did succeed in also maintaining some historical sense of creation even before history was understood in its full modern meaning.[46] Both as a genre as well as thematically, the "new story" would seem to belong, therefore, within what the West has understood as religious history.[47] The fact that the universe was included as history is a recovery of an earlier tradition that had become eclipsed with the emergence of modern human-centred historical consciousness.

As religious history, the "new story" fits H. Richard Niebuhr's category "internal history."[48] As such, it attempts to include the reader in the story itself. The story becomes identifiable as "my story." A case in point is the notion of the revelatory experience mentioned above. Berry interpreted the events described by science as disclosures of a relationship also recognizable within the human psyche. A second more pervasive example is the rhetoric of the story itself.

One way in which Berry thematized the relationship between scientific discovery and intuitive awareness of the human relationship to the earth was by associating the term "revelation" with the idea of a dream, giving the latter its two common meanings:

We are, of course, using this term not only as regards the psychic process that takes place when we are physically asleep, but also as a way of indicating an intuitive, nonrational process that occurs when we awaken to the numinous powers ever present in the phenomenal world about us, powers that possess us in our high creative moments.[49]

He continued by comparing these numinous powers not just to the productive imagination of artists and poets, but to shamanic personalities, who "more than any other of the human types concerned with the sacred... journey into the far regions of the cosmic mystery and bring back the vision and the power needed..." This power of the shaman was a dimension of the psyche itself. The activation of this dimension of the psyche was also referred to as "intimacy with our genetic endowment and through this endowment with the larger cosmic process." Whereas in primal peoples this was a spontaneous process, in modern humans it required a post-critical intentionality, or second naivete. "We need to become sensitized to these spontaneities," he said, "not with a naive simplicity, but with critical appreciation." "What earlier peoples did immediately and intuitively in establishing their identity we must do deliberately."[50]

The discoveries of science, constituting a narrative as they do, gave voice to the mythic presence of the cosmic process in the human psyche. The integral relationship of the human to the rest of the universe was now supported by empirical evidence, but it was the "new story" only to those who could empathetically and imaginatively understand the meaning inherent in the evolution of the universe.[51] Berry further insisted that a particular meaning was revealed; namely, that the universe was characterized throughout its entire process by differentiation, subjectivity and communion, the precise definitions of which we will return to below. This particular meaning was seen as analogous to human experience. So, both in the experience of intimacy with the natural world and in the particular meaning assigned to, or extrapolated from, that experience, humans could identify with the "new story" from the beginning and not just with the account of the emergence and development of their species.

Besides presenting the argument for the inclusion of humans within the entire "new story" directly, *The Universe Story* used a rhetoric that aimed to create a sense of intimacy between humans and the rest of the universe. In internal history, as Niebuhr described it, the readers identified with the story, empathized with the characters and found solidarity between life as they experienced it and the events of the story.[52] Note how these elements are present in the following descriptions of the mechanisms of evolution in *The Universe Story*:

Stochastic points to the experience of moving toward a goal, but in darkness and thus with a great deal of groping and multiple approaches... *Error* refers to the experience of drifting and changing directions, all in the hope that if one continues to wander, one might stumble upon what is desired.

[I]n a searing lightning flash [Earth] witnessed the emergence of a profoundly novel event—Aries, the first living cell... Aries emerged from the cybernetic storms of the primeval oceans and found itself alone, in a sea devoid of other life forms. But Earth would never again be the same.[53]

Goals, wandering, drifting, direction, aloneness, risk and radical change were constitutive of the human existential experience of history. According to this story, they were also cosmic experiences.

The metaphors mentioned immediately above suggested the existential experience of the individual, the loner or even the heroic initiator of change. This was one aspect of identification the story of the universe invited; the other was community.

Each member of the community makes ultimately the same demands on the new population: "If you are to stay, we must become related and not just externally. We must become kin, internally related. We live here. Our meaning is here. Our identity comes out of this place of togetherness. If you wish to join us we will work to provide everything you might need. But you must first demonstrate your willingness to let go of your previous accomplishments and enter our world freshly."[54]

The immediate interest in this passage was to establish an understanding of natural selection. It is not difficult, however, to feel both an indictment on the human species ("If you are to stay"), as well as an invitation to community ("place of togetherness," "let go... and enter"). It is in this community that humans belong and, by implication, they ought to behave in the appropriate manner.

In terms of rhetoric and identification, how the story speaks of the emergence of the human is truly significant. In that event "the universe, as a whole, turned back and reflected on itself."[55] The image connotes a double mirror; humans see themselves in the history of the universe up to their own emergence and the story of the universe is seen in the human. The language suggests that humans arrived on the planet already possessing a meaningful past. The familiar concept of tradition is conjured in the notion of turning back and reflecting.

As will become clearer in the discussion of the cosmogenetic principle, there was a strong impetus toward identification, communion, similarity and wholeness within Berry's notion of the "new story." Community often meant communion. Berry went beyond the notion of interrelatedness as a social contract to an organic sense. This becomes clear if we contrast Berry's notion with the contention by Ricoeur that history, through repetition, reveals other to self but for the sake of community.[56] According to this sense, the founding acts of a community are communicated and in that communication the listener or reader is inserted into the otherness of these acts; hence, into community. While one could argue that the events of cosmogenesis in their otherness are so communicated as to insert the human into that community, the horizon of the ecological crisis functioned in such a way for Berry that, with the possible exception of his description of differentiation, any sense of otherness seems to play second fiddle to the stronger sense of organic union. Difference is real, but it does not preclude the strong organic bond that inheres among all dimensions of the universe. We are different insofar as cousins are different.

The Cosmogenetic Principle

Berry and Swimme gave the cosmogenetic principle a central ordering role in the "new story." The cosmogenetic principle assumed "that every point in the universe is the same as every other point and additionally, that the dynamics of evolution are the same at every point in the universe." The principle further stated that "the evolution of the universe will be characterized by differentiation, *autopoiesis* ['subjectivity' in Berry's other works] and communion." Of all the configurational elements that entered into the story, this one was the most overtly intentional. "The sequence of events in the universe becomes a story precisely because the events are shaped by these ordering tendencies," Berry and Swimme stated. [57]

These features of cosmological evolution belonged to Berry's thought prior to the writing of *The Universe Story*. They are related to ideas associated with the tradition of the one and the many and the notions of plenitude. What is most important, however, is what is meant by the terms as they later apply to the construction of the universe story as elements within the cosmogenetic principle as a whole.

The cosmogenetic principle is concerned with the form-producing dynamics of evolution. It arose from observation of the present universe and the awareness of its long emergence over time: "We find ourselves in a universe that has over fifteen billion years given birth to an astounding development. What can we say about this?"[58] One thing said about this was that the universe seemed to exhibit intentionality or bias in the production of structures. The example given by Swimme and Berry was that of the formation of amino acids. It was estimated that to get random collisions of atoms to form a molecule would take at least "a hundred times more than fifteen billion years [the estimated age of the universe]." Yet, amino acids formed throughout the entire Milky Way galaxy. The activation of the interaction, in this case, of electromagnetic, gravitational, and strong and weak nuclear forces produced amino acid. The "algorithm for weaving these interactions" in precisely the way necessary to produce amino acids was referred to as a form-producing power. In other words, the universe displayed agency prior to the emergence of the human species and, therefore, possessed a relative independence from human history. It could not be correctly characterized as a neutral, dead object.

The form-producing power such as that of the galaxy was not magical, however. What looked like bias toward a certain structure, or an intention to produce in one direction, rested on the fact that previous chance occurrences set the stage for other even less likely happenings; less likely, that is, had the first occurrence not taken place. Branches, or pathways, were established. With each further branching, some options were eliminated; with each further development, commitment to a certain direction was gradually established. Scientists expect that this is a generic characterization of what takes place everywhere in the universe. It is generic with respect to a generalization from a few places to many, as well as with respect to the evolution of the dynamics themselves at different levels in the evolutionary process. Hence, the isomorphism, or similarity of form, that seems to exist over space in the universe is also held to exist over time.

Differentiation, subjectivity (*autopoiesis*) and communion were exhibited then in the form-producing structures of the universe that were characteristic of the evolution of the universe; they referred to the "governing themes" or "basal intentionality of all existence." They were "primordial orderings." They spoke of "the nature of the universe in its reality and its value." The most minimal meaning of these characteristics was given in this description of the consequences of their absence:

> Were there no differentiation, the universe would collapse into a homogeneous smudge; were there no subjectivity, the universe would collapse into inert, dead extension; were there no communion, the universe would collapse into isolated singularities of being.[59]

Thus, Berry and Swimme referred differentiation, subjectivity (*autopoiesis*) and communion to the physical dynamics by which the universe existed at all. Each of the terms, however, admits a surplus of meaning that extends beyond this minimalist meaning and requires further examination. It is in the investigation of their surplus of meaning that their function as value referents within the particular horizon of the ecological crisis becomes apparent.

What Berry spoke of as "differentiation," at one level, was the fact that we see differences around us and infer that evolution produced great variety among species, beings and kinds of relationships. It also related, however, to the fecundity and indescribable nature of divinity. It was integral to human language and imagination and constituted the beauty and celebratory nature of the universe.[60] Furthermore, differentiation formed the basis for powerful arguments, beyond human usefulness, for the preservation of biodiversity. As it operated within the "new story" itself, it also provided accounts of natural beings that enchanted, provoked wonder and engendered shame over human destructiveness.[61] Finally, differentiation was employed within the story to preserve the sense of the otherness and ultimate mystery of beings in an atmosphere clearly committed to establishing the unity that exists within the universe. Swimme and Berry wrote about this quality of difference, as follows:

> To be is to be a unique manifestation of existence... Science deepens our understanding of a thing's structure and its ineffable uniqueness. Ultimately each thing remains as baffling as ever, no matter how profound our understanding.[62]

That difference and baffling individuality existed primarily, however, for the sake of the integrity of the whole. Nothing was absolutely individual.

"Subjectivity" is a problematic term when applied to the non-human world because the word refers to properties that are so characteristically and distinctly human. Together with the term "communion," however, it recurs like a refrain in Berry's works: "The universe is a communion of subjects and not a collection of objects... "[63] The juxtaposition of subjects and objects obviously reflects the agenda of his program: uproot old assumptions and replace them with different, even opposite assumptions.

The major flaw in modernity's treatment of the natural world was the distorted notion that the natural world was merely a "collection of objects," deriving its value from its usefulness to humans. Berry was interested in overturning that attitude. Hence, his elaborations (sentience, voice, interiority, interior identity, self-determining force, numinous mystery) of the term "subjectivity" were intended to instill those attitudes toward the natural world that were more commonly held toward human subjects. It was, in this sense, more concerned with the creation of value than with a precisely defined content with respect to the non-human world.

Berry did give some clues as to how he understood the subjectivity of the non-human world in a manner applicable beyond the horizon that most concerned him. In one place, he said the term was to be understood analogically. Diagramatically, therefore, this means that there exists some *x*, such that

x is to a non-human being as subjectivity is to a human.

As we have seen, on one level *x* is what scientists describe as *autopoiesis*, as controversial as that theory may be. In various places, Berry associated the experience of the subjectivity of the natural world with the Platonic tradition in its various expressions. This would seem to suggest that the sense of numinous mystery encompassed in his term "subjectivity" was some sort of anima, vitalistic principle or ideal form. Berry did not himself understand subjectivity in this sense, however. In the philosophic tradition, he contended it was close to Aquinas' use of Aristotle's notion of intelligible form, but within a dynamic or developmental perception of reality.[64] Norris Clarke has suggested that "in a broadly analogous way" the Aristotelian idea of form and matter seem "to be indispensable for a reflective understanding" especially of nature today. He wrote:

> [T]he world of nature [is] understood non-reductionistically as composed of levels of being where lower elements are integrated into higher unities or natures, which become new centers or subjects of characteristic new properties and actions.[65]

Clarke's extension of the traditional meaning of "form and matter" does seem to give some sense of agency ("new centers or subjects") to the universe, and Berry's notion of subjectivity certainly does. While he wished to escape the dualism and idealism of the Platonic heritage, the language by which subjectivity was characterized suggests an agency or intelligence that was not implied in the Aristotelian category of intelligible form. Aquinas did hold, however, that God gave to each creature a viability and an integrity, a freedom to be itself.[66] Thus, creation was considered to have intrinsic and not merely extrinsic or instrumental value. For Berry, non-human nature did not have the self-reflective subjectivity of humans, but it had some power of agency that increased in its degree of freedom as the higher plants and animals evolved. This would seem to be a stronger assertion than either Aristotle's philosophy or Aquinas' theology could support, but is closer to Teilhard's view.

The problem that Berry attempted to negotiate under the horizon of the ecological crisis was the subject/object duality of the post-Cartesian world. Nature as object was considered sheer extension in space. The entire realm of affective relationships and of values was associated with the subjective. Likewise, the process of objectification or objectivity was understood as a kind of knowing from which subjectivity (hence, feeling and valuation) was removed.[67] While, theoretically, the notion remains problematic, the application of the term "subjectivity" to nature was designed to change the perception of nature in the attitudes of the reader or listener. The difficulty of arriving at a precise term to describe a reality that is neither "object" in the post-Enlightenment sense nor fully "subject" in its accepted meaning is perhaps what Berry pointed to in his view that our language is no longer adequate to describe the realities we confront.[68]

In *The Universe Story*, the third characteristic of evolution, "communion," was associated with the patterns of interconnections within which the components of the universe evolved. As each phase of the story was related, new beings were seen to emerge from patterns of forces that made their emergence possible and more probable. As soon as a being emerged, it became involved in changing the pattern to suit its own survival. This in turn created a new pattern often conducive to further creativity. The emergence of amino acid molecules was one example. Another was the adaptation of living organisms to changing niches through capitalization on mutations, or the often simultaneous process of modifying the niche to suit changing needs. Communion was also associated with mating patterns, symbiosis, predator-prey relationship and the functioning of ecosystems. It referred to the assumption of contemporary cosmology that the energy in the universe was a quantum, all generated by a singular beginning, to the forces of attraction, such as gravity, that hold the universe together and to the genetic unity of the living world. This scientific support gave credence to the organic metaphor invoked by the idea of communion.

Despite all this scientific support, however, some assertions about communion seem to say more. "The universe is the communion of each reality in the universe with every other reality in the universe."[69] While there is some scientific evidence that subatomic particles have unmediated effects on each other, it is difficult to see how this statement of Berry is *literally* true;[70] while all realities share energy and matter, for example, a particular free-standing carbon atom would seem to be related to a particular plant or animal in only a very minimal and indirect sense, at least insofar as we know. Of course, some carbon atoms are integral to the life of that organism.

Communion seems to be an overriding paradigm for the understanding of the universe in Berry's thought. Even conflicts, as in
predator-prey relationships or the turmoil of volcanoes or earthquakes,
were seen as self-sacrificial elements from which greater creativity,
beauty and the well-being of the whole emerge. The whole possesses
an agency greater than that of the parts.[71]

It bears repetition that horizon is extremely significant in understanding any of Berry's concepts and, hence, the import of the idea of
communion. The question that arises is why communion as paradigm for the interrelatedness within the natural world is better than
the traditional Darwinian notion of competition, for example. Berry
saw different consequences of the two for human-earth relationships.
There were, he felt, historical instances to support his claim. The
North American native peoples lived in communion with the North
American continent, in contrast to the "mechanistic exploitation" of
the continent by the European colonizers. Their rituals accompanying hunting and even warfare attested to the sense of communion
they felt with their prey as well as with their enemies. "The sacred
function of enemies," Berry wrote, "was to assist one another to the
heroic life by challenge, even by the challenge to death."[72] Thus,
Berry applied the paradigmatic notion of communion to the interrelationships within the natural world because it was shown to support
more effectively a sound ecology than would other notions, such as
survival of the fittest.

The "new story" sought to establish this sense of communion.
Images of some aspects of existence, which humans already regarded
with a sense of reverence and awe, were associated with images of
other aspects that had been interpreted mechanistically. Hence, Berry
and Swimme wrote:

> The thinking taking place within a human is distinct from the
> activity within an isolated carbon atom. Yet there is some awesome
> relationship between the roaring activities in the carbon atom and
> the activities taking place in the thinking human...[73]

The appeal was primarily to affect; the goal, to change perceptions,
attitudes and ultimately values.

While differentiation, subjectivity and communion worked together (within the cosmogenetic principle) in configuring the events
of evolution in the universe story, there is no doubt that Berry's
overall emphasis was on wholeness. From the beginning of his writings, he confronted alienation and fragmentation as existential human experience, as religious exclusivity, as the rift between religion
and the modern world, as the alienation of humans from the natural

world and as the fragmentation of the natural world itself (atomism, for example).[74] Therefore, his thrust had been to build connections and to create syntheses. The "new story" continued that thrust. In doing so, the organic metaphor was maintained.

As a root metaphor, organicism underlines strong interrelationship and bondedness. The emphasis is on the whole. Traditionally, the questions raised to its proponents dealt with freedom and otherness, especially as the metaphor included human society. While Berry did include humans within the organic bondedness of the universe, he did maintain that they possessed a special self-reflective capacity. Berry's presentation of this issue was supported by the views of some contemporary scientists and futurists who held that a new organic sense of society was emerging. While organicism was usually strong on world view but weak on empirical evidence, some scientists felt that science had now put together enough details that a whole world view could be constructed. Such a view was based on the reciprocity of the whole and the individual, of "particle and field, freedom and order, at each and every level."[75] Human liberties could be ensured on the basis of a scientific underpinning. The freedom and creativity so evident in humans was inherent in the whole process of evolution.

As noted above, it is difficult to find in the "new story" a clear articulation of the notions of otherness and difference in most of the applications of these terms: the otherness of the Divine from the universe, of human subjectivity from the agency within the universe, of evil from good. While these issues will be investigated more thoroughly below, it is helpful at this point to locate Berry's ideas of relatedness and difference within two contrasting mainline conceptions (those of Paul Ricoeur and Karl Rahner) of how images mediate meaning.

For Ricoeur, metaphors set up a tension by bringing together two unrelated terms and, hence, projecting a new and possible world.[76] The emphasis is on the newness of the world, which shocks the reader/listener into a realization that one could live as if the world were this way. According to this line of thinking, the metaphoric description of the universe as story, cells as agents, the universe as subjective, the universe as revelation or genes as codes of human behaviour work because they juxtapose non-related terms and project a possibility in which humans may freely choose to live. They provoke (more than evoke) human feeling toward creating a new world in which they live "as if" and hence make that world a reality. Likewise, the physical universe, itself a metaphor for divine nature and action, would manifest the Divine only in the sense that it raises a possibility for living "as if" the Divine were this way. Here again, the difference of God from God's creation is pre-eminently preserved. The linguistic image, metaphor, is a construct within which Ricoeur can protect both the difference of human worlds from the embedded nature of physical processes and the unbreachable difference between God and the created world.[77]

In Rahner's theological presentation, symbol or sacrament offers the construct for understanding the relationship of God to the creation, including humans as creators (more correctly co-creators) of their worlds.[78] While the concept of creation itself also implies a difference between God and the physical and human worlds, nonetheless, these worlds are expressions of primordial being. As symbol or sacrament of God, the universe is sacred. In the symbol, the human can recognize (in a cognitive sense) dimensions of the nature of God and can experience (affectively and existentially) God's presence. The very notion of Trinity itself as self-expressive divinity undergirds Rahner's (following Thomas Aquinas') ontology of symbol and image. The unity in plurality that characterizes all beings is not simply an aggregate or association of parts, but stems from an original unity that is expressed in each of the parts. So, Rahner concluded that "the symbol is the reality, constituted by the thing symbolized as an inner moment of itself, which reveals and proclaims the thing symbolized and is itself the thing symbolized, being its concrete form of existence." Further he writes, "The unity is more original than the distinction, because the symbol is a distinct and yet intrinsic moment of the reality as it manifests itself." Images then, for Rahner, refer to a prior ontological unity. They mediate God in a real (ontological) and not only existential sense. While metaphors may well provoke an existential change in the world, they primarily evoke a recognition of a prior unity between the terms.

Berry's understanding of differentiation, subjectivity and communion was more closely allied with Rahner's notion than with Ricoeur's. It is Rahner's rather than Ricoeur's understanding of the referential character of language and human understanding that is reflected in such statements of Berry as:

> If God is speaking to us through the universe and if we are now seeing that the universe functions differently from what earlier Christians thought, then we must have a different way of articulating our Christian belief.[79]

Hence for Berry, as for Rahner, what we know to be true about the universe reveals something about the nature of God.

In Berry's expression of the organic and sacramental understanding of reality there is a strong sense of unity. To repeat, communion

is organic connectedness and not "social contract." Under the horizon of ecological disaster, it seems crucial that the whole is greater
(meaning for Berry, in both fact and value) than the parts. The consequences of difference are value-laden in that they apply to the main-
tenance of biodiversity, but, primarily, because each part contributes
to the well-being of the whole. In the organic developmental metaphor, all is subservient finally to the good of the whole.

Berry's organicism, then, can be seen as a new expression of a
traditional Christian understanding of reality. The "different way of
articulating Christian beliefs," in the freedom of the human person
and the nature of evil, however, is not worked out within the "new
story" itself. Any references in Berry's works to the problems regarding human evil and social action in the world themselves reflect an
impatience with human concerns about the social problems of the
human community to the virtual exclusion of the natural world.[80]
This is consistent with his contention that redemption (as compared
to creation) has been overemphasized in Christianity. Yet there are
references that reflect a sensitivity to the plight of poor nations and
to the pathology that leads the Western world to think it is helping
the poor while it devastates their natural environment.[81] Furthermore, there was no naivete about the destructive nature of human
history, thus far. The question, of course, is not whether Berry believed that real evil or genuine human freedom exists (he obviously
did), but whether the organic metaphor by which the "new story"
was configured adequately grounds these realities.

A final comment with respect to the intended audience of the
"new story" sheds some light on some of the significant lacunae,
such as the concrete implications of organicism as Berry uses it. Berry
intended that the "new story" supply a context for a wide range of
cultures. Throughout his academic career, he spoke of the emergence
of a global culture. This was a story, then, for the global culture. It
was not to replace the other great narratives, but to provide a context,
an enrichment, a conversation partner for each, so that their effectiveness could be expanded and intensified. Religions, as they are
presently, do not have the adequate resources to confront the ecological crisis, he said, but we cannot confront the crisis adequately
without them.[82] The "new story," thus, sought a completion within
particular religious expressions and even within a more systematic
treatment by theology, without which, he said "the entire project of
an ecological age is insecure."[83] Hence, terms such as differentiation,
subjectivity and communion (like others noted above, such as revelation and religion) take on more specific meanings within the tradition
that appropriates the story.[84] North American natives, for instance,

are likely to understand subjectivity in quite a different fashion than European Christians would.

In reaching out to a global community, Berry relied on the growing universal awareness of the ecological crisis and the necessity for a co-operative worldwide approach, on the incursion, for better and for worse, of Western science on most world cultures and, if he was right, on traditional universal experience of some form of intimacy with the natural world. The particular appropriation of the "new story" within specific cultures and religions is the challenge he offered.

Primarily, then, the "new story" is concerned with meaning and value. By restoring meaning to the physical universe, Berry believed, he could enable people to see intrinsic value in the physical universe. The present modern assumption that sees the natural world as a resource for the myth of progress, or a commodity for consumption, would be dislocated. If the "new story" formed the basis of culture, people would be moved to act according to the values it carried. In that sense, it would supply a functional cosmology for a viable human existence within the limitations of the natural world.

Can this story (or history) as presently configured also provide a context for a Christian theology of ecology as Berry himself hoped? The remaining chapters will use the explanatory categories derived by the Catholic theologian and philosopher Bernard Lonergan, who was also interested in the reformation of theology, to confront this question.

Notes

1.   Bernard Lonergan, *Insight: A Study of Human Understanding. Collected Works of Bernard Lonergan. Vol. 3*, ed. by Frederick E. Crowe and Robert M. Doran (Toronto, Buffalo, London: University of Toronto Press, 1992 and Toronto: Lonergan Research Institute of Regis College, 1992), 273, 316-317. Henceforth, Lonergan, *Insight*.

2.   Ibid., 273.

3.   Cf. *The Dream of the Earth*, 117.

4.   Berry's critique and recovery parallels Paul Ricoeur's hermeneutics of suspicion and hermeneutics of recovery (or affirmation). Cf. Paul Ricoeur, "The Critique of Religion," in *The Philosophy of Paul Ricoeur*, ed. by Charles E. Reagan and David Stewart (Boston: Beacon Press, 1978), 215.

5.   Berry, "Seminar," 8.

6.   *The Dream of the Earth*, 25.

7.   Cf. Berry, *The Dream of the Earth*, 187-190; Swimme and Berry, *The Universe Story*, 3. See also Eliade, *The Sacred and the Profane*, 20-65, and Paul Ricoeur, "Metaphor and Symbol," trans. by David Pellauer, in *Interpretation Theory: Discourse and the Surplus of Meaning* (Fort Worth, TX: Texas Christian University Press, 1976), 58-63.

8.   Cf. Stanley Hauerwas and L. Gregory Jones, "Introduction: Why Narrative?" in *Why Narrative? Readings in Narrative Theology* (Grand Rapids, MI: William B. Eerdmans Publishing Company, 1989), 1-18, for an overview of the various standard positions with regard to narrative, its relationship to experience and its relevance to dimensions of religiosity.

9.   Swimme and Berry, *The Universe Story*, 241.

10.   Berry, *Befriending the Earth*, 26.

11.   Swimme and Berry, *The Universe Story*, 22.

12.   Cf. Berry, "Individualism and Wholism in Chinese Tradition," *Riverdale Papers IX* ; and *Cosmogony and Ethical Order*, ed. by Robin W. Lovin and Frank E. Reynolds (Chicago and London: University of Chicago Press, 1985).

13.   Berry, *The Dream of the Earth*, 88.

14.   Ibid., 80.

15.   Ibid., 55-57, 75.

16.   Cf. N. Max Wilders, *The Theologian and His Universe: Theology and Cosmology from the Middle Ages to the Present*, trans. by Paul Dunphy (New York: Seabury Press, 1982).

17.   Berry, *Befriending the Earth*, 20-21, 80.

18.   Berry, *The Dream of the Earth*, 125-126.

19.   Ibid., 115. Cf. Vine Deloria, *God Is Red*, 91-109; Roderick Nash, *Wilderness and the American Mind* (New Haven: Yale University Press, 1976, 1st ed., 1967), 24-25, 31, 36; and Lynn White, "The Historical Roots of Our Ecological Crisis," *Science* 155 (March 10, 1967): 1203-1207.

20.   Cf. Wilders, *The Theologian and His Universe*, 80-82; and Alexander Koyré, *From a Closed World to the Infinite Universe* (Baltimore: Helicon Press, 1957), 1-3.

21.   Cf. Michael Buckley, *The Origins of Modern Atheism* (New Haven and London: Yale University Press, 1987), for a similiar critique of the split between religion and science.

22.   Berry, "Economics: Its Effect on the Life Systems of the World," 16, *Befriending the Earth, 79.* See also Matthew Lamb, *Solidarity with Victims. Toward a Theology of Social Transformation* (New York: Crossroad, 1982), 2-7.

23.   Berry, *The Dream of the Earth*, 92.

24.   Ibid., 201.

25.   Ibid.

26.   Ibid., 202.

27.   Ibid., 95.

28.   Berry, *Befriending the Earth*, 110-111; *The Dream of the Earth*, 50-69, 70-88.

29.   Berry, "Individualiam and Wholism," 17.

30.   Cf. Berry's reference to David Ehrenfeld's *The Arrogance of Humanism* (New York: Oxford University Press, 1981), *Befriending the Earth*, 113.

31.   Cf. Caroline Richards, "The New Cosmology: What It Really Means," in *Thomas Berry and the New Cosmology*, 100.

32.   Berry, *The Dream of the Earth*, 123.

33.   Cf. Hauerwas and Jones, "Introduction" *Why Narrative?* 65-88; Happel, "Metaphors and Time Asymmetry: Cosmologies in Physics and Christian Meanings,"

Quantum Cosmology and the Laws of Nature: Scientific Perspectives on Divine Action, ed. by Robert John Russell, Nancey Murphy and C.J. Isham (Vatican City State: Vatican Observatory Publications, 1993), 103-134.

34.   Berry, *Befriending the Earth,* 132.

35.   Swimme and Berry, *The Universe Story,* 248.

36.   Ibid., 47.

37.   Ibid., 47-48. For other examples, see 100-102, 105-107, 110, 116.

38.   Ibid., 72.

39.   Paul Ricoeur, *Time and Narrative,* vol. 1, trans. by Kathleen McLaughlin and David Pellauer (Chicago: University of Chicago Press, 1984), 31ff, 208.

40.   Berry, *Dawn Over the Earth: Our Way into the Future,* Tape W3 (Laurel, MD: Earth Communications Center, no date), videocassette.

41.   Swimme and Berry, *The Universe Story,* 250.

42.   Ibid., 223, 255; See also Berry, *The Dream of the Earth,* 211 and passim.

43.   Ibid., 198. See also H. Paul Santmire, *The Travail of Nature: The Ambiguous Ecological Promise of Christian Theology* (Minneapolis: Fortress Press, 1985), esp. 35-41, 60-68.

44.   Berry, *Befriending the Earth,* 13.

45.   Berry, *The Dream of the Earth,* 20.

46.   Cf. M.D. [Marie-Dominique] Chenu, *Nature, Man and Society in the Twelfth Century* (Chicago, London: University of Chicago Press, 1968), 165-177; and Santmire, *The Travail of Nature,* 62-64.

47.   Cf. Stephen Dunn, C.P., "Needed: A New Genre for Moral Theology," in *Thomas Berry and the New Cosmology,* 76.

48.   Niebuhr, "The Story of My Life," *Why Narrative?* 31-32.

49.   Berry, *The Dream of the Earth,* 211.

50.   Ibid., 21, 65-69, 163-170.

51.   For the continuity of this concept with Vico's thought and subsequent notions of knowing as *Einfühlung* and *Verstehen,* see chapter one above.

52.   Niebuhr, "The Story of My Life," 32.

53.   Swimme and Berry, *The Universe Story,* 86, 126-127.

54.   Ibid., 133-134.

55.   Ibid., 143.

56.   Ricoeur, *Time and Narrative,* vol. 1, 194-197.

57.   Swimme and Berry, *The Universe Story,* 66-69, 71, 92. This principle added a second clause to the cosmogenetic principle, which assumed that all places are alike. A principle as understood here is a "reasonable assumption" based on available evidence. It was also complementary to the Second Law of Thermodynamics. The Second Law dealt with the dynamics that break down order in the universe; the cosmogenetic principle with the dynamics that build up order.

58.   Ibid., 69. See pp. 69-73 for the explanation of "form-producing powers" that follows here. Cf. p. 287, chapter four, bibliography, for dependence on Ilya Prigogine and Erich Jantsch for this concept.

59.   Ibid., 73.

60.   See chapter two above for discussion of the relationship of this principle to the traditional notions of the one and the many and of plenitude.

61.   Cf. Swimme and Berry, *The Universe Story*, 127, 136-138.

62.   Ibid., 74.

63.   Ibid., 243. See also *Befriending the Earth*, 96, 104; "The Cosmology of Religions," 108 and passim.

64.   Berry, interview by author, telephone and written account, Halifax, NS, October 1, 1993. The movement toward a more Aristotelian-Thomist understanding detectable in his latest works was probably due to his professed renewed interest in Aquinas. See also Swimme and Berry, *The Universe Story*, 230.

65.   Norris Clarke, "Form and Matter," in *The New Dictionary of Theology*, ed. by Joseph A. Komonchak, Mary Collins and Dermot Lane (Wilmington, DE: Michael Glazier, 1987): 403.

66.   See Thomas Clarke's response to Berry in *Befriending the Earth*, 31.

67.   Cf. Frederick Lawrence, "Self-knowledge in Gadamer and Lonergan," in *Language, Truth and Meaning*, ed. by Philip McShane (Notre Dame, IN: University of Notre Dame Press, 1972), 169-170.

68.   Cf. Berry, *The Dream of the Earth*, 209-210.

69.   Ibid., 45.

70.   Cf. M. Kafatos and R. Nadeau, *The Conscious Universe: Part and Whole in Modern Physical Theory* (New York: Springer-Verlag, 1990).

71.   Cf. Anna Bramwell, *Ecology in the 20th Century*, 39-63, for a discussion of the prevalence among ecologists of holistic biology, within which this idea of Berry was prevalent.

72.   Berry, *The Dream of the Earth*, 190.

73.   Swimme and Berry, *The Universe Story*, 38.

74.   Cf. Berry, "The Catholic Church and the Religions of the World," *Teilhard Perspective* 18,1 (August 1985): 2. See also David Bohm, "Fragmentation and Wholeness in Religion and Science," *Zygon* 20, 2 (June 1985):125-127, for a similar expression of concern.

75.   Cf. Arthur Fabel, "The Organic Society: A Search for Synthesis," *Teilhard Perspective* 17,1 (June 1984): 1-7.

76.   Paul Ricoeur, "Metaphor and Symbol," 46-53.

77.   Cf. Happel, "Metaphors and Time Asymmetry," 115-120.

78.   Karl Rahner, "The Theology of Symbol," in *Theological Investigations*, vol. 4, trans. by David Bourke (London: Darton, Longman and Todd, 1969), 221-252.

79.   Berry, *Befriending the Earth*, 55.

80.   Cf. Colloquium 1993, Holy Cross Centre, Port Burwell, Ontario, Audio-tape, June 1993. See also James Farris, "Redemption: Fundamental to the Story," in *Thomas Berry and the New Cosmology*, 68-70.

81.   Berry, *The Dream of the Earth*, 5-8. See also *The Universe Story*, 217-218 and *Befriending the Earth*, 81-82.

82.   Berry, *Befriending the Earth*, 54-55 and passim.

83.   Berry, "Perspectives on Creativity," 17.

84.   Cf. Lonergan's similar concept of general categories for theology in *Method in Theology* (Minneapolis, MN: The Seabury Press, 1972), 288-293.

CHAPTER SIX

BERNARD LONERGAN
AND EMERGENT PROBABILITY

Introduction

The previous chapters have been an attempt to understand Berry's response to the ecological crisis in the context of the genetic development of his thought and under the horizon that attracted him in the later years of his work. In moving the horizon to Christian theology, we move beyond the question of what Berry himself meant or intended to the further question, What aspects of his work are going forward with respect to a reform of Christian theology in the light of the ecological crisis? Bernard Lonergan's compelling and inclusive account of emergent probability is especially suited as a framework within which to address these questions. Lonergan's account is heuristic, in that it is a method for discovery or investigating solutions to various problems. The structural outline of world process is provided and the invitation is to test its validity with content specific to the problem at hand. The expectation is that Lonergan's heuristic account of world process and Berry's narrative account will complement and give credibility to each other. Furthermore, Lonergan will provide general categories for mediating Berry's descriptive proposal into the explanatory discipline of Christian theology.

As mentioned previously, Lonergan was himself greatly concerned with the growing irrelevance of Christian theology to the contemporary world. He was particularly aware of the seemingly irrevocable dualisms developing between scientific and humanistic methodologies, theory and common sense, theology and praxis, the human and the universe. He sought the solution in a phenomenology of human knowing itself and its place in the universe as modern science explained it. Emergent probability is the all-encompassing name of the solution he proposed. Because of how emergent probability overcomes the relevant dualisms, it is particularly appropriate to bring it into dialogue with Berry's ecological proposal. This chapter will examine categories from Lonergan's thought that are helpful in understanding Berry's contribution to Christian theology. The first of these is a classification of the nature of language according to its purposes.

Description and Explanation

As briefly explained in the previous chapter, Lonergan used the terms "description" and "explanation" to distinguish two kinds of language: language that relates things "to us" and language that relates things "to each other," respectively. Hence, when we speak of the "setting" sun, for instance, we are speaking descriptively of how the sun appears "to us." The explanation on the other hand is that the sun does not "set" at all; it is a matter of how the earth and the sun relate to each other.

Lonergan's viewpoint moves, develops and deepens throughout his work; this can be especially observed from the beginning of *Insight* to the end of *Method in Theology*. This designation of the two kinds of language is a case in point. Descriptive and explanatory language gain in significance both in themselves and in relation to each other as Lonergan presents and argues his viewpoint in the progression of his work.[1]

Lonergan maintained that description relates to explanation in two ways. The first way is best seen within science. A scientist selects descriptive accounts of experience (data) that are relevant to a particular problem and likely to assist in leading to a theory or solution. Here description acts as a "tweezers," holding on to aspects of experience in anticipation of an explanation. The explanatory account does not replace the descriptive one, however. The latter remains important as the control against which the theory is tested, retested and often discarded in favour of one that is more adequate.[2]

The second relationship is more indicative of what Lonergan called "the two universes of discourse" represented by these terms. Both forms of discourse refer to the same "universe of being," but they work from different viewpoints. By universe of being, Lonergan meant the sum total of all that is intelligently grasped and reasonably affirmed. It is not the "already out there now real" of the empiricists, nor the ideal of the idealists.[3] The operations of knowing that give rise to both viewpoints are the same: descriptive accounts, like explanatory ones, result from attention to data, a reasonable grasping of the intelligibility in the data and a responsible affirmation that what is grasped is, in fact, so. The criteria for the judgments involved differ, however. The descriptive account is concerned with the practical consequences in the world of human concerns; it is driven by the question, What is the good of it? The explanatory account is concerned with the universals, the general truths, the abstract, the ultimate; it relates to the ancient question, What is the nature of...? Science and philosophy, the world of theory, generally yield explanatory accounts; the whole domain referred to as "common sense," the world of human affairs, yields descriptive accounts.

Emergent Probability and the "New Story"

This preliminary account of the relationship of description to explanation discloses neither the full import of Lonergan's presentation nor the full significance of Berry's work as a work of description. It does, however, suggest an instance of mutual confirmation between the two realms of discourse. On the one hand, Berry's "new story" proves to be a concrete example of Lonergan's heuristic account of world process. On the other hand, Lonergan's theory of emergent probability provides an explanatory grounding for Berry's work and the science on which it is based.

As shown above, contemporary scientific accounts of evolution contain concepts and theories that explain aspects, at least, of the "new story." While scientific categories explain the evolutionary narrative, however, Lonergan's account of world process explains both the evolutionary narrative and the construction and telling of the "new story." In other words, emergent probability explains world process—the evolution of the universe, including the human and the emergent process by which humans come *to know* the universe and *to act* within it.

The Intelligibility of the Universe

Emergent probability shows, first of all, how classical laws and statistical laws reveal the inherent intelligibility of the universe. Classical laws grasp the necessary, causal and deterministic qualities and functioning of the universe. They are what scientists traditionally aimed for and understood to be possible for every aspect of physical reality. Statistical laws, on the other hand, grasp the probable occurrence of events, their coincidence, the likelihood of their survival and such other qualities of the universe that, as contemporary science has shown, are not subject to classical laws. They refer to the radical contingency, freedom and creativity that also inhere in the universe but that do not, thereby, render the entire process chaotic and unintelligible.

Lonergan did not invent the idea of statistical laws and their relevance to the universe. What he did was to show that these laws result from the same acts of human knowing as classical laws do.[4] Both kinds of laws express an abstraction from data of an intelligibility inherent in the data. What differs is the kind of data. Classical laws ignore the concrete occurrences and define relationships, "other things being equal." Statistical laws deal with the data of concrete happenings, the "other things" that are almost never equal. So, while a classical law assures us that at 0° Celsius water freezes, statistical law states the likelihood of such occurring within the atmosphere of a particular geographic region.

We can observe in retrospect that world process is also emergent.[5] Whole new realities come to be. Lonergan moved away from speaking of the emergence of individual things (as Darwin had done) to consider the emergence and survival of schemes. A thing does not emerge independently; it is already embedded in a cyclic relationship within which it is dependent on surrounding events and things, as they are dependent on it. Each cyclic scheme (Lonergan called them schemes of recurrence) is also embedded in other schemes or sets of schemes. Schemes of recurrence explain why highly improbable events occur and even survive, even though the probability of occurrence and survival is hardly ever the same.

Simply stated, a scheme can be represented as follows: if A occurs, then B will occur and then C; but if C occurs, then A will continue to occur, initiating the whole cycle again. Thus, if B, considered independently, is a highly unlikely event, it becomes almost assured by the occurrence of A. Once B has occurred, the probability of its survival is dependent on the probability of the occurrence of some other scheme that destroys, replaces, changes or otherwise interferes with its integral functioning. A series of schemes is conditioned if the concrete possibility of a particular scheme occurring depends on the actuality of other schemes. Hence, while schemes in the plant world are not generally conditioned by schemes in the animal world, the reverse is true.

Contemporary scientific discussions provide concrete examples of the emergence and survival of interrelated schemes. Those that enter into the story of the universe, as Berry and Swimme told it, include the nature of subatomic particles as energy events, the fundamental interrelatedness of all the components of the universe, self-organizing dynamics, the Gaia theory and the nature of ecosystems.[6] Evolution, as scientists presently understand it, exhibits qualities of contingency. At any one point in time the future looks radically open and unpredictable, but in retrospect the occurrence of events satisfies the laws of statistical probability, within which classical laws define terms and relations.

Emergent probability is an account of the intelligibility of world process of which the intelligibility of the physical universe is one instance. Lonergan showed that statistical laws, as well as classical, indicate intelligibility. The universe is not a lock-step, mechanical design as Darwin had already discovered, but neither is it an unknowable, merely chaotic set of discrete events.

World process also exhibits a vertical finality, which Lonergan defined as a relationship to an end, rather than as an end itself.[7] He distinguished absolute finality, which is to God; horizontal finality, which is to the proportionate end; and vertical finality, which is to an end higher than the proportionate end and thus operates in evolution. Vertical finality is characterized by a dynamic climb upward to ever more complex levels of reality. Emergent probability, thus, displays a hierarchy. It is not, however, a static hierarchy nor is it one that necessarily imputes higher intrinsic value to each successive level. It is rather a dynamic process of sublation in which lower levels are instrumental in the emergence and survival of higher levels, but the lower level is participative in the process and, in fact, often creates a mutually beneficial situation.[8]

At the physical level, energy coalesces into events or particles that comprise schemes we call atoms and molecules; atoms and molecules form more complex schemes within chemical compounds and then living organisms. While the more complex schemes integrate the lower into functioning wholes, the integrity of the lower level is also maintained. The description of the dimensions of the carbon atom in *The Universe Story* is an illustration of this dynamic sublation.[9] To be fully appreciated in all its potential, the carbon atom must be seen in its functioning in the human brain. Yet, the carbon atom is its own entity as well. The brain is comprised of atoms, but a full knowledge of those atoms does not exhaustively explain the reality we call the human brain.

The notion of sublation confronts the mistakes of reductionism on the one hand and of instrumentalization on the other. "Wholes" that emerge in the universe are not merely the sum of their components; some new dimension is achieved. While the components are instrumental in that achievement, they retain an identity that is not fully explainable in terms of their usefulness in particular cases.

Emergent Probability Grounds a Story

So emergent probability is an explanatory account of those characteristics of the universe that make a story of the universe possible at all. This is because emergent probability grounds the inherent intelligibility of time as it applies to the evolution of the physical universe. It shows how time is constructed through the unfolding of events characterized by an interaction of necessary and contingent happenings that can be understood in terms of a relationship between classical and statistical laws. Lonergan's notions of vertical finality and sublation explain the temporal constitution of the universe: the present is different from the past, but is both genetically related to it and a further development from it. Furthermore, past events play a purposeful role in the present but maintain their own integrity apart from it. Thus, Lonergan's ontology can ground scientific accounts of evolution.[10]

Scientific accounts add an empirical concreteness to emergent probability but are also explanatory, that is, concerned with the "nature of" the universe and its components. Berry's account is different again; it is concerned with the "good of" these explanations in confronting the ecological crisis. As illustrated, theories that imply contingency, creativity and agency within the evolution and functioning of components of the universe were interpreted, by Berry, as continuous with human history, and images were purposefully chosen to evoke affect and empathy toward other members of the universe.

The three kinds of accounts, then, are related as the expression "emerging scheme of recurrence" (Lonergan) is related to "self-organizing dynamics of a cell" (scientists) and further to "the mysterious creative efforts of a fragile being" (Berry). Lonergan's expression is heuristic and formal, grounded in the isomorphism between human knowing and what is known. It refers to the nature of everything that can be known, that is to the nature of being itself. The scientific phrase refers to the nature of a concrete known, a cell. Berry's phrase is not inconsistent with the nature of a cell; it uses the notion of self-organization in a cell and sets it in metaphoric relationship with mystery, creativity and fragility. The "good of" the explanation to Berry is that it supports (even suggests) the kind of rhetoric he considered powerful in the overturning of post-Enlightenment conceptions of the natural world as static and mechanistic. Therefore, it works toward establishing an ecological ethic. While they refer to the same universe of being, these expressions clearly belong to different universes of discourse. The significance of their distinctive functions and their interdependence are further clarified within the account of emergent probability as it applies to the role of humans in the world.

Human Knowing in Emergent Probability

According to Lonergan's heuristic account, world process is intelligible. Within the human, that process also becomes intelligent. The human role consists in the exercise of the transcendental operations of knowing and meaning-making. When authentically performed, these operations contribute to the intelligibility and meaningfulness of the world.

Of course, human knowing is not the only dimension of human activity that is significant within world process; nor does human knowing occur apart from the concrete life context of human subjects. It is only within this larger context that it achieves (or does not achieve) its authenticity. Lonergan's account of authenticity and its relationship to knowing will be further explicated below.

In Lonergan's words, "The advent of man does not abrogate the rule of emergent probability." Human activity follows classical and statistical laws that produce concrete sets of schemes of recurrence. The unique situation of humans is that, while they are subject to emergent probability, they also can take initiative in influencing probabilities. As Lonergan explained:

> The specific difference of human history is that among the probable possibilities is a sequence of operative insights by which men can grasp possible schemes of recurrence and take the initiative in bringing about the material and social conditions that make these schemes concretely possible, probable and actual.[11]

Lonergan saw the process of human knowing to be a practical activity within emergent probability.[12] When authentically exercised, the operations of human knowing, attention to data, grasp of intelligibility by insight (or of non-intelligibility, in the case of inverse insights) and responsible judgment regarding the adequacy of the insight yield a succession of higher viewpoints. Higher viewpoints sublate former (now lower) viewpoints just as molecules sublate atoms, cells sublate molecules and organisms sublate cells. When effectively mediated into the culture and the society, these higher viewpoints function as emergent schemes of recurrence. High probability of such schemes emerging and surviving constitutes the conditions for what Lonergan called progress; the opposite is decline. It should be noted that Lonergan did not mean by progress the liberal approach of the nineteenth century that fueled the materialist, techno-industrial revolution. For Lonergan, progress was connected to the authentic lives of persons and communities, where authenticity is understood as a number of conversions to be discussed below. In effect, Lonergan's departure from the liberals rests on what counts as the criteria for progress.

As mentioned above, human knowing occurs within different realms, designated as the realms of theory and common sense, each with its own dynamic exigence. When progress is occurring, these realms interrelate in dynamic fashion. Explanation integrates the images supplied by description into higher viewpoints that understand the process as a whole and produce long-range views that guide common-sense decisions and actions. Description not only provides the data that explanation integrates, but also provides the images that mediate explanatory views within the realm of common sense. Decline is evident in a breakdown in this dynamic interrelationship.

Decline and Its Solution

The Longer Cycle of Decline

Common sense is often subject to individual bias that results from egotism. It is also subject to group bias in which the social groups refuse compromise and work for their own objectives over and above that of any others. When not successfully negotiated, both of these biases inhibit the successful functioning of human society. It is general bias, however, that is the most serious and results in the longer cycle of decline.[13]

General bias arises from the ambiguity of common sense.[14] Common sense is defined by its attention to the immediate, the here and now and the practical solution. This is both its strength and its limitation. The limitation becomes dysfunctional, however, only when

refuses to acknowledge it and to allow an effective
Then the higher explanatory viewpoints and longer
hould play a highly functional role in promoting
enter the realm of real possibility. Higher explana-
are the theoretic integrations that explain historical
ght not to be repeated. Longer views would preclude
be practical in the immediate present but would be
he long run. Besides disregarding higher viewpoints,
may also consciously refuse insights deemed to be
ontrary to immediate interests.[15] As Lonergan admit-
alism has its role and is often correct in its negative
heories. Over the course of time, however, a constant
omission or refusal of more comprehensive explana-
results in a long process of decline with recognizable

xclusion of more comprehensive viewpoints in one
is that these ideas are not readily available to the next
even less so to the next. In the development of West-
n was the case with the gradual hegemony of materi-
science and its partnership with technology and in-
shing the norms of so-called "progress."[16] To a large
iation can be seen to result from the exclusion of
hilosophical insights regarding what constituted the
ancy of Cartesianism and the refusal of its adherents
y the traditions that Vico and his followers repre-
in the increasing marginalization of a set of insights
elped avert the fragmentation of modern scholarship
living. According to Lonergan, when comprehensive
integral functioning of society are consistently re-
, less and less available, the society stagnates. Then
igible is the balance of economic pressures and na-

ture is isolated from social reality. In an unintelligible society, religion is relegated to personal life. Art, which nor-
mally embodies the insights of artists and often points symbolically
to the intelligible, assumes trivial, decorative and elitist roles.[17] The
academy is instrumentalized for the support of the status quo. The
theoretic disciplines, capable of uncovering the relationship of culture to the concrete, practical life of society, are paralyzed in that
effort, since the exclusion of the necessary theoretic viewpoints has
made the society itself unintelligible. To return to our example of the
first characteristic, if any notion of the real other than the empiricist,
materialist conception of modern science has become inoperative in

society, then art, religion and academic pursuits can be considered relevant to common sense only if they cater to the technocratic, industrialist and consumerist society. They are admitted to that society only if they do not interfere with its agenda.

Seeking intelligibility in an unintelligible society would be akin to solving a problem in which many of the data are unrelated. Such data constitute an empirical residue. Lonergan called the increasing unintelligibility, the growth of irrationality and incoherence within society, "the social surd."

Third, humans operating within the increasingly unintelligible situation become victims of their own creation. Not only do those in the realm of common sense arduously defend things as they are, but those operating at the speculative level capitulate to common sense. The capitulation consists in rejecting what they denounce as "apriorist, wishful thinking," to consider "things as they are." (Statistical descriptions, for example, are seen as normative.) While this sounds admirable, "things as they are" often means things as the present common sense sees them. The defect is the rejection of the normativity of authentic human knowing, which recognizes that experience itself is not explanatory. (Statistics are merely data, the meaning and value of which are subject to human understanding and judgment.) Hence, there is no critical basis for culture.[18]

Lonergan's understanding of the transcendental structure of values and meanings lay the building blocks for his solution to the problem of decline. That solution rests on the authenticity of the human operations whereby meaning and value are established. The following sections present those building blocks and show how they relate to the authenticity required to avoid or overturn decline.

Values and Moral Self-Transcendence

There is no "pure form" of speculative reason, Lonergan said; knowing happens within human subjects. Hence:

> Scientific or philosophic experiencing, understanding and judging do not occur in a vacuum. They are the operations of an existential subject who has decided to devote himself to the pursuit of understanding and truth and with greater or less success, is faithful to his commitment.[19]

So a presentation of the human role in emergent probability, of the conditions for decline and the possibility of progress, must include an account of authenticity. As indicated above, the classical and statistical laws of emergent probability also operate in the human sphere.

Other things being equal, humans are free. This is what is known as essential freedom. In actual, concrete human life, however, this freedom is always conditioned. This is called effective freedom. The relationship of essential to effective freedom can be seen as analogous to the relationship of classical and statistical laws as Lonergan explained it.[20]

Effective freedom is always conditioned by the group, society and culture that one more or less appropriates.[21] So if a civilization is in decline, the patterns of thinking and behaviour that are appropriated are those characteristic of this cycle; hence, the probability of the exercise of human freedom toward progress is small indeed, but never zero. This raises the question as to how, concretely, human decisions and actions can be directed toward the reversal of decline. While the full answer to this question, for Lonergan, was a religious one, he understood it to be mediated within the context of human freedom. Furthermore, freedom is not an arbitrary exercise of will; rather it consists of decisions and actions that arise in a context of values and meanings that are originated or appropriated by human subjects in various stages of moral self-transcendence.

The notion of values is a transcendental notion. While this may sound like an abstraction, Lonergan's understanding was that transcendental notions are always concrete. According to this notion, values are apprehended in feelings and confirmed as good or not in answers to questions for deliberation.[22] It is important to be aware that for Lonergan the transcendental operations were posited on the basis of a phenomenology of human knowing. *Insight* is an examination of how knowing operates within the theoretic disciplines and within common sense; it is also an exercise for the observation and appropriation of the reader's own knowing. Likewise, all transcendental notions represent patterns of concrete behaviours. Furthermore, they include an invitational element. To say that values have a transcendental structure does not imply that they are automatic; experience invites the authentic operation of understanding and so on.

The term "feelings" in the context here refers to a class of intentional feelings. In general, feelings include non-intentional states, such as anxiety, and trends and urges such as hunger. While states are "caused by" something, trends and urges are "toward goals" but are not necessarily consciously intended. Intentional feelings, however, are consciously directed toward objects and belong to one of two classes. One class refers to objects as "agreeable or disagreeable, satisfying or dissatisfying." The other (the class of primary interest to Lonergan and to this discussion) concerns objects as valuable, whether agreeable or disagreeable, satisfying or dissatisfying; they relate instead to self-transcendence. For Lonergan, "response to value both carries us toward self-transcendence and selects an object for the sake of whom or of which we transcend ourselves."[23] One's capacity to judge what is valuable or good, then, depends upon a number of factors, but in particular upon the achievement of moral self-transcendence, which Lonergan thematized in several ways.[24]

First, feelings apprehend values according to a scale of preference. Hence we have vital, social, cultural, personal and religious values. Vital values respond to basic needs; social values to the good of order, whereby the vital needs of a community are met; cultural values refer to the shared values by which communities live; personal values refer to the self-transcendence of the individual as the originator of values; religious values stem from the operative love of God in one's life. The scale of values is hierarchically arranged in that greater self-transcendence is required as one makes decisions relative to each succeeding level, vital to social and so on.

Lonergan's theology of values and of growth in moral self-transcendence implies a progress up the scale of values from vital to religious, where the supreme value is love of God and all other values are seen as expressions of God's love in the world. At such a summit of self-transcendence, genuine values are whatever one loves. This is the meaning of authenticity at its limit. Such a development of moral self-transcendence is the ideal, however, and hardly ever happens in a continuous and uninterrupted fashion.

Second, moral self-transcendence does not operate in a vacuum. In judgments of value, three components unite: knowledge of our human reality, intentional response to value and a thrust toward moral self-transcendence constituted by the judgment itself (the existential discovery of oneself as a moral and responsible being). Knowledge of human reality provides a context and content for judging moral action and is a safeguard against moral idealism. An intentional response to value refers to a prior apprehension that consistently draws one toward self-transcendence. The judgment itself or the actual thrust toward moral self-transcendence becomes the existential discovery that one is, in fact, a moral and responsible being. Finally, it is in the actual "doing" of moral acts that one progresses in moral self-transcendence.

Third, while the probability of moral self-transcendence in an individual is subject to the social, cultural and religious heritage in which one attempts to live, all values do originate in persons. As Lonergan contended,

> That human world does not come into being or survive without
> deliberation, evaluation, decision, action, without the exercise of

freedom and responsibility. It is a world of existential subjects and it objectifies the values that they originate in their creativity and their freedom.[25]

Thus, Lonergan upholds the relevance of personal freedom, however small effectively, in the achievement of authenticity.

The achievement of values is an accomplishment in the first place, then, of the freedom and responsibility of individual subjects in acts of self-transcendence. Thus, the statistical element of emergent probability refers not just to the *failures* of human subjects as agents of world process, but also to their free and responsible *choices* that affect the probability of emergence and/or survival of schemes of recurrence.

Finally, moral self-transcendence relates to moral conversion. Human schemes of recurrence sometimes require radical change, a reorientation or change in horizon that is not accomplished by genetic development. Hence, the necessity of moral conversion is indicated. All conversions are changes in horizon. In the case of moral conversion, the criterion of decisions and actions changes from satisfaction to value. Then one enters a lifelong process of further developing the three components of moral judgments outlined above.[26]

Just as a life of pure intellect would be, in Lonergan's words, "something less than the life of a psychopath," so the notion of the will as arbitrary power refers simply to unauthenticity. Willing refers not to arbitrariness, but to the concrete decisions and actions with which human subjects negotiate the "highly complex business" of authenticity and unauthenticity.[27]

The Structure and Stages of Meaning

What is meaning and how does it function in individuals and communities in history? As was the case with values, Lonergan answered this question with an account of the invariant structure of meaning-making.

Once humans leave the immediacy of the world of young infants, they live in a world mediated by meaning.[28] The world of immediacy refers to the sum total of both the data of sense, which, in principle at least, are open to public inspection, and the data of consciousness, which constitute human subjectivities and are not open to inspection. The world of immediacy is the world of experience not yet subject to human questioning. The world mediated by meaning consists of all that is to be known from one's questioning of the world of experience; in other words, it is the interpreted world.

"Meaning," Lonergan said, "is an act that does not merely repeat but goes beyond experiencing." He continued:

> For what is meant is what is intended in questioning and is determined not only by experience, but also by understanding and, commonly, by judgment as well. This addition of understanding and judgment is what makes possible the world mediated by meaning, what gives it its structure and unity, what arranges it in an orderly whole of almost endless differences partly known and familiar, partly in a surrounding penumbra of things we know about but have never examined or explored, partly an unmeasured region of what we do not know at all.[29]

While humans construct a meaningful world, they do not do so in isolation. Meanings are carried from one to another and over time in quite distinct carriers: intersubjectivity,[30] art, symbols, language and the fullness of persons' lives (incarnate meaning).

Meanings also function differently within human society and culture; they can be cognitive, efficient, constitutive and communicative. Cognitive meaning results from questions for understanding (what is and why), the questions that move one out from the world of immediacy into the world mediated by meaning. Meaning as efficient refers to the intentionality and mindfulness of human work. Constitutive meanings are the meanings around which social and cultural institutions are constructed. They are the "intrinsic components" of religions, arts, literature, sciences and of the family, the state, the law and the economy. Finally, meaning is communicative. By means of intersubjectivity, art, symbol, language and whole lives, humans share meanings. Thus, there result common meanings transmitted from individual to individual and over the generations especially by education. The meanings, of course, can change as new meanings originate within persons and are likewise communicated. They can be enriched and transformed by additions, refined formulations and so on. They can also become deformed and impoverished by the same process.

To a large extent, humans construct their lives from a given set of common meanings. Thus, as Lonergan indicated in his discussion of values, the human struggle for authenticity is very much conditioned by the state of progress or decline that presently exists. From the other side, traditions enter decline when unauthenticity occurs among individuals on a massive scale. Then functions and rituals may remain, but the meanings have gone. In this latter assessment, Lonergan referred to meaning as content. "Meaning," he said, "has its invariant structures and elements, but the contents of that structure are subject to cumulative development and cumulative decline."[31]

While the structures of meaning seem to have been consistent over time, there was also a discernible series of genetically related differentiations of consciousness resulting in different stages of meaning. Lonergan distinguished among four realms or stages of meaning that have developed, namely, common sense, theory, interiority and transcendence.[32]

The first three realms of meaning refer to differentiations of consciousness whose development can be recognized over history. There is a fourth realm, transcendence, which will be discussed later in this chapter. The realms of meaning are existentially cumulative, that is, one has to be in the first stage to advance to the second and in the second to advance to the third. They are, however, also ideal constructs and there is no precisely identifiable transition point from one to another. They are also not chronologically sequential, since theory does not replace common sense, nor interiority the other two.

Primitive humans operated within the mode of common sense. Consciousness had not been differentiated. Relying on the research of anthropologists, Lonergan pointed out how primitive groups constructed their world according to the same conscious and intentional operations as modern humans do; meaning fulfilled all the functions: cognitive, efficient, constitutive and communicative. The differences in the functions were not clearly understood and defined, however. Myth, for example, resulted from the blending of the constitutive and cognitive functions.

Primitive humans gave constitutive meaning not only to their society and culture, but also to the account of the origin, nature and destiny of the universe. It was the constitutive meaning of the universe that made it a functional cosmology in Berry's terms. The entire cosmos was meaningful, not only with cognitive meanings such as modern science supplies (and which at the time were also present from other sources), but with values and directions for life. Myth also supplied the basis for magic; words and rites derived from the myths were considered powerful strategies for control over forces that impinged on human life. Hence, its meaning was effective.

Within the context of the primitive construction of the world, intelligence progressed, however. Great civilizations grew up within a cosmological vision of homogeneity among cosmos, society and divine being.[33] Undifferentiated consciousness does not mean lack of intelligence; the achievement of differentiated consciousness was a slow and cumulative process.

The transition from the first stage of meaning to the second is marked by the discovery of mind, recognizable in the West (Lonergan did not deal with Eastern cultures) in the ancient Greek philosophers. This transition is characterized by a growing awareness of such distinctions as those of image from the thing imagined, representation from real perception, wish from fulfillment, dreams from waking consciousness. The awareness of the inefficacy of magic compared to human ingenuity, the weakness of humans in controlling divine power and questions demanding general definitions as to the nature of things were all developments that led to the emergence of theoretic consciousness and the second stage of meaning. A succession of Greek philosophers dispelled the magical character of knowledge and upheld more empirical and humanly controlled notions of knowledge. Eventually, within this context, modern science as we know it emerged.

The transition from common sense to theory meets the systematic exigence. The systematic exigence inquires about common meanings, internal relations, congruencies and differences. The questions arise in common sense, but the answers are to be found in theory. Whereas the mode of expression at the level of common sense was description, at the level of theory it is explanation.

In the second stage of meaning, common sense continues to operate alongside theory. It is characteristic of this stage, however, that neither the theoretic mode of consciousness nor the common-sense mode understands the relationship between the two. Hence, there are the mistaken beliefs that science as a way of knowing will replace common sense, that the knowledge acquired by science is the only true knowledge and that mathematics alone can claim the certainty of truth. According to this way of thinking, all other expressions of knowledge are trivialized.

These are the assumptions that created the reaction of the counter-Enlightenment described in the earlier chapters of this book. Science's exclusivist claim to knowing contributed largely to various expressions of materialism, empiricism and rationalism that had their results in the instrumentalization of the natural world, to which Berry drew attention. The gap between science and the humanities and between science and religion, in particular, was also a result of confusion over what constituted real knowledge.[34]

The Third Stage of Meaning—Intellectual Conversion

A new stage of meaning emerged in response to the confusion over the nature of knowing evident in such epistemological questions as: Is common sense only nonsense, or is it actually what knowing really is? Does science reveal the nature of the universe or does it merely supply sophisticated techniques for its control? Can humans really know anything? And if they do, how do they know that they do?

Lonergan associated the emergence of this stage with a series of developments that centred around the human as subject of knowledge and action. These included Immanuel Kant's account of the conditions of human knowing, the existentialist philosophers and theologians and intentionality analyses. With these (and other) developments, attention moved from the contents of knowledge to knowing itself. The self-understanding of scientists changed. Instead of seeing their goal as the stating of truth, they now saw it as "an ever better approximation of truth" attained by "an ever fuller and more exact understanding of all the relevant data."[35] Theory and common sense were not seen as competitive modes of consciousness, but rather as different viewpoints directing different tasks and fulfilling complementary roles.

The third stage of meaning is Lonergan's way of grounding the possibility of any human knowing at all.[36] It corresponds to the level of judgment, making possible the critical human judgment, "I am a knower." Applied to the two preceding stages of meaning, this stage enables the subject to see common sense and theory as corresponding to the levels of experience and understanding, respectively. In other words, while common sense and theory both employ experiencing, understanding and judging, common sense has not appropriated or objectified the operations of understanding and judging, nor has theory appropriated or objectified the operation of judging.[37]

The movement from one realm of meaning to another is characterized by the appropriation of another operation of knowing. Therefore, from the perspective of interiority, one could judge that at the theoretic level one understands what was experienced at the level of common sense. When the data examined is the data of one's own consciousness, then the third stage of meaning rests on the judgment that at the level of common sense "I experience knowing" and at the theoretic level "I explain it." To repeat, this judgment can only be made once one has reached the stage of interiority in which the operations of experiencing, understanding and judging have been experienced, identified, appropriated and objectified as dynamic dimensions of one's own knowing.

Attempts at the theoretic level to understand the relationship between common sense and theory proved inadequate.[38] Thus, a new stage of meaning arose (and still arises) from the need to determine the relationship of the previous stages to each other and to the question of what knowing really is.

The third stage of meaning consists in "the appropriation of one's own interiority, one's subjectivity, one's operations, their structure, their norms, their potentialities."[39] The process begins with a heightening of self-presence, that is the experience of the subject-as-subject, a self-presence that precedes any cognitional operations and is presupposed in every act of the subject intending an object. Lonergan related the subject to the object (the knower to the "to be known") with his phenomenological account of the dynamic structure involved in the directional, intentional self-transcendence that constitutes the process of knowing and is intrinsic to the human subject.[40] Interiority is a heightening of intentional consciousness, "an attending not merely to objects, but also to the intending subject and his acts."[41] *Insight* was an invitation to the reader, gradually, step by step, to pay attention to one's own knowing, to understand the operations by which one came to know and to affirm that one is "in fact" a knower.

Interiority is manifested in the performance thus envisioned by *Insight*. It is the grounding in one's own experience of the structures, operations and norms of knowing. These are recognized in the objectification of these structures, operations and norms at the theoretic level. Interiority results in a critical realist position. A critical realist understands and judges the real to be the result of experiencing, understanding and judging. Furthermore, in this position, what one calls objectivity is understood to be the authentic exercise of these operations.

Later, Lonergan called the third stage of meaning an intellectual conversion. As in all conversions, there is a shift in horizon, in this case from theoretic knowledge as the basis of normativity to interiority as the basis of normativity. Hence, there is a change between the second and third stage in how meaning is controlled. The control of meaning by theories and logic in the second stage gives way to the control of meaning by the operations of human consciousness. The latter is possible because what is achieved by the third stage is a self-knowledge and a consequent ability. Subjects gain control of a method by which they can relate the procedures of their own knowing to the different realms of meaning, relate the realms to each other and "consciously shift from one realm to another by consciously changing [their] procedures."[42] Furthermore, it is the careful and attentive exercise of this method in the experience of life, individual and communal (societal and cultural), that initiates schemes of recurrence that constitute authentic progress and, if necessary, confronts the longer cycle of decline.

Psychic Conversion and the Third Stage of Meaning

Relying on Lonergan's notion of the role of the human psyche in the creation of meaning as well as on the insights of Carl Jung, Robert

Doran developed the concept of psychic conversion as constitutive of the third stage of meaning. Doran's analysis is particularly relevant to the analysis of Berry's proposal because of the significance Berry gives to the role of the psyche.

Doran maintained that a full recovery of human subjectivity and the achievement of interiority require an appropriation of operations at the level of the psyche. Besides the conscious capacities such as inquiry, insight, reflection and decision, there exists within human subjectivity an "elemental symbolic function" that constantly supplies data for consciousness in the form of motifs and symbols. There also exists a "preconscious collaboration of imagination and intelligence" that acts as a censor in seeking out and selecting from this imaginal flow (symbols, dreams, images) what will be admitted to consciousness and, hence, become subject to the intellectual operations.[43]

The symbolic function is, first of all, an internal communicator. It reveals organic and psychic vitality to intentional consciousness and vice versa. Second, symbols both embody the objects of feelings and evoke feelings. In these capacities, as elemental, the meaning of the symbol is not yet objectified. It is, Lonergan said, "like the meaning of the smile prior to the phenomenology of the smile." It is in its contact with intentional consciousness that the symbol becomes objectified. Symbols, however, defy logical reduction. They embody multiple meanings, tensions, conflicts and even contradictions. So they always remain even after they have been objectified in consciousness.[44]

In concrete human existence, the organic, psychic and intellectual levels of human subjects co-operate to create a pattern of human living. As each level is sublated by the other, the function of sublation is not merely one of integration, but also one of dynamic operation. The psychic level works within the organic, selecting, transforming and repressing the exigencies that arise from there. Likewise, the intellectual operator actively receives, selects and transforms data arising from the psyche. So while the symbols that inform human life arise from below, they are always subject to dynamic activity from above downward. Hence, not only the invariant operations of human knowing, but also the personal, intersubjective, social and cultural influences bear on the symbolic composition of human life, individually and communally.[45]

Psychic conversion focuses on the process of censorship at the level of the psyche. It reorients and transforms that process from habitual repression to a liberated construction. Thus, it releases the flow of images and sensitivities to become data for the insights that govern human life. It enables human life to better reflect its nature as unity-in-tension. It does so by establishing and maintaining an integral dialectic between limitation and transcendence within the human psyche.[46]

Under a religious horizon, the integration (psychic conversion) is the result of a healing or soteriological vector. Not every dialectic is healed by integration, however. Departing from Jung, Doran pointed out that dialectics that relate to good and evil can only be healed by replacing evil with good. The integral dialectic between limitation and transcendence to which Doran refers depends first on the resolution of the good-evil dialectic (dialectic of contraries) in favour of the good. Then the good itself consists in the "unity-in-tension" (dialectic of contradictories) of limitation and transcendence. These two kinds of dialectic represent a clarification of the two ways in which Lonergan used the term.

While all values are personal before they are incorporated into the larger community, our interest is in values at the cultural level, since that was Berry's primary focus. His critique and recovery centred on culture as the locus for the mediation of values throughout society. So our question regards the interaction of psychic conversion and culture. Doran thematized that relationship in terms of limitation and transcendence and Lonergan's stages of meaning.

Historically, the censorship of the imaginal flow within the human psyche reflected the stages of meaning. Within the primal world, the censorship operated in favour of limitation, that is, toward a capitulation to the biological exigencies and an embeddedness in the cosmological and planetary cycles and seasons. Within the primal cultures, there is evidence of an ecological differentiation. There seems to have been a high valuation of nature by primal groups. With the emergence of the anthropological differentiation, conditioned by a transcendent differentiation, there resulted a high concentration on human history. With that occurrence, the censor tended to operate more generally in favour of transcendence, human freedom and control of nature to the consequent near (if not total) elimination of cosmological consciousness. Therefore, one can see that the results of the psychic operations were a constitutive and functional cosmology among primal peoples, followed by a gradual replacement of cosmology by historical consciousness as the second stage of meaning developed.[47]

The conversion to a more constructive role for the psychic censorship would result in the restoration to consciousness of images arising from sensitivities to earth and cosmos, not to replace those geared to human history, but to exist in an integral dialectic with them. Psychically converted subjects can be expected to initiate values of respect for the natural world that will consequently bear fruit in many different schemes of recurrence to meet decline as it is presently manifested by ecological devastation.[48] This new ecological differentiation would be quite different from that of earlier ages because it would include a differentiation between the rhythms of the sensitive psyche and the exigencies of conscious intentionality, which have since been achieved. Such an ecological differentiation is something yet to be accomplished.

Doran's account of psychic conversions further delineates and clarifies the structure of human authenticity as Lonergan understood it. For Lonergan, the mediation of human authenticity in society and culture constitutes the solution to decline. He used the symbolic term *cosmopolis* to designate that solution.

Cosmopolis

The Heuristic Structure of Cosmopolis

The symbol *cosmopolis* functions in Lonergan's work as the place holder x functions in mathematical equations. The solution set expands as one moves from integers to rational numbers to real numbers, but each greater set includes the previous and, hence, does not cancel out the truth of the previous solutions. In Lonergan's moving viewpoint, the meaning of *cosmopolis* expands as well without canceling out former meanings. While *cosmopolis* ultimately indicated a divine solution to the problem of decline, Lonergan understood that solution to be mediated within the bounds of human freedom.

Cosmopolis is first of all "a withdrawal from practicality to save practicality."[49] In other words, *cosmopolis* is concerned with the cultural meanings and values. The purpose of such values is to provide critical and long-range viewpoints capable of overturning decline and guiding progress within the common-sense affairs of the world. Since *cosmopolis* is a cultural intervention, it is worth looking at what Lonergan calls the two levels of culture. They are the superstructure, which is a theoretic differentiation, and the infrastructure, which consists of the shared meanings and values and their carriers within common sense.[50] While the superstructure is the locus of the critical views to be mediated by *cosmopolis*, the actual mediation occurs within the infrastructure. The infrastructure consists of the arts, the media, the school and the university; it is the arena of communication.

The theoretic views arise, are appropriated and shared in the second stage of meaning, but it is within the third stage that *cosmopolis* becomes possible. This is because *cosmopolis* is an intentional construction; it relies on the ability to distinguish the previous stages of meaning and, hence, to exercise control over both theory and common sense. The end of this function of *cosmopolis* is to influence the probability of the emergence of appropriate schemes that could meet decline.

The critical viewpoints (meanings and values) to be appropriated are those judged true and relevant. Such a judgment is founded on the application to history of dialectical methods under a hermeneutics of suspicion regarding *disvalues* and a hermeneutics of recovery regarding *values*. Again, it bears repetition that always in Lonergan's schema values and disvalues are apprehended not in abstract isolation, but rather in the concrete problems at hand.[51] But the actual appropriation within common sense depends on a further task of mediating those meanings and values. The object is to re-establish the integrity of the scale of values, the ordering of which is skewed under decline.

The possibility of *cosmopolis* relies on a series of conversions. First, it relies on intellectual and psychic conversions, which ground command of its method. Second, it relies on moral conversion, which grounds the discernment of value in the apprehension of the good over mere satisfaction. As will be indicated below, it ultimately requires a religious conversion, which grounds universal willingness and action.

Cosmopolis, as an intervention in the world of common sense, depends primarily on descriptive language for its effective and practical edge.[52] In Lonergan's words:

> man's explanatory self-knowledge can become effective in his concrete living only if the content of systematic insights, the direction of judgments, the dynamism of decisions can be embodied in images that release feeling and emotion and flow spontaneously into deeds no less than words.[53]

Cosmopolis, then, consists in a set of interwoven images within culture that function in the world of common sense in communicating values and motivating action in the direction of progress, that is, toward the authentic operation of human responsibility for history.[54] Its full meaning for Lonergan, however, is uncovered only under the religious horizon. That meaning is further specified under a Christian horizon.

Cosmopolis Under a Religious Horizon

For Lonergan, the problem of decline and its solution opened onto questions of ultimate concern. *Cosmopolis* is, in the end, a religious solution to evil, especially when evil is understood as the longer cycle of decline. The human society and culture in which decline occurs are a concrete empirical society and culture of human history. An examination of that concrete empirical reality reveals the general incapability of humans to deal with the social surd. The self-transcendence and willingness required are only possible within the existential stance of persons possessed by an ineffable love, which Christians call God.[55] Lonergan contended, further,

> a religion that promotes self-transcendence to the point not only of justice, but of self-sacrificing love, will have a redemptive role in human society inasmuch as such love can undo the mischief of decline and restore the cumulative process of progress.[56]

The religious conversion involved in this existential, religious stance is not to be understood, however, as a simple and naive replacement for the difficult work envisioned by Lonergan's account of *cosmopolis* thus far. It rather sublates the work; as stated before, he enhances and makes more effective the preceding levels and does cancel out preceding levels, as he understood Hegel to mean by sublation.

Religious conversion begins with the "word of God [speaking] to us by flooding our hearts with love." While this experience, Lonergan claimed, is unmediated, the outward word of tradition and culture plays a constitutive role in the "unfolding of [the] life-long implications" of God's love and the human response.[57] As in the case of human love, it is *the expression of* the love of God that "brings about" a new situation and with it new discernment and judgments of value. Thus, the mediation of religious experience in the various carriers of meaning and, in particular, in linguistic expression, is key to its effectiveness in personal, communal and social life in their various geographical and historical contexts.[58]

Because of the constitutive role of religious language, Lonergan emphasized the importance of recognizing how it moves through the different realms of meaning. The source and core of religious expression is the religious experience itself, which belongs to the realm of transcendence. The first linguistic expression of religious experience is descriptive. It is characterized primarily by images that flow from the experience of mystery as *mysterium tremendum* and *fascinans* and more often than not issues directly into decisions and actions without the aid of the other realms of meaning.[59] For imaginal language is connected to willingness. In Lonergan's words, "Your willing is efficacious in your living insofar as what you will can be connected with images that are efficacious for you... It is the image that is efficacious for you that works."[60] Thus, the meaningfulness of the image is emphasized.

The technical or explanatory unfolding of religious language belongs to the realm of theory, where, in Western religion, for instance, theological understandings of Christian religious experience developed. In this realm, the vibrant images, vital stories and poetic forms of descriptive expression are not replaced, but sublated and enriched by the addition of intellectual insight and its expression in explanation.

The foundation of religious language lies in the realm of interiority, where its basic terms and relations and its method can be differentiated.[61] The method made possible by the third realm of meaning grounds the understanding of the dynamic relationship that exists between explanatory and descriptive languages and (as seen above) provides the tools for the beneficial amplification of that relationship within *cosmopolis*.

Finally, religious language communicates through teaching and preaching, not only the religious experience, but also the results of its theoretic mediation. "As explanation is reached through description," Lonergan wrote, "so it must be applied concretely by turning from explanation back to the descriptive world of things for us."[62] When governed by the methodology of interiority, descriptive religious language embodies the practical and effective edge of *cosmopolis*, which under the religious horizon is itself the mediation of the salvific power of God's word of love.[63] Thus, the communicative role of descriptive religious language in *cosmopolis* must not be understood as merely making theories or doctrines understandable or adapting them to different situations. The language embodies the meanings discerned at the theoretic level, but also constitutes the experience, the belief and the action engendered by that meaning. The language has a cognitive reference derived from the theoretic level, but also an existential constitutive reference in the possibilities for life that it opens up.

The question of how imaginal language constitutes and mediates the experience and understanding of God has been the subject of much discussion that cannot be dealt with here.[64] Of more specific interest for our purpose is Lonergan's notion of mystery and its relationship to images.[65]

Mystery is a notion that refers to two aspects of humanness, the unrestricted openness of intelligence and reasonableness, as well as a corresponding orientation to transforming change at the level of sensitive living. Lonergan's account of mystery in *Insight* highlights the relationships among human knowing, images, mystery and the question of God. The universal phenomenon of images, especially as they relate to religion, indicates the human desire to represent that which is beyond human knowing. While humans question and find answers to their questions, the answers can never keep up with the questions. Mystery designates that "known unknown," that which is known insofar as it is intended in questions, but is unknown in that the questions have not been satisfied. The advance of knowledge is grounded in this finality or dynamic orientation of human questioning, but mystery does not refer to gaps that will eventually be filled in. It is, rather, the transcendent answer to all questions that lies beyond human capacity to achieve in this world.

Even if the quest for knowledge could achieve a full explanation and, thereby, a full satisfaction of all human questions, "explanation does not give man a home," Lonergan said. The need for images that partly are symbols and partly are signs will always remain. As signs, images are linked to an interpretation designed to reveal their import; as symbols, they embody the paradox indicated by the "known unknown." As signs, they relate to the self-transcendence inherent in human knowing; as symbols, they relate to the rootedness of human experience in *bios* and *cosmos.*

In its function as symbol, an image can also block development. This happens when the sign dimension is cut off. Then, instead of raising questions for intelligence, the experience expressed by the image is taken to be the explanation. The result of this is what Lonergan called myth and, far from being an outdated mode of expression, myth always remains a possible option for humans.

Mystery and its attendant images, then, are to be distinguished from myth and its attendant images. Mystery incorporates the human exigence for the continued quest for being that is evident in consistently bringing judgment and decision to bear on the results of understanding. Myth arises when the data of sensible consciousness are considered explanatory of reality. The notion of mystery captures the full orientation of humans to the advance of truth. Because both remain possible options throughout history, *cosmopolis* is associated with mystery and directed against myth (as Lonergan understood it).

In *Method in Theology*, Lonergan emphasized that mystery does not relate only to knowing in its strict sense; it includes the full range of human meaning. In Lonergan's words, "Just as our unrestricted questioning is our capacity for self-transcendence, so being in love in an unrestricted fashion [love of God] is the proper fulfilment of that capacity." In the first place, this dynamic state of being in love with God is an *experience* of mystery. The mystery inherent in all knowing grounds intellectual operations. So, too, the mystery, as experienced, grounds the concrete living out of the willingness involved in deliberation, judgment, decision and action "with the easy freedom of those who do all good because they are in love."[66]

In the dialectic involved in the authentic expression of religious experience, the reference of images to mystery is maintained in the integral dialectic of transcendence and immanence. When transcendence, as encompassed in the sign dimension of images, is overemphasized, God becomes irrelevant and remote. When immanence, as encompassed in the symbolic dimension, is overemphasized, then the symbols, images and rituals become mere idols and myths, or the Divine is identified with the universe itself.[67]

Cosmopolis Under a Christian Horizon

We have been discussing religious conversion understood in Lonergan's sense of a dynamic state of being in love with God.[68] The implication of Lonergan's discussion of such concepts as the transcendence and immanence of God under the religious horizon (rather than the specifically Christian horizon) is that they are notions that need to be thematized across all religions in order to adequately mediate human experience. This is because, for Lonergan, the transcendence of God grounds moral self-transcendence. *Cosmopolis*, under a Christian horizon, however, rests not only on the effectiveness of God's love in a general sense, but on the actualization of that love in a specific historical event, God's incarnation in Jesus and his redemption of the world. "What distinguishes the Christian," Lonergan wrote, "was not God's grace [the gift of God's love], but the mediation of God's grace through Jesus Christ our Lord."[69] It is from this specific mediation that Christianity receives its distinctive history, beliefs and social forms.

God's redemption in Jesus is the solution to the problem of decline, understood as sin. The implications of Jesus' redemption are universal and account for the world-communal dimension of *cosmopolis*. Within a Christian context, specifically, those values are thematized in relationship to the experience recounted in the Gospels and the community that embodies that experience throughout time. Indeed, in this context, the authentic mission of the Church, in its expressions and actions, is to generate (or to be) *cosmopolis* in the world.[70]

In the full context of Lonergan's thought, it is necessary to keep in mind that the mystery of the Incarnation means that God became subject to the universal process of emergent probability. Furthermore, redemption, while divinely originated itself, does not abrogate the initial creation. To do so would be to admit a mistake on God's part. God created, willed and embraced the order of the universe both in creation and in redemption. Thus, while the full solution is ultimate and final, it becomes effectively probable within the emergent nature of the universe. The relevant probability is that which relies on the exercise of effective human freedom.

If *cosmopolis* is a critical mediation of redemption, then it does, as we have already seen, stand in opposition to the evil inherent in the longer cycle of decline. In its Christian expression, it will carry not only the values (such as charity, justice, peace, respect for creation), but also the Christian images which keep alive the concrete embodiment of these values. Hence, *cosmopolis* includes the preaching of the gospel. In its critical mediation, however, *cosmopolis* must make the gospel relevant to the concrete reality of history in each age. The *cosmopolis* of the present must confront the particular way in which decline operates in the present, both in the world in general and within the Christian community itself.[71] Its heuristic structure stays the same, but its content must constantly undergo reform, while maintaining a cognitive connection to the Christian originary experience in history.

Lonergan's heuristic account of emergent probability, the dialectic of progress and decline and *cosmopolis*, as the mediation of redemption sets the stage for a theology of redemption that is integral to the entire world process. A theology that participates in and is constitutive of *cosmopolis* would meet the problems that Berry critiqued as stemming from a creation-denying, individualist, otherworldly and totally human-centred understanding of redemption; likewise for the historical forms through which the Gospels are preached and lived.

Notes

1.   Cf. Bernard Lonergan, "Bernard Lonergan Responds," *Language, Truth and Meaning: Papers from the International Lonergan Congress, 1970*, ed. by Philip McShane (Notre Dame, IN: University of Notre Dame Press, 1972), 310; and Frederick E. Crowe, *Lonergan. Outstanding Christian Thinkers Series*, ed. by Brian Davies (Collegeville, MN: A Michael Glazier Book, Liturgical Press, 1992), 74.

2.   Lonergan, *Insight*, 316-317.

3.   Ibid., 317, 375-376.

4.   Ibid., 128-138. Cf. Patrick Byrne, "God and the Statistical Universe," in *Zygon* 16, 4 (December 4, 1981): 345-363.

5.   For a discussion of the significance of the term "emergent" compared to "evolutionary," see Patrick Byrne, *Randomness, Statistics and Emergence* (Notre

Dame, IN: University of Notre Dame Press, 1970), 171-205; Stephen C. Pepper, "Emergence," *Journal of Philosophy* 23 (1926), 244; and David Oyler, "Emergence in Complex Systems," *Journal of Lonergan Studies* 1,1 (Spring 1983): 47-59.

6.   Swimme and Berry, *The Universe Story*, 27-29, 77-78, 81-95 and passim.

7.   Lonergan, "Mission and the Spirit," *A Third Collection*, ed. by Frederick E. Crowe (New York and Mahwah: Paulist Press, 1985), 24.

8.   Philip McShane, "*Insight* and the Strategy of Biology," in *Lonergan's Challenge to the University and the Economy* (Lanham, MD: The University Press of America, 1980), 42-59.

9.   Swimme and Berry, *The Universe Story*, 36-38.

10.   Cf. Lonergan, *Insight*, 415-421 and Happel, "Metaphors and Time Asymmetry," 124-125.

11.   Lonergan, *Insight*, 235, 252.

12.   The word "practical" is used here in relationship to praxis and not as related to instrumentalization. Cf. David Tracy, "Theologies and Praxis," in *Creativity and Method: Essays in Honor of Bernard Lonergan, S.J.*, ed. by Matthew L. Lamb (Milwaukee: Marquette University Press, 1981), 49.

13.   Lonergan, *Insight*, 247-250. For the account of the longer cycle of decline that follows, see *Insight*, 251-257 and *Method*, 52-55, 242-244.

14.   While Lonergan began his account of general bias by locating its source within common sense, it would seem that the source can be located in the ambiguity of all human knowing (and not only common-sense knowing). Lonergan also allowed for the inauthentic operation of theory; blindspots, inattention and ivory-tower attitudes were attributed to the theoretic level. He did, however, begin with and emphasize (perhaps, even overemphasize) the role of common sense in causing decline.

15.   Cf. Hugo Meynell, *An Introduction to the Philosophy of Bernard Lonergan* (London and Basingstoke: The Macmillan Press, Ltd., and New York: Harper and Row, Publishers, Inc., 1976), 118.

16.   Cf. Matthew Lamb, *Solidarity with Victims: Toward a Theology of Social Transformation* (New York: Crossroad, 1982); Robert Doran, *Theology and the Dialectics of History* (Toronto, Buffalo and London: University of Toronto Press, 1990); William P. Loewe, "Toward a Responsible Contemporary Soteriology," in *Creativity and Method: Essays in Honor of Bernard Lonergan, S.J.*, ed. by Matthew L. Lamb (Milwaukee: Marquette University Press, 1981), 213-227; and Tracy, "Theologies and Praxis," in *Creativity and Method*, 35-51.

17.   Lonergan, *Insight*, 244-245, 647-649.

18.   Ibid., 255-256. Cf. Kenneth Melchin, *History, Ethics and Emergent Probability* (Lanham, MD: University Press of America, 1987).

19.   Lonergan, *Method*, 340.

20.   Lonergan, *Insight*, 643-647; Melchin, *History, Ethics and Emergent Probability*, 144-157.

21.   Cf. Lonergan, *Method*, 27-28; Melchin, *History, Ethics and Emergent Probability*, 125-128.

22.   Lonergan, *Method*, 27.

23.   Ibid., 30-34.

24.   This summary follows Lonergan, *Method*, 73-85. For explanation of his notion of the good as concrete, see Lonergan, *The Subject* (Milwaukee: Marquette University Press, 1968), 24.

25.   Lonergan, *The Subject*, 30.

26.   Lonergan, *Method*, 240.

27.   Ibid., 119-120.

28.   Ibid., 57-99.

29.   Ibid., 77.

30.   By intersubjectivity Lonergan meant the phenomenon by which humans are "we" before they are "I." It is the vital and functional unity and communication of feeling and meaning that precedes the differentiation of subject-object. The meaning communicated is of the subject as subject, as the smile communicates something of the self. Lonergan, *Method*, 57-61. Cf. Mary E. Frohlich, *Intersubjectivity and the Mystic* (Missoula, MT: Scholars' Press, 1994).

31.   Lonergan, *Method*, 76-81.

32.   Ibid., 81-99. The following account of stages of meaning follows these pages.

33.   Cf. Eric Voegelin, *Order and History, I. Israel and Revelation*, (Louisiana State University Press, 1956), 14, 27.

34.   Cf. Langdon Gilkey, *Religion and the Scientific Future* (New York, Evanston and London: Harper and Row, Publishers, Inc., 1970).

35.   Lonergan, *Method*, 94.

36.   Cf. Matthew Lamb, *History, Method and Theology: A Dialectical Comparison of Wilhelm Dilthey's Critique of Historical Reason and Bernard Lonergan's Meta-Methodology* (Missoula, MT: Scholars' Press, 1978), 290. Henceforth, Lamb, *History, Method and Theology*.

37.   There is also the operation of deciding which is appropriated at the stage of transcendence. Since we are dealing only with the third stage of meaning, interiority, deciding is not considered at this point. It should also be noted that understanding and judgment are operative at the level of common sense from the perspective of relationship to the practical affairs of life, that is, "to us." At the theoretic level, understanding and judgment are of "things to themselves." They are equally valid forms of understanding and judgment.

38.   See Lonergan, *Insight*, 320, 362-366, and *The Subject*, 17-18.

39.   Lonergan, *Method*, 83.

40.   Lamb, *History, Method and Theology*, 290-291.

41.   Lonergan, *Method*, 83. See also *The Subject*, 13-18.

42.   Lonergan, *Method*, 84, 241.

43.   Doran, *Theology and the Dialectics of History*, 661.

44.   Ibid., 286. See also Lonergan, *Method*, 66.

45.   Ibid., 59-63.

46.   Ibid., 186-187 and passim. It should be noted that Doran used the term "dialectic" in Lonergan's sense and that it is not the same as Hegel's dialectic of ideas. Cf. Lonergan, *Method*, 235-266.

47.   Ibid., 533, 541-544, 650. Doran's idea of the displacement toward transcendence and its effects on modern culture is very closely in tune with Berry's hermeneutic of suspicion focused on the notion of transcendence.

48.   Ibid., 332-349. Such schemes of recurrence could include those envisioned by Berry in *The Dream of the Earth*, 50-69, 138-170.

49.   Lonergan, *Insight*, 266.

50.   Lonergan, "Belief: Today's Issue," *A Second Collection*, ed. by William Ryan and Bernard Tyrrell (Philadelphia: Westminster Press, 1974), 91. Note that superstructure and infrastructure overlap; in other words, they do not consist entirely of different people. Scientists, for example, live in both. Cf. Lonergan, *Insight*, 261.

51.   Lonergan, *Method*, 245-249.

52.   Cf. Lonergan, *Method*, 61-69, for a discussion of other mediators.

53.   Lonergan, *Insight*, 570.

54.   See Happel, "Metaphors and Time Asymmetry," 126.

55.   Cf. Lonergan, *Insight*, chapter 19, 657-708, for the development of his thought connecting emergent probability to the fact and nature of God. See also Patrick Byrne, "God and the Statistical Universe," and Bernard Tyrrell, *Bernard Lonergan's Philosophy of God* (Notre Dame, IN: University of Notre Dame Press, 1974).

56.   Lonergan, *Method*, 55.

57.   Ibid., 115. For further explication of the immediacy of religious experience, see Sebastian Moore, *The Fire and the Rose Are One*, (New York: Seabury Press, 1981), esp. 22-23, 32-38; Vernon Gregson, *Lonergan, Spirituality and the Meeting of Religions*, The College Theology Society: Studies in Religion 2 (Lanham, MD: University Press of America, 1985), esp. 60-78. For discussion and controversy around Lonergan's foundationalism, in general, see Richard R. Topping, "Transcendental Method and Private Language," in *ARC: The Journal of the Faculty of Religious Studies, McGill University* 21 (Spring 1993). See also the interchange between Charles C. Hefling, Jr., "On Understanding Salvation History," in *Lonergan's Hermeneutics: Its Development and Application*, ed. by Sean E. MacEvenue and Ben F. Meyer (Washington, DC: The Catholic University of America Press, 1989), 221-275, and his respondents in the same text.

58.   Lonergan, *Method*, 112-115. See also Stephen Happel, "The Sacraments, Interiority and Spiritual Direction," in *A Promise of Presence: Festschrift in Honor of David Power, OMI*, ed. by Michael Downey and Richard Fragomeni (Washington, DC: The Pastoral Press, 1992), 139-161. Happel showed how, for Lonergan, the inner word (the operation of mind itself or, religiously, God's word of love) and the outer word (linguistic expression or, religiously, God's revelation) are one. Hence, he argued "private" and "public" are coincident in Lonergan.

59.   Ibid., 106; reference to Rudolf Otto, *The Idea of the Holy* (London: Oxford University Press, 1923).

60.   Lonergan, *Understanding and Being. The Collected Works of Bernard Lonergan*, vol. 5, ed. by Elizabeth A. Morelli and Mark D. Morelli, rev. and augmented by Frederick E. Crowe et al. (Toronto, Buffalo and London: University of Toronto Press, 1990), 219.

61.   Lonergan, *Method*, 114-115.

62.   Lonergan, *Insight*, 570.

63.   The methodology of interiority also includes the concrete application of dialectical methods to the discernment of values and disvalues. The authentic resolution of dialectics is, however, also dependent on the third stage of meaning. Lonergan, *Method*, 235-266.

64.   Although the words "constitute" and "mediate" refer to different operations, in reality they operate together. It is the mediation of the religious experience in language (or other expression) that constitutes the meaning, and moves the decisions and actions in the ongoing development of the experience itself. See Lonergan, *Method*, 28.

65.   Lonergan, *Insight*, 554-572; *Understanding and Being*, 217-219. Our discussion will follow Lonergan's presentations in these texts.

65.   Lonergan, *Method*, 106-107.

67.   Ibid., 110-111.

68.   Ibid. See also Gregson, *Lonergan, Spirituality and the Meeting of Religions*, 47-49.

69.   Lonergan, "The Future of Christianity," *Second Collection*, 151.

70.   Lonergan, *Insight*, 718-725; *Method*, 364-368 and passim. Cf. Loewe, "Lonergan and the Law of the Cross" and "Toward a Responsible Contemporary Soteriology."

71.   Lonergan, *Insight*, 743.

CHAPTER SEVEN

A THEOLOGICAL ANALYSIS
OF BERRY'S PROPOSAL

Introduction

If theology is, as Lonergan described it, a mediation "between a cultural matrix and the significance and role of a religion in that matrix,"[1] then there are two major questions that arise in considering Berry's contribution to Christian theology: (1) The methodological question: How is Berry's "new story" situated in terms of mediating between Christianity and culture? In Lonergan's terms, this is to ask whether methodologically the "new story" belongs to *cosmopolis*, since *cosmopolis* is the symbolic name for the mediation of authentic meanings and values to aid progress or to meet decline. (2) The content question: If the "new story" does belong to *cosmopolis* methodologically, is its mediation Christian? In other words, is its cognitive reference consistent with the Christian story?

The Methodological Question

As already indicated, *cosmopolis* is constituted by authentic persons and communities and, therefore, is dependent on moral, intellectual, psychic and, ultimately, religious conversions, which sublate the others. Under a Christian horizon, it is also dependent on Christian conversion and mediates a set of meanings that is specific to Christianity. So the task is to establish whether or not (or to what extent) Berry's proposal meets these criteria.

The "New Story" and Moral Conversion

In his hermeneutics of suspicion, Thomas Berry painted (in broad strokes, at least) a picture of many aspects of the longer cycle of decline as Lonergan explained it. Berry's particular focus, however, was on the breakdown of a comprehensive vehicle (story) for the mediation of meaning, especially the meaning of the physical universe. While, in his view, there had been for some time a set of meanings to be gleaned from scientific theories about the universe, they did not enter into common-sense living except in the form of an instrumentalized "know-how" fueled by distorted myths. The reason was that the new cosmology was left to science (the world of theory), while religion and the humanities were concerned with human affairs.

What Berry proposed, then, as the new story, was intended to meet those aspects of decline that he identified, just as Lonergan's *cosmopolis* was designed to meet his heuristic account of decline. As indicated at the beginning of chapter five, we are dealing, however, with two different realms of discourse, descriptive (Berry) and explanatory (Lonergan). So, while Lonergan presented theory about how decline happens and what is to be done, Berry presented a description that itself is designed to bring about the solution he saw as appropriate. (It ought to be noted with respect to Lonergan that his intention in *Insight* went beyond presenting theory to an expectation that the reader become intellectually converted, a condition he also admitted was very rare, however.)

Berry was not concerned, then, with giving an account of human authenticity. He did not explicitly deal with moral self-transcendence. He was not engaged in an explanation of precisely how humans originate and appropriate values, as Lonergan was. Nevertheless, he was concerned with values. The subtitle of Berry's first published edition of *The New Story* was *Comments on the Origin and Transmission of Values*. In that essay, he took note of the passage from the classical perception of values to the existential view. He wrote:

> Whereas formerly values consisted in the perfection of the earthly image of an external Logos in a world of fixed natures, values are

now determined by human sensitivity in responding to the creative urgencies of a developing world.[2]

The example that Berry gave of response to "creative urgencies of a developing world" was that of the scientist drawn unconsciously by "the mystical attraction" of the emerging process that is the universe.

Berry spoke often of the relationship between the natural world and human affect and psyche. It is clear that he understood the affect and psyche to be the domains where a revaluing of the natural world can originate, a revaluing because the present culture does not associate positive values with the physical universe. Human sights have been trained away from whole dimensions of the physical universe, which was the domain of a "value-free" science. He used the images of blindness and autism to describe modern humankind's unawareness of the damage done to the natural world and of the aesthetic and spiritual qualities present there.[3]

At the same time, Berry continued to insist on the importance of culture in the transmission of values. With regard to confronting the ecological crisis, however, culture must be infused with new values. That is the role of the "new story." But the "new story" itself originated in persons (notably Berry himself) making judgments that the values of beauty, creativity and intrinsic worth apprehended in nature were indeed so, that the scientific account of evolution opened onto a spiritual dimension, that the "new story" was the best medium for transmitting the new values and so on. His own advertence to the necessity of critical judgment is also apparent; "we must respond critically" on the basis of our spontaneous relationship with the natural world, he wrote.[4] Berry's words and performance imply a concrete instance of Lonergan's account of values, which are first apprehended in feelings, but then subject to understanding and judgment.

What is more significant, however, with regard to laying the basis for an evaluation of Berry's contribution to theology, is that Berry's proposal requires not only a moral self-transcendence, but also a moral conversion, in Lonergan's sense of these terms. The genetic development of the culture as Berry understood it would almost certainly not result in the ecological way of life he called the Ecozoic Era. A radical change, a change in horizon described variously, from human-centred to earth-centred or from human community to life community, is implied. There are indications in his writing that suggest such a conversion.

In writing about economics and ecology, Berry spoke of the radical change required as "changes in the deep structure of our sense of reality and of value and in the practical adaptation to lifestyles."[5] In another place, he wrote: "All the great transition moments are sacrificial moments. Our present transition will not be accomplished without enormous sacrifice" and "the reshaping of the human face of the planet... is not going to be without its negative, sacrificial, entropic aspects. But that is what we must willingly undertake."[6] What is required involves sacrifice of satisfactions for the sake of higher, long-term values (moral self-transcendence). While these may be forced upon the human community in some cases, the transformation, Berry said, requires a willingness.

Berry's thematization of sacrifice sometimes suggests a kind of inevitability in which the human is fatefully a part of the sacrificial aspects of the universe, death giving way to life. He was also critical of a moral tradition that made "morality" a mark of the great gap that separated humans as moral beings, from the perceived amoral (chaotic and meaningless) physical universe.[7] Yet the theme of human freedom and the unique role of the human in assuming responsibility for the further evolution of the universe are also present in his writings. He challenged the spiritual and moral traditions to deal with the ecological problem.[8] In speaking of the present as a new "Exodus moment," he said, "If we do not perceive the sacred nature of our journey [including the whole evolutionary process], we will not be able to bring about the salvific transformation needed." For Berry, this salvific process would lead not only to "eternal beatitude," but also to "an earthly situation" of a more fulfilling and delightful human-earth relationship.[9]

As crucially centred within a heuristic account of the emergent universe and of the whole human subject, Lonergan's explanation of values and moral self-transcendence meets the problem of alienated moral human beings within a chaotic universe. This is so not only because human freedom is understandable within the overall process, but also because values and facts, as virtually true and normative, result from the authentic engagement of the same transcendental human processes of experience, understanding and judging. The effective edge of moral self-transcendence consists in human decision and action toward promoting progress and overcoming decline. While not so clearly developed by Berry, this notion of moral self-transcendence is indicated in his work and given a concrete application in his proposal for meeting the ecological crisis.

The "New Story" and Intellectual Conversion

To summarize briefly, intellectual conversion, also called interiority, is manifested in a critical realist position with respect to knowing and in a method that the conversion enables. The critical realist position relies on an explanatory account of the terms and relations of one's own consciousness. Critical realism moves beyond both empiricism, which holds that knowing consists in "taking a look," and idealism, which concedes to the empiricists that the real is what one "sees," but maintains that the object of knowledge is not this "real," but the ideal. The critical realist recognizes that knowing involves the transcendence of the operating subject and that the real is "what we come to know through a grasp of a certain type of virtually unconditioned."[10] By "certain type of virtually unconditioned," Lonergan meant the result of a judgment based on the satisfaction of all available and relevant questions. The method of which one gains control through intellectual conversion is the ability to identify the operations of one's own knowing, to distinguish description from theory and to intentionally move from one to the other.

Does Berry's proposal display the position and method that are the results of intellectual conversion? A consideration of this question cannot be a direct examination of whether or not Berry himself was intellectually converted. The data of one's consciousness are not publicly available, and Berry did not explain the conscious procedures that ground his work. Furthermore, discerning a consistent position from descriptive language is problematic. Descriptive accounts are not systematic. Berry's writings are characterized by multivalent images, rhetorical devices of various kinds and often spontaneous diversions geared to specific audiences. Images arising from diverse cultures, historical movements and religions often run together, blurring the distinctions and creating new connections.

Despite the difficulties, however, there are aspects of Berry's work that indicate his position on knowing. On the one hand, Berry purported to find in many expressions of the idealist tradition forerunners of the ecological movement. He listed Plato, Plotinus, neo-Platonists, romantics and transcendentalists among those who maintained a tradition against the empiricists and materialists. Like Teilhard, he spoke of a consciousness within the whole physical universe. On the other hand, he criticized Teilhard and Hegel for overemphasizing the "spirit" of the universe at the expense of the concrete universe itself. In his latest writings, not unlike other contemporary nature writers, references to idealists were less frequent and seem to have been replaced by appeals to scientists and contemporary ecologists.[11] The change in perception regarding the nature of scientific knowing, at least, and in the meaning of objectivity is certainly alluded to many times in *The Universe Story*.[12] So, while there is no clear indication of a full critical realist position in Berry's writings, it is obvious that he considered scientific knowing to include more operations than intuition of sensory experience. He clearly also presumed that the universe is knowable; knowledge has a referent that is not merely a human construction.

Berry's work does display the interaction of theory and common sense. His primary focus was the arena of common sense, but he showed a respect for the role of theory. His own project was based on scientific theory especially, but also upon theories of history and religion as shown in the early chapters above. Furthermore, he called on theology to provide the critical basis needed in the recovery of creation themes.[13] What he was keenly aware of, however, was the practical edge of theory when mediated in the world of common sense, as well as the need within common sense for this mediation of authentic theory. This awareness is evident in his early work on world religions, where his challenge to scholars was to consider the relevance of their work to the enrichment of world spirituality and to provide a critical control of new movements in spirituality. The same concern is evident behind his comment that there is no longer a story that adequately carries the common meanings and values for the human tasks required at present. His own life's project was to identify the medium, a story and its content, cosmology, that could be such a carrier within the world of common sense. Hence, his focus was on speaking to the public, not only to the professional scientist or the professional religionist. He warned society against the folly of the short-term practical solution that generally disregards the insights of science as far as ecology is concerned. His emphasis on education in general and on the university, in particular, also points to this concern.[14]

One of the factors that no doubt affected Berry's articulation of the human role and his attention to the human process of knowing was a reluctance to concentrate efforts in that direction because of his charge (and that of many ecologists) of anthropocentrism against the Western tradition. Statements regarding changes in notions of objectivity and scientific knowing were set in the context of assertions about human inclusion in the universe process, as in the following passage:

> Scientific knowledge in a developmental universe is no longer understood as information about an objective world out there. Scientific knowledge is essentially self-knowledge, where self is taken as referring to the complex, multiform system of the universe... The human is not simply noting an external design [in the universe] but is participating in the creation of the design.[15]

In fact, the full recovery of the human subject involved in Lonergan's notion of intellectual conversion seems diametrically opposed to Berry's project. But is it?

While there are many different positions held by ecologists, the charge of anthropocentrism by Berry and others generally refers to the exaltation of the human species over and above the rest of the natural world. The human sphere becomes the only realm of meaning; nature is the merely materialistic stuff that fuels the machines of an industrial-technological "progress" intended to enhance human life. In this kind of anthropocentric world, however, the human subject is not enhanced, but alienated. While the natural world is instrumentalized, the human is "at sea" in a meaningless universe.

Lonergan's recovery of the human subject within emergent probability was a recovery of the universe as well. The phenomenology of human knowing grounded the meaningfulness of the entire universe process. One might argue from Berry's position that beginning with the human is inherently anthropocentric and, in the literal meaning of the word, it is so. The critical mistake of the past leading to the alienation of the human from nature, however, was a mistake in the perception of human knowing and the related notions of objectivity, subject-object relationship and the normativity of so-called "non-empirical" knowledge. In facing these mistakes, Lonergan dealt with the very bases of anthropocentrism. Thus, his recovery of the human subject is not vulnerable to the ecologists' charges. In fact, the recovered human subject of Lonergan is a requirement if one is to judge that a story of the universe refers (however conditionally) to some reality outside human perception and that that reality is worthy of human action on its behalf. This grounding seems presumed in Berry's proposal but is not clearly articulated.

The "New Story" and Psychic Conversion

We have noted in several places above that Berry consistently associated the human psyche with the origin of the values he wished to recover. There is a notable relationship between this notion in Berry and in Doran's account of the psychic conversion in the third stage of meaning, where the transparency of the operations of the psyche enables the subject to intentionally incorporate these operations into the creation of meaning. Doran's presentation of the psychic differentiations (cosmological and anthropological) over the history of the Western world supports Berry's critique of the same tradition and the separation of what he called cultural and genetic codings. It also supports the significance Berry gave to the richness of natural images that the earth, especially, presents to the human psyche. "If we lived on the moon," Berry wrote, "our mind and emotions, our speech, our imagination, our sense of the divine would all reflect the desolation of the lunar landscape."[16] If such relevant data from the sensitive flow and the unconscious were selected out at the psychic level, there was little chance that schemes of recurrence initiated by humans into world process would include those appropriate to a form of human life integral with natural ecosystems; hence, the distorted notion of human progress as it relates to human-earth relations.

Likewise, in the recovery of a viable relationship between humans and the natural world, Berry considered the human psyche to have a crucial role. The construal of the scientific account of the events of evolution as the story of the universe, Berry said, was a result of experiences at the level of the human psyche. Recent scientific cosmology receives a fuller significance when the psychic dimension is taken into account, he said. The psyche apprehends aspects of the universe that must be incorporated into the scientific account in the construction of the new story. Human intimacy with the natural world is identifiable in the archetypes, dreams and images that emerge in the human psyche.[17]

In the methodology he inherited from Vico (and others), Berry's cultural history admitted the cyclic rise and decline of civilizations and the renewal required as a civilization is in decline. That renewal, he argued, requires a return to primal sources for a vibrancy of presence to the natural world and a recovery of values. The question of whether or not he meant a romantic return or a capitulation of historical process to an undifferentiated mythic embeddedness in cosmic cycles has already been raised. Based on Berry's own contention and on the main thrust of his work, we have contended that this interpretation of his work cannot be sustained. The passages in his writings that seem to indicate a naive return to a previous form of consciousness (if such were even possible) are best understood as a what Lonergan calls a "heaping up of images" in an attempt to reorient the human psyche and affect toward biological and cosmic sensitivities.[18]

When Berry spoke of a return to primal consciousness, he meant a critical return in order to recover the values lost with the passage from cosmological to anthropological consciousness. He was not advocating what Doran described as a mixture of cosmological and anthropological consciousness within either individuals or the human community as a whole.[19] Rather, the mainstream of Berry's thought advocated a new form of consciousness (again in Vico's sense) according to which the cosmos again becomes part of the constitutive meanings for human living, but not to the exclusion of historical consciousness. His own project relied on the extension of history to include the evolution of the universe. He called on humans not only to be aware, but also to celebrate the great historical moments in the evolution of the universe.[20]

The understanding of the cosmos as itself historical is, however, only a partial solution to the problem of whether or not by a new consciousness Berry meant a naive return to primal consciousness. The self-reflective capacities of the human are what essentially constitute the full meaning of historical consciousness. The process of extending history to include the natural world is a human process of which the rest of the natural world (so far as we know) is incapable. As a product of cosmic and earth processes, the human is still differentiated by a peculiar capacity for freedom, the inauthentic exercise of which created the ecological crisis. It is the authentic exercise of freedom that can work toward overturning it. Berry referred to both these consequences of human freedom in his notion of cultural coding. Furthermore, his own proposal presupposed the responsible and effective engagement of human freedom in changing the present state of human-earth activity. Nevertheless, his full proposal *as presented* requires a greater explication or even imaging of the relationship of the human psyche to the responsibility of human freedom in order to avoid the misunderstandings that presently arise with respect to this aspect of his work.[21]

What then is the relationship of Doran's notion of psychic conversion to Berry's emphasis on the role of the psyche in the emerging new consciousness? The phenomena described variously by Berry as "the deeper spontaneities" of the universe present in the human psyche, genetic coding, archetypal images, dreams and shamanic aspect of the psyche, refer to different aspects of the organic base, to internally communicating symbols and to data from the unconscious. His claim that an adequate response to the ecological crisis calls for a new attention to and valuation of the elemental symbols that were repressed under anthropological consciousness and Doran's claim that psychic conversion is constitutive of a new form of consciousness are mutually confirming.

Influenced by the thought of Carl Jung and of Mircea Eliade, Berry consistently, throughout all the phases of his work, insisted on the role of the human psyche as establishing an invariant base for a world spirituality. As Doran concluded (confirming Jung), wherever there is human subjectivity, there are the elemental symbols and their mediating structures and functions. In his proposal for confronting the ecological crisis, Berry spoke of the necessity of listening again to the spontaneities embodied in the images presented to the human psyche: of evoking, or waking up, psychic sensitivities to the natural world by being more attentive to its beauty, diversity, creativity and history; and of integrating the dreams and symbols of the psyche into our conscious and responsible decisions and actions. These, in descriptive language, indicate control of the methodological moves issuing from psychic conversion in the third stage of meaning.

That Berry's account of the transformation of psychic consciousness, with the further clarifications suggested, is confirmed by Doran's explanation of psychic conversion is significant for our purposes because it locates Berry's notion of the role of the psyche as post-naive. The role of the psyche in the reform of ecological attitudes rests on what Doran called a conversion with all the presuppositions of critical dialectical methods involved.

Berry's Proposal and the Methodology of *Cosmopolis*

On the methodological level, at least, Thomas Berry's proposal of a "new story" to confront the ecological crisis is a contribution to *cosmopolis*. He proposed a set of interwoven images within a narrative intended to intervene in the world of common sense at the infrastructural level of culture.

While Berry did not give an explanatory, self-conscious account of the method characteristic of the third stage of meaning, his descriptive expression reveals many of the characteristics stemming from the series of conversions (moral, intellectual and psychic) grounding that method.[22] He focused on the relevance of theoretic cosmology and ecology to the affairs of the world, such as law, economics, politics, medicine and lifestyle. The values and meanings he wished to communicate rest on a hermeneutics of suspicion and recovery applied to history. The application rested on the basis of disvalues (such as the instrumentalization of nature) and values (such as a desire to preserve nature) apprehended within the present human-earth relationship. While the task of the full dialectical investigation of history with regard to the ecological problem still continues, it does seem from the attempts, to date, that Berry succeeded in outlining the main contours of that investigation.[23]

As a contribution to *cosmopolis*, Berry's work is both a weaving of images to communicate the cognitive and constitutive meanings of the natural world that will work to overturn the present crisis and a rhetorical performance focused on the appropriation of these meanings and values by his audience. While a large portion of his work is a low-key descriptive presentation of the why, what and how of the ecological crisis, he was also on a mission of reform. Like a prophet, he cajoled, persuaded, appealed to emotions, but also shocked and perplexed his readers or listeners. They must be awakened from the trance of the Technozoic Era! It is in this context that some of the more troublesome statements and notions that we attempted to clarify in the previous chapter are to be understood. Statements that function rhetorically include: "It is time to listen to the gene." "We must re-invent the human at the species level." "We should put the Bible on the shelf for a while." "We must blow the bridges!" or, more positively, "...we participate in the original dream of the earth."[24] They do have cognitive reference within Berry's thought, but the real point of their intent is not a literal adherence to what they say, even if it were possible. These statements function like parables; they break open the present world.[25] On the one hand, they engender discomfort and force a re-examination of the status quo; on the other, they enable the hearer to reimagine the world as one in which the "new story" is the context of meaning and value. The scientific cosmology relies for its effectiveness in mitigating ecological attitudes on the performative dimensions of the rhetoric. This is the mediating function of *cosmopolis*. It remains to investigate Berry's contribution to *cosmopolis* under its religious horizon.

The "New Story," *Cosmopolis* and Religious Conversion

For Lonergan, religious conversion begins as an experience of divine love prior to its thematization. At the same time, however, its expression, especially in linguistic form (but also in other forms, notably action), becomes constitutive of the experience. While Berry did not speak in those terms of religious experience, he considered the "new story" to result from an experience of the universe that he called religious. Furthermore, he held that the "new story" would enable its listeners/readers to share in that religious experience. In this sense, as for Lonergan, religious experience grounds the willingness required for the moral transcendence (we also contended conversion) that Berry's Ecozoic Era requires. Does this "new story," then, mediate the sense of mystery that Lonergan saw as a key indicator of the images that would characterize *cosmopolis*? Recall that images that mediate mystery embody an integral dialectic of the transcendence and immanence of the Divine.

Like Lonergan, Berry spoke about mystery and myth. He did not distinguish between the two terms as Lonergan did but often used them interchangeably.[26] Occasionally, however, he did speak of mystery in the two senses (that which grounds knowing *per se* and that which grounds concrete living) used by Lonergan:

> The term "God"... refers to the ultimate mystery of things, something beyond that which we can understand adequately... At every moment we are experiencing the overwhelming mystery of existence. It is that simple, but that ineffable. What is the divine? It is the ineffable pervasive presence in the world about us.[27]

God as ultimate mystery is that for which the understanding reaches but never adequately attains and that which we experience in the world around us.

Throughout most of his work, however, it was the *experience* of mystery and its relation to immanence that Berry emphasized. This was to offset what he claimed was an overemphasis in the Christian tradition on the transcendence of God and the transcendent nature of human activity. More specifically, he sought to reawaken religious sensitivities to the mediation of mystery in the multiform universe and particularly in the earth. Following a sharp-edged observation that the failure of religions to take effective responsibility for the earth was a failure of religious responsibility to the Divine as well as to the human, he exclaimed:

> Why do we have such a wonderful idea of God? Because we live in such a gorgeous world. We wonder at the magnificence of whatever it is that brought the world into being. This leads to a sense of adoration. We have a sense of immense gratitude that we participate in such a beautiful world. This adoration, this gratitude, we call religion.[28]

Berry's work is replete with images of the beauty of the universe. Many such passages indicate a mediation of religious experience through the aesthetic, even hierophanous, qualities of nature, such as one would find in kataphatic mysticism. The Divine envisioned here is a god of plenitude. Notably, Lonergan also commented on the relevance of kataphatic mysticism to questions about the relationship of God to the universe.[29]

For Berry, however, immanence of the Divine did not simply mean that natural beauties are mere pointers toward the Divine. He accused Christians of moving too quickly from the natural forms to the adoration of God, so that even spirituality reduces nature to a tool of human development. Berry challenged humans to think more deeply about nature and its relationship to both humans and God. He emphasized inner connectedness and manifestation. His pervasive use of the organic metaphor was an attempt to create a bond between humans and nature and to reduce human arrogance by emphasizing the utter dependence of humans on nature. Differentiation, subjectivity and communion carry a surplus of meaning regarding some immanent human-like or god-like quality of agency embodied in evolution. He suggested that together they provide a cosmological model of Trinity.[30] References to the many selves—personal, communal, societal and cosmic—and to genetic codings mandate a mode of human presence within natural systems and the cosmos in general. The "new story" is "my" story; the energy generated in the Big Bang is the same energy "I" use in physical, emotional and psychic activity. All of these images pertain to that symbolic dimension of images that bind humans to *cosmos* and *bios*. Under a religious horizon, they refer to the immanence of God.

Is there, then, an integral dialectic of transcendence and immanence in relationship to God in Berry's work?[31] Berry tended to correct distortions by highlighting them, particularly in their concrete expression in common sense, and then emphasizing the neglected dimensions. Hence, he emphasized God's immanence and even then nature itself as having a spiritual dimension (rather than merely pointing to an external God). His sense of nature was sacramental, in the full sense of embodying that which it symbolizes. Furthermore, he was not addressing Christians specifically, and so notions of divinity from many religions are blended together or placed side by side without integration. For some of these religions (Buddhism, North American native religions), the Divine, or ultimate, is not transcendent in the Christian sense.[32] Moreover, because he wished the "new story" to be a world-communal story, he attempted to use images and notions that could be "filled in" differently in different traditions. For example, at the end of *The Universe Story*, he indicated how the sense of the sacredness of the universe community has been celebrated differently by native American peoples, Chinese religions, Hindus, Buddhists and Christians.[33] The result is that under a religious horizon, we cannot find in Berry's work a consistent sense of the dialectic of transcendence and immanence as it applies to God.

The reference above to God as "something beyond that which we can understand adequately" is, of course, a traditional Christian attempt to speak of God's transcendence. It occurred in one of a series of talks in which Berry addressed Christian themes. Even there, Berry did not give any sense of how a doctrine of God's transcendence and immanence might be reconstructed in relation to new scientific understandings of the universe. The whole intent of his work under a religious horizon was to *mediate* the experience of God in the created universe in the descriptive rhetoric of story and metaphor. This is what he referred to as the revelatory nature of the universe and its story. Berry himself wrote of the doctrine of immanence and transcendence as follows:

> There is indeed a difference, a distinction [between God and creation], but if there were a difference in the sense of separation, the created world would not be... There is always the mystery of things and the mystery of existence can be given the name divine, it can be called God or immanence or whatever one wishes... I do not perceive a great problem with this immanence and transcendence issue. It does seem, however, that our excessive emphasis on transcendence is leading us to destroy the planet.[34]

Hence, in Berry's mind, at least, the "new story" would not exclude an understanding of God as transcendent, even though the rhetoric of the story itself is much more easily understood in terms of God's immanence.

Thomas Clarke suggested that the "new story," as Berry understood it, did not require any additions to the doctrines of the immanence and transcendence of God, but a recovery of their true meaning.[35] In relationship to creation, it is God's transcendence that allows creation to operate according to the intrinsic nature of its own being. The contemporary scientific accounts of the intricate self-organizing aspects and statistical nature of universe process would seem to mediate more clearly the notion of the relative independence of creation from God. The doctrine of God's immanence maintains that God is not distant from creation, but that all creation participates somehow in the divine reality. It grounds a sacramental approach to all things as sacred. Hence, an integration of the two modes of divine presence to creation (in their recovered meaning) would seem to ground Berry's "new story" more adequately than an emphasis on immanence alone. In particular relationship to humans, the experience of mystery as transcendent grounds the self-transcendence required by all the conversions that are constitutive of *cosmopolis*. As shown above, these conversions are at least indicated by Berry's proposal, if not clearly articulated.

The central focus of Berry's religious concern is that language about the universe and the experience of the religious dimensions of the universe it mediates become explicitly and intentionally constitutive of understandings of the Divine. While this notion was not foreign to the Christian tradition, it had become marginal in modern theology. Berry pointed out that Aquinas dedicated much of his effort to "defending the reality, goodness and efficacy intrinsic to the natural world."[36] Lonergan's work is in this tradition and certainly shows an integral relationship between creation and understandings of God.[37]

The significance of Berry's contention that our understanding of the universe be constitutive of our understandings of God rests on the fact that understandings of God ground the normativity of human praxis. In the biblical tradition, the Exodus and other events of human history reveal a God of liberation and justice, thus grounding the normativity of a social ethic of justice and empowerment. So, too, Berry argues, acts of God in creation reveal God as beneficent, playful, imaginative, artistic, intelligent and so on and thus ground not only an individualized personal spirituality, but a normative respectful ethic of relationship to the universe. The time dimension added to the universe establishes that action of God in creation, not as a once-and-for-all act, but as constant and new (in the sense of confirming) revelatory action over time, as is the case in human history. This in religious terms is the meaning of a functional cosmology. It is the concretization of God's plenitudinous care in the world both in creation and in human presence to and acts toward creation.[38]

While, in Berry's understanding, the doctrine of God's immanence could best ground human responsibility within the universe, Lonergan showed that the transcendent dimension also has normative implications for the very kind of responsible decision and action that Berry called for in the "new story." Again, the reluctance by Berry to deal adequately with the human subject is the likely cause of the virtual exclusion of discussion in his work relating God's transcendence to the experience of mystery in the universe.

This emphasis on new images, pre-eminently a "new story," as constitutive of our understanding of the Divine and hence, normative for human activity is, however, what seems to be "going forward" in Berry's religious language. While this emphasis relates to the actual content of Berry's proposal, it is, however, also significant methodologically because *cosmopolis* is grounded in religious conversion. Religious conversion is not an abstraction, but a concrete lived experience mediated in particular religious expressions (hence, meanings) of the mystery experienced.

The Content Question: The Christian Horizon

Under a Christian horizon, *cosmopolis* becomes understood as the mediation of redemption, the divine solution to the evil, which is decline. This does not change the essential methodology of *cosmopolis*, since the conversions that constitute it already rest on the resolution of the dialectic of contradictories in favour of the good. It does mean, however, that the thematization of the conversions will be in terms of a specific act of redemption within history and its interpretations and expressions in the history of a particular tradition. Under the Christian horizon, then, we will examine Berry's proposal for meanings relevant to Christian themes, notably of the historical reality of redemption in Jesus.

There is no sustained treatment of Christian redemption themes in the "new story" or the rhetoric in which it was presented. Following the corrective style of his presentation, Berry dealt with what had been de-emphasized or ignored without rehabilitating, in any adequate fashion, what was distorted. Again, he was not an apologist for the Christian tradition, so the story of the universe itself did not pay attention to the significance of Jesus or to redemption. The same is true for the related themes of sin and grace.

When Berry did mention the doctrine of redemption, it was generally to indicate that the cosmic dimension of Christ as found in the Gospel of John (Jn.1) and the Letters to the Corinthians (1 Cor. 15:22-28), Colossians (1:15-20) and Ephesians (1:10 and 4:10) ought to be re-emphasized, but in the developmental mode of consciousness as in Teilhard's presentation of the cosmic Christ. He spoke positively of Teilhard's understanding of the universe as Christocentric. The notion of subjectivity was related to the cosmic person archetype and thus to the cosmic Christ in the Teilhardian sense. His emphasis, like that of Teilhard, on the magnificent and celebratory aspects of creation was much more congenial to an idea of cosmic fulfilment in Christ than to the historical realism characteristic of the mainstream of Christian teaching on redemption. We must point out, however, that interpretations of the cosmic Christ in the tradition have been ambiguous and more often than not support an excessively spiritualized and "high descending" Christology, rather than an earth- or even human-centred approach. Berry was correct in that Teilhard's interpretation associated the cosmic Christ with the material universe, but this is not a consistent, nor even common, interpretation of the relevant Johannine and Pauline texts.[39]

While Berry acknowledged that in the human world, the "tragic and sacrificial dimension" of the universe takes on "a special moral sense," the full dimensions of the human problem of evil were not thematized. The problem of the relationship between natural evil and the possibility of moral evil is inherent in the idea of plenitude and was a consistent theme wherever Berry spoke of evil.[40] In some places, the Western conception of evil is critiqued as a preoccupation with tragedy and refusal to accept the human condition. Here evil (in the sense of moral evil) and the whole sense of human mortality seem to be conflated. On the other hand, Berry spoke approvingly of the power of the Christian story in empowering the early Christians in their struggle against the evil of a declining Roman civilization. Furthermore, he compared the ecological crisis to that particular time in history and insisted that the present crisis is much greater, since the whole planet is threatened. Yet, he insisted, the "ultimate word" for Christianity is resurrection, not evil. That resurrection applies to the whole world and the paradox of Christianity is that the temporal damage we do is also eternal. The new resurrected world will bear the distortions humans have caused.[41]

Is Berry then open to the same charge as that laid against Teilhard de Chardin and some process theologians, of an inadequate or ambiguous treatment of the problem of evil? In terms of what he actually said about evil and redemption, the evidence is too scanty to be conclusive.[42] The indications, as just mentioned, are that the relationship between human responsibility and ecological disaster, for instance, would require a clearer distinction between issues of moral evil and those that refer to either natural evil or human finitude. While Berry did speak about the extension of the concept of sin to include biocide and geocide, the grounding of the morality was in the same concepts (genetic coding, communion with the earth) as mentioned previously and not in theological and philosophical terms of good and evil. His presentation of the story of the universe, the influence of the organic metaphor in its Whiteheadian development, the Jungian and Eastern religious influence and the emphasis on human tragedy and sacrifice as integral to the tragic and sacrificial aspects of the universe leave his work open to the charge of diminishing the reality of human evil. It is this reality that the concrete historical basis for the mystery of redemption in the Jesus of history offers a powerful thematization. Berry saw this to be the case with Augustine's *City of God*. However, it is not the content, but the genre of story that he adopted from Augustine. This he saw to be an effective tool in confronting the ecological crisis.[43]

The Christian understanding of redemption is that the solution to evil does not allow for a dialectic of contraries of good and evil, in Jungian or Chinese yin-yang terms, or in the sense that the evolution of physical universe involves false starts and dead ends. It is rather a dialectic of contradictories. Hence, the Christian story has engendered powerful human efforts against evil and on behalf of good throughout history. The problem to which Berry alerted his readers is the distortion that resulted from this dualism when evil was associated with this world or, in what was more often the case, the good was considered a purely spiritual and otherworldly reality and the natural world valueless, except as it served human concerns. The distortion, however, does not prove that the dualism of good and evil itself is a distortion, but it points to the necessity of the authentic mediation of its meaning.

There is an important and relevant difference with regard to the theme of good and evil, however, between Berry's work and that of Teilhard, for example. Berry, unlike Teilhard, was not primarily concerned with the reconciliation of theories of evolution and Christian teaching. He was responding to a crisis, which we have identified within Lonergan's thought as a dimension of decline. The sense of "automatic" progress toward spiritualization of all human effort is not present in Berry's work. There is, as there is in Lonergan, the underlying perception of God's action in the universe as respectful of the original creation and of human freedom. The concrete reality to which he was responding is always close to the surface. "God is not going to save the planet if we decide to destroy it," he warned. "Until enough people realize we are in a crash situation, they are not going to do what needs to be done."[44]

The "new story" was engendered by the awareness, motivation and praxis implied in these warnings. It would be, he believed, an effective medium for rendering the new scientific cosmology "functional," that is, constitutive of human history. The dialectic in Berry's work is closer to that of Lonergan in its historical concreteness than to the Hegelian sense present in Teilhard. Furthermore, concerning human change and action on behalf of ecological meanings and values, evil (or in his words, the supreme pathology) is identifiable and not a matter for compromise.

Berry's own performance in terms of his rhetoric and methodology, as well as that envisioned by his proposal, is itself a praxis that is a participation in *cosmopolis* and thus can be understood under a Christian horizon (which was not his own) as mediating redemption in an effort to meet the moral evil inherent in the ecological crisis. The "new story" was an attempt to ground a willingness that is at once self-transcendent and practical.

Methodologically, at least, Berry's work belongs within *cosmopolis*. Insofar as it engenders meanings and values that evoke a new experience and understanding of God and the relationship of that experience and understanding to ecological praxis, it also belongs thematically within *cosmopolis* under religious and Christian horizons. As performative, the "new story" attempts to mediate religiously interpreted scientific cosmology and render it constitutive of human history. Under a Christian horizon and to the extent it is effective, it thereby mediates redemption and also renders it constitutive of human progress. As specifically thematized in terms of Christian conversion on the part of the human subjects engaged in this praxis and as offering a descriptive language for theoretic mediation in Christian theology, a clarification of the dialectic of good and evil is necessary.

In summary, under a Christian horizon, the "new story" attempts to engender decisions and actions that would create authentic relationships between humans and the rest of God's creation. This performance can be understood as a mediation of Christian redemption and thematized in Christian theology as such. As a context for other stories (including the Christian story), as Berry suggested, the actual story as told requires clarification of the human role in evil, not just as part of a kind of pathological drift of culture, but also as subject to the relative freedom (however small effectively) of humans from the natural cycles of the universe and from the culture of which they are an integral part. It is in this margin of freedom that the love of God mediated in the redemption wrought by Jesus in history can be effective. No matter how gloriously God's love is manifested in the non-human world, if the effective freedom of humanity is not converted then the "new story" itself will soon become an instrument in the longer cycle of decline that Lonergan explicated.

More specifically, the ambiguous presence of humans within the universe, as Berry presented it, would have to be understood not only as a dialectic of cultural and genetic coding, but also as a dialectic within human freedom between sin and the universal willingness grounded in God's gift of redemption. Such images as the numinous and mysterious origin of the universe, the transcendent upward reaching of the evolutionary process itself, the subjectivity of the universe and the self-reflective role of humans within the universe require further articulation in terms of the transcendent dimension of mystery. Finally, the psychic energy and hope that would motivate the issuing of the "new story" into the constitution of human history require an articulation in terms of the appropriation of the redemption wrought in Jesus and the concrete, authentic praxis that was generated by the historical reality of Jesus in history.

Notes

1. Lonergan, *Method*, xi.

2. Berry, *The New Story: Comments on the Origin and Transmission of Values. Teilhard Studies*, Spring 1970 (Chambersburg, PA: Anima Publications, 1970).

3. Cf. Berry, "The Gaia Theory: Its Religious Implications," 7-19.

4. Berry, *The Dream of the Earth*, 196.

5. Ibid., 84.

6. Berry, *Befriending the Earth*, 132, 134.

7. Ibid. See also Berry, "Science and Technology for Development," *Riverdale Papers on the Earth Community*.

8.   Berry, *The Dream of the Earth*, xv, 111 and 119, and "Ethics and Ecology," *Teilhard Perspective 24*,1 (June 1991): 1-3.

9.   Berry, *Befriending the Earth*, 51.

10.   Lonergan, *Method*, 76. See also 239-240 and 264.

11.   Cf. Douglas Burton-Christie, "Mapping the Sacred Landscape: Spirituality and the Contemporary Literature of Nature," *Horizons* 21,1 (Spring 1994): 44.

12.   Cf. *The Universe Story*, 1, 26, 28, 66-67, 167, 234 and 251.

13.   Cf. Berry, *Befriending the Earth*, 10, 27-28, 67.

14.   Berry, *The Dream of the Earth*, 89-108. An interesting comparison of the role of education in reform can be made, methodologically, at least, between Berry's essay "The American College" and Robert Doran's "Education for Cosmopolis," in *Method: Journal of Lonergan Studies* 1,2 (Fall 1983): 134-157.

15.   Swimme and Berry, *The Universe Story*, 40.

16.   Berry, *The Dream of the Earth*, 11.

17.   Ibid., 212.

18.   Cf. Lonergan, *Method*, 66.

19.   Doran, *Theology and the Dialectics of History*, 545. See also Berry, "Individualism and Wholism in the Chinese Tradition," *Riverdale Papers IX*.

20.   Cf. Swimme and Berry, *The Universe Story*, 267.

21.   Cf. Gregory Baum, "The Grand Vision: It Needs Social Action," and James Farris, "Redemption: Fundamental to the Story," in *Thomas Berry and the New Cosmology*, 51-55 and 65-82, respectively.

22.   The third stage of meaning, like any stage, is a gradual acquisition on the part of individuals or culture and rarely ever clearly and definitively indicated. Bernard Lonergan, *Doctrinal Pluralism* (Milwaukee: Marquette University Press, 1971), 33-39.

23.   For parallel or confirming accounts, cf. Santmire, *The Travail of Nature*; Rosemary Radford Ruether, *Gaia and God. An Ecofeminist Theology of Earth Healing* (San Francisco: HarperCollins Publishers, 1992); John Haught,*Cosmic Adventure: Science, Religion and the Quest for Purpose* (New York: Paulist Press, 1984); Carolyn Merchant, *The Death of Nature* (San Francisco: Harper and Row, Publishers, Inc., 1980).

24.   Berry,*The Dream of the Earth*, 197, 208, 223; and *Befriending the Earth*, 75, 112.

25.   Cf. Ricoeur, "The Metaphorical Process," *Semeia*, 95, for analysis of this existential-referential dimension of parables.

26.   Most scholars use "myth" to cover both meanings delineated by Lonergan. Doran, *Theology and the Dialectics of History*, 124.

27.   Berry, *Befriending the Earth*, 11.

28.   Ibid., 9. Compare Lonergan, "Man's response to transcendent mystery is adoration," *Method*, 344.

29.   Cf. Lonergan, *Method*, 341-342.

30.   Berry, *Befriending the Earth*, 19, 27.

31.   We are using the term "dialectic" here in Lonergan's sense (clarified by Doran) as "dialectic of contraries" in which the terms are not mutually exclusive, but can be reconciled in a higher synthesis. Cf. Doran, *Theology and the Dialectics of History*, 10, 14, 64-92.

32.   It is the case that Lonergan saw the necessity of an integral dialectic of transcendence and immanence within the divine reality for all religious expressions. He

did not contend, however, that this dialectic actually existed within all religions, or, for that matter, that it existed in authentic fashion in the concrete (actual lived) Christian tradition.

33.   Swimme and Berry, *The Universe Story*, 266.

34.   Berry, *Befriending the Earth*, 7, 19. Berry also indicated that he does not identify the Divine with the universe itself. He contended, convincingly, that no religion ever identified the Divine with components of the universe.

35.   Thomas Clarke, *Befriending the Earth*, 31-33.

36.   Berry, *The Dream of the Earth*, 81. For recent efforts to produce new metaphors for God, cf. Sallie McFague, *Models of God* (Philadelphia: Fortress Press, 1987).

37.   Cf. Lonergan, *Method*, 342. For an analysis of the mediation of an understanding of God through understandings of the universe in Lonergan's work and the tradition to which he belongs, see Happel, "Metaphors and Time Asymmetry," especially pp. 122-127.

38.   For reference to the theme of "cosmic caringness" in Berry's works, see John Haught, *The Promise of Nature* (Mahwah, NJ: Paulist Press, 1993), 14.

39.   Berry, *Befriending the Earth*, 66-82. Cf. Santmire, *The Travail of Nature*, 210-218 and footnotes.

40.   Cf. Rosemary Radford Ruether's discussion of the ambiguous relationship between finality and evil in the Christian tradition in *Gaia and God*, 126-139.

41.   Berry, *Befriending the Earth*, 49-51, 82.

42.   The text to which we are referring here is a transcript of a series of conversations. There are no well-developed passages on this theme in Berry's work. The video presentation of the same conference on which the book is based gives a better sense of the context of the ideas we are using here since it is actual footage of the conference. See *Befriending the Earth*, 13-part video series (Mystic, CT: Twenty-Third Publications, 1991).

43.   Cf. Berry, *Befriending the Earth*, 27, 80.

44.   Ibid., 46.

SUMMARY
AND CONCLUSIONS

This work originated in a desire to discover the relationship between two urgencies of our times. The first was the ecological crisis and the second, the reform of Christian theology. The preliminary, largely untested insights that moved the project into actuality were that (1) as Thomas Berry had loudly and clearly proclaimed, the ecological crisis was also religious; it had religious roots and it required a religious solution, and (2) a theology that did not serve to increase hope in the possibility of authentically negotiating the major crises of our time had already died. Bernard Lonergan seemed to corroborate this latter premonition, and also to meet the challenge with the assertion that theology can still be an effective mediator of hope in the contemporary world.

Hence, we began with an investigation into the formation of Berry's convictions that the ecological crisis was first and foremost a cultural crisis requiring a cultural solution. Religion, for Berry, operated most prominently at the level of culture. Chapters one to four traced the genetic development of his thought from his early study of Vico to his consuming interest in the ecological crisis. We found that Berry inherited from Vico (or found resonant with him) a methodology of cultural history and a counter-Enlightenment stance. Like Vico, he displayed a penchant for large synthetic views and organizing principles. He saw history as a succession of identifiable ages, which in their states of decline required some kind of return to the primal stages of humankind for the renewal and rejuvenation of history itself. The emergence of new ages were not merely adaptations of human ingenuity, but were characterized by a radical change in human consciousness. Thus, Berry would later postulate the emergence in our times of the Ecological Age (Ecozoic Era), accompanied by a psychic transformation that would be expressed in human culture as a new contextual story. This transformation would require some kind of recovery of primal sensibilities.

If Vico was the precursor of a counter-Enlightenment tradition, as scholars maintain, then Berry was its inheritor. Throughout his career he found support for his developing ideas in a smorgasbord of groups and individuals (neo-Platonists, Renaissance Platonists, alchemists, romantics, transcendentalists, natural historians, humanists and existentialists) in the Western tradition, whose common trait was sometimes not much more than their insistence on an alternative to developing mainstream Enlightenment notions. They were anti-materialist, anti-empiricist and anti-mechanist (many were organicist and idealist) in their conceptions of the natural world. Because of their high valuation of nature, Berry saw in them forerunners of the contemporary ecological movements. That he would find support (and perhaps solace) in the alternative visions of the past was not surprising in the light of his own conviction that Western society was not working.

Berry's interest in world religions grew, he admitted, from his desire to find out why Western society and Christianity were not working. His writings in that area attest to his concern that religious scholarship be effective in society. He interpreted the role of religions within cultures as existential meaning-making. He consistently challenged Christianity and theological scholarship, in particular, to examine the religions of the world with a view to self-criticism and fruitful collaboration for the sake of renewing contemporary culture. Notions of plenitude and organicism were organizing principles for his own conception of the interrelationship among religions. His particular fondness for the religion of the North American natives attested to his Vichian conviction that primal consciousness held a wisdom that was lost, but urgently needed, in the present world. He concluded from his investigations into religion that the contemporary world needed a myth that would guide it and motivate it as the religious myth of the past had done for former times.

Aware from the beginning of the hegemonic role modern science commanded in Western society, Berry found in Teilhard de Chardin a religious interpretation of science. Furthermore, Teilhard, like Berry, was concerned with the growing irrelevance of religion, in particular Christianity, to the contemporary world. Even further, he had composed a modern story, a grand narrative, that reinterpreted both mainstream science and Christian beliefs. This story, Berry felt, was in the tradition not only of the great myths of all the religions, but also of Augustine's *City of God* and Dante's *Divine Comedy*. These, in his view, had been epochal stories that incorporated the cosmologies of their day into Christianity, provided effective cultural remedies for abuses and created meanings for life. Berry distanced himself from Teilhard's exclusive focus on Christianity, his low valuation of the past and other cultures than Western, his naive faith in Western progress, and, under the ecological horizon, his overspiritualization of nature. Yet Teilhard's evolutionary story continued to be for Berry a paradigm of a story that would render cosmology (scientific and religious) functional for the contemporary world.

For Berry, science was a cultural construct. It not only emerged from a religious and mythic setting that was conducive to the nature it assumed, but it amplified, secularized and even technologized those myths. Berry found support for his conception of science in a growing number of scientists (like Prigogine and Stengers) who were becoming increasingly aware of the tenuous assumptions on which their epistemology and methods were based. Furthermore, he was attracted by new theories that tended to provide scientific support for ideas that Berry had already encountered in the counter-Enlightenment tradition with which he identified. Such theories as self-organization dynamics, the anthropic principle and the Gaia theory were also very conducive to a more ecological perception of human relationships to the rest of the universe. Ecologists provided actual strategies (such as bioregionalism) for the practical implementation of new ways of relating to nature.

Chapter five dealt with Berry's proposal for the ecological crisis. It began with an account of Berry's critique of Western culture. While broad-stroked and sweeping, his critique was characterized by what Ricoeur called a hermeneutic of suspicion and a hermeneutic of recovery. It unmasked the myths that informed Western culture's conception of nature. His proposal found within that same tradition, however, the seeds of a new future.

Primarily, Berry was concerned with the creation of a meaningful story, a cosmology, that would effectively revalue the universe as intrinsically worthy of human respect and mediate the appropriate new values and meanings into society. He was convinced that the latest scientific account of cosmology was not only open to religious interpretation, but also evoked a religious experience of the universe. The very scientific discovery itself involved psychic intuitions and a religious revelation of the numinous dimensions of the universe. This story, which brought together scientific findings and religious sensitivities, held the power to effect a new age in the Vichian sense.

Berry challenged all human disciplines, in particular Christian theology, to do the critical work necessary to ensure the effectiveness of this "new story" in contemporary societies. The story was not in itself a theology; it was addressed to the general public. Berry believed that its configuring principles, such as the cosmogenetic principle, could be contextualized within different cultures and religions.

Berry's work was not easily systematized. Some images carry surpluses of meaning that conflict or contradict what seemed to be Berry's overall intentions. Thus, there was difficulty in sorting out images that connoted reminiscences of idealism, romantic return to primal consciousness, sense of agency in the universe, iconoclastic attitudes toward modern technology and Christian tradition, within a contention that we cannot be idealist or romantic and that both modern technology and Christian tradition are essential elements of recovery. Much of the difficulty in interpretation and systematization stemmed from the nature of Berry's work. It is located primarily within what Bernard Lonergan called the realm of descriptive discourse. The full impact of that categorization as explanatory of Berry's project and of the contribution it can make to Christian theology was considered in the final chapters.

Categories from the thought of Bernard Lonergan were selected with a view to assessing whether or not Berry's proposal could contribute to the renewal of Christian theology in the light of the ecological crisis. Lonergan confronted the epistemological basis from which many of the problems concerning the status of theology in modern society emerged. His distinction between explanation and description as representative of two different universes of discourse each with its own exigencies by itself enabled a clarification of the role of work such as Berry's and its relationship to theoretic discourse, such as theology. Lonergan's recovery of the human subject as knower, lover and actor, integral with, but also potentially free within overall world process grounded a method from which theology functioned as a mediation of the religious experience of God's love and redemption within a cultural matrix. This was the kind of theology that could meet Berry's challenge.

Lonergan's methodological categories enabled us to form the following conclusions with respect to Berry's contribution to a Christian theology that takes seriously the ecological horizon.

(1) Insofar as Berry's "new story" is an interweaving of images and rhetoric designed to meet aspects of the longer cycle of decline, it is a candidate for *cosmopolis.*

(2) Insofar as the conversions (moral, intellectual, psychic and religious) are indicated as necessary for the praxis for which the "new story" calls, the foundational requirements of *cosmopolis* are met. As descriptive discourse, the "new story" does not consciously and systematically articulate the role of these foundations. This is seen in the ambiguity around the dialectic of transcendence and immanence, for example. Nevertheless, there is enough evidence to conclude that Berry's project is open at least to an interpretation as a post-critical intervention in culture engendering a new future and that he is not simply advocating a naive return to some primal consciousness.

(3) Under a Christian horizon, then, the "new story" is already a mediator of redemption, since in the performance it engenders it meets aspects of decline, understood within this horizon as sin. As such, it invites Christian thematization in terms of the redemption wrought in Jesus.

(4) In turn, Lonergan's interpretation of redemption as effectively operative within the gift of creation and respectful of its integrity offers a thematization of Christianity that meets Berry's suspicion of the mythic aspects of redemption and its virtual exclusion of the creation myth in recent Western tradition.

(5) Berry's piling up of images on the side of aspects of religious and specifically Christian traditions that he wished to recover often confuses distinctions that are crucial to Christian praxis and hence to theology. Issues of moral evil are not clearly articulated and distinguished from those dealing with natural evils and finitude, despite the call for moral responsibility for ecological recovery. Hence, the settlement of the dialectic of good and evil on the side of good, so central to the mediation of God's love in the world, requires the clarity that Lonergan (through Doran) provides. Then the concrete meaning of Christian redemption is manifested more clearly.

(6) The predominant strengths of Berry's "new story", from a theological perspective, are (a) that it raises the challenge to make understandings of the universe constitutive of our understanding of God and hence normative for our praxis, and (b) that it is methodologically located as a mediator of meanings and values that see the universe as religious, in a manner largely supported by Lonergan's theory of emergent probability.

(7) From a Christian theological perspective, the major source of the weaknesses in Berry's proposal is an ambiguity with respect to

the human subject. The general reluctance to deal adequately with the human subject is no doubt due to the suspicion of anthropocentrism cast by ecologists. Lonergan's work offers a recovery of the human subject in a manner that confronts the distorted relationship between humans and the rest of the natural world. The effectiveness of the "new story" as a mediation of Christian meanings and values would be enhanced by imaginal expressions of Lonergan's theoretic account of the human subject within emergent probability.

The "new story" is a story evoked by the awesome discoveries of scientists and perhaps the mystical experience of the universe by Berry and some of his sources. Nevertheless, it is a human construction, which requires for its effectiveness or functionality the decisions and actions of authentic human persons who understand their roles as integral to the emergent process of the universe. Humans who are confused about their ability to know, what knowing actually is, what the real is and whether or not their insights bear any relation to the universe as it is are poor candidates for the task engendered by the "new story". Likewise, humans who cannot find assurance that the universe is an intelligible place in which their decisions and actions, their love and praxis count in an ongoing and meaningful emergent process cannot accept a story that relies on these grounds. Hence, the reclamation of the human subject within emergent probability provides a necessary critical basis for both the ecological agenda and Christian theology.

BIBLIOGRAPHY—WORKS CITED

Primary Sources

A. Thomas Berry

"The American College in the Ecological Age." *Religion and Intellectual Life* 6, 2 (Winter 1989): 7-28.

"Authenticity in Confucian Spirituality." *Monastic Studies* 8 (Spring 1972): 153-158.

Befriending the Earth. Co-authored with Thomas Clarke. Ed. by Stephen Dunn, C.P. and Anne Lonergan. Mystic, CT: Twenty-Third Publications, 1991. Also a 13-part video series.

Buddhism. New York: Hawthorn Books, 1967.

"The Catholic Church and the Religions of the World." *Teilhard Perspective* 18,1 (August 1985): 1-5.

"Christian Missions in the Twentieth Century." Talk given to a meeting of Mission Societies of America. Laurel, MD: Earth Communications. Audiocassette.

"Contemporary Spirituality: The Journey of the Human Community." *Cross Currents* (Summer/Fall 1974): 172-183.

"Cosmic Person and the Human Future." Paper presented to the Symposium for the American Teilhard Association for the Future of Man and the C.G. Jung Foundation of New York, International House, New York, 1975. Published in *Anima* 3,1 (1975): 20-35.

"The Cosmology of Religions." *Pluralism and Oppression. The Annual Publication of the College Theology Society* 34 (1988): 100-113.

Dawn Over the Earth: Our Way into the Future. Tape W3. Laurel, MD: Earth Communications Center. Videocassette.

The Dream of the Earth. San Francisco: Sierra Club Books, 1988.

"The Dynamics of the Future: Reflections on the Earth Process." *Monastic Studies* 12 (1976): 159-174.

"The Ecozoic Era." E.F. Schumacher Society Lecture, Oct. 19, 1991. Great Barrington, MA: E.F. Schumacher Society and Thomas Berry, 1991.

"Ethics and Ecology." *Teilhard Perspective* 24,1 (June 1991): 1-3.

"The Gaia Theory: Its Religious Implications." *ARC: The Journal of the Faculty of Religious Studies, McGill University* 22 (1994): 7-19.

The Historical Theory of Giambattista Vico. Washington, DC: The Catholic University Press of America, 1949.

Human Presence in the Earth Community. Talks given at a conference. Five audiocassettes. Sonoma, CA: Global Perspectives, 1989.

"Introduction." *The Breathing Cathedral: Feeling Our Way into a Living Cosmos.* By Martha Heyneman. San Francisco: Sierra Club Books, 1993.

Management: The Managerial Ethos and the Future of Planet Earth. Teilhard Studies Number 3. Chambersburg, PA: Anima Books, 1980.

The New Story: Comments on the Origin and Transmission of Values. Teilhard Studies Spring 1970. Chambersburg, PA: Anima Books, 1980, rep.

"Oriental Philosophy and World Humanism." *International Philosophical Quarterly* 1,1 (February 1961): 5-33.

"Perspectives on Creativity: Openness to a Free Future." In *Whither Creativity, Freedom, Suffering?: Humanity, Cosmos, God. Proceedings of the Theology Institute of Villanova University.* Ed. by Francis A. Eigo. Villanova, PA: Villanova University Press, 1981. Pp. 1-24.

Reinventing the Human. Friends of Creation Spirituality. Videocassette.

Religions of India: Hinduism, Yoga, Buddhism. 1st ed. New York: Bruce Publishing Co., and London: Collier-Macmillan, 1971. 2nd ed. Chambersburg, PA: Anima Publications, 1992.

Riverdale Papers. Vols. I-IX. Essays and papers delivered on different occasions, some of which have since been published. Compiled by Riverdale Centre for Religious Research, Riverdale, NY, 10471.

Riverdale Papers on the Earth Community. Essays and papers related to ecology and religion, some of which have since been published. Compiled by Riverdale Centre for Religious Research, Riverdale, NY, 10471.

"The Spiritual Form of the Oriental Civilizations." In *Approaches to Asian Civilization*. Ed. by T.[Theodore] deBary. New York and London: Columbia University Press, 1964.

"The Spirituality of the Earth." In *Liberating Life: Contemporary Approaches to Ecological Theology*. Ed. by William Birch, William Eakin and Jay B. McDaniel. Maryknoll, NY: Orbis Books, 1990. Pp. 152-157.

Teilhard in the Ecological Age, Teilhard Studies Number 7. Chambersburg, PA: Anima Books, Fall 1982.

Thomas Berry and the New Cosmology. Ed. by Anne Lonergan and Caroline Richards. Mystic, CT: Twenty-Third Publications, 1990.

"Traditional Religions in the Modern World." *Cross Currents* 22 (Spring 1972): 129-138.

The Universe Story. Co-authored with Brian Swimme. San Francisco: Harper-Collins Publishers, 1992.

"The Viable Human." *Revision* (January 1987): 1-10.

"Wonderworld as Wasteworld: The Earth in Deficit." *Cross Currents* 35 (Winter 1985-1986): 408-422.

B. Bernard Lonergan

"Belief: Today's Issue." *A Second Collection*. Ed. by William Ryan and Bernard Tyrrell. Philadelphia: Westminster Press, 1974.

"Bernard Lonergan Responds." In *Language, Truth, and Meaning: Papers from the International Lonergan Congress, 1970*. Ed. by Philip McShane. Notre Dame, IN: University of Notre Dame Press, 1972. Pp. 306-312.

"Dimensions of Meaning." In *Collection: Papers by Bernard Lonergan*. Ed. by Frederick E. Crowe. New York: Herder and Herder, 1967. Pp. 252-267.

Doctrinal Pluralism. Milwaukee: Marquette University Press, 1971.

"The Future of Christianity." In *A Second Collection*. Ed. by William Ryan and Bernard Tyrrell. Philadelphia: Westminster Press, 1974.

"Healing and Creating in History." In *A Third Collection*. Ed. by Frederick E. Crowe. New York and Mahwah: Paulist Press, 1985. Pp. 100-112.

Insight: A Study of Human Understanding. Collected Works of Bernard Lonergan. Vol. 3. Ed. by Frederick E. Crowe and Robert M. Doran. Toronto, Buffalo and London: University of Toronto Press and Toronto: Lonergan Research Institute of Regis College, 1992.

Method in Theology. Minneapolis, MN: The Seabury Press, 1972.

"Mission and the Spirit." In *A Third Collection*. Ed. by Frederick E. Crowe. New York and Mahwah: Paulist Press, 1985. Pp. 23-31.

"Reality, Myth and Symbol." In *Myth, Symbol, and Reality*. Ed. by Alan M. Olson. Notre Dame, IN: University of Notre Dame Press, 1980.

"Religious Knowledge." In *Lonergan Workshop*. Vol. 1. Ed. by Fred Lawrence. Missoula, MT: Scholars' Press, 1978. Pp. 309-327.

The Subject. Milwaukee: Marquette University Press, 1968.

Understanding and Being. The Collected Works of Bernard Lonergan. Vol. 5. Ed. by Elizabeth A. Morelli and Mark D. Morelli. Rev. and augmented by Frederick E. Crowe et al. Toronto, Buffalo and London: University of Toronto Press, 1990.

C. Pierre Teilhard de Chardin

Activation of Energy. Trans. by René Hague. New York and London: Harcourt, Brace, Jovanovich, 1970.

The Divine Milieu. New York: Harper and Row, Publishers, Inc., 1965.

The Heart of the Matter. Trans. by René Hague. New York and London: Harcourt, Brace, Jovanovich, 1978.

Phenomenon of Man. Trans. by Bernard Wall. New York: Harper Torchbook, 1965.

Science and Christ. Trans. by René Hague. New York and Evanston: Harper and Row, Publishers, Inc., 1968.

Toward the Future. Trans. by René Hague. New York and London: Harcourt, Brace, Jovanovich, 1975.

D. Giambattista Vico

The New Science of Giambattista Vico. 3rd ed. Rev. and trans. by Thomas Goddard Bergin and Max Harold Fisch. Ithaca, NY: Cornell University Press, 1968.

Secondary Sources

Adamson, Joy. Born *Free: A Lioness of Two Worlds*. New York: Pantheon Books, 1960.

Armstrong, Edward. *St. Francis: Nature Mystic, The Derivation and Significance of the Nature Stories in the Franciscan Legend*. Berkeley, CA: University of California Press, 1973.

Barrow, John D., and Frank J. Tipler. *The Anthropic Cosmological Principle*. Oxford, UK: Clarendon Press and New York: Oxford University Press, 1986.

Barrow, John D., and Joseph Silk. *The Left Hand of Creation*. New York: Basic Books, 1983.

Bateson, Gregory. *Mind and Nature: A Necessary Unity.* New York: Bantam Books, 1988.

Baum, Gregory. "The Grand Vision: It Needs Social Action." *Thomas Berry and the New Cosmology.* Ed. by Anne Lonergan and Caroline Richards. Mystic, CT: Twenty-Third Publications, 1990. Pp. 51-55.

Beney, Guy. "Gaia: The Globalitarian Temptation." Interview with Guy Beney. In *Global Ecology: A New Arena of Political Conflict.* Ed. by Wolfgang Sachs. London and New Jersey: Zed Books, and Halifax, NS: Fernwood Publications, 1993. Pp. 179-191.

Benfey, Theodor. "A Scientist Comments." *Religion and the Intellectual Life* 6, 2 (Winter 1989): 63-68."

Bergson, Henri. *La pensée et le mouvant en œuvre.* Paris: Éditions du Centenaire, PUF, 1970. English. *The Creative Mind.* Trans. by Mabelle L. Andison. Totowa, NJ: Littlefield, Adams, 1975.

Bergstrasser, Arnold. *Goethe's Image of Man and Society.* Freiburg, Germany: Herder, 1962.

Berlin, Isaiah. *Against the Current: Essays in the History of Ideas.* New York: The Viking Press, 1980.

_____. Preface to *The Mind of the European Romantics* by H.G. Schenk. London: Constable and Co., Ltd., 1966.

Bernstein, J.M. "Grand Narratives." In *On Paul Ricoeur: Narrative and Interpretation.* Ed. by David Wood. New York: Routledge, Chapman and Hall, Inc., and London: The University of Warwick, 1991. Pp. 102-123.

Berry, Wendell. *The Unsettling of America: Culture and Agriculture.* New York: Avon/Sierra Club Books, 1978.

Bloom, Harold. "Lying against Time: Gnosis, Poetry, Criticism." In *Rediscovery of Gnosticism I—The School of Valentinus.* Ed. by Bentley Layton. Leiden, Netherlands: E.J. Brill, 1981.

Bohm, David. "Fragmentation and Wholeness in Religion and Science." *Zygon* 20,2 (June 1985): 125-127.

_____. *Wholeness and the Implicate Order.* London and Boston: Routledge and Kegan Paul, 1980.

Bonifazi, Conrad. *The Soul of the World: An Account of the Inwardness of Things.* Washington, DC: University of America Press, 1978.

Bowden, John, and Alan Richardson, eds. *New Dictionary of Christian Theology.* 2nd ed. London: SCM Press, 1983. S.v. "Romanticism," by Stephen Happel.

Bramwell, Anna. *Ecology in the 20th Century: A History.* New Haven and London: Yale University Press, 1989.

Buckley, Michael. *The Origins of Modern Atheism.* New Haven and London: Yale University Press, 1987.

Burton-Christie, Douglas. "Mapping the Sacred Landscape: Spirituality and the Contemporary Literature of Nature." *Horizons* 21,1 (Spring 1994): 22-47.

Bury, J. *Idea of Progress*. New York: Macmillan Publishing Co., 1932.

Byrne, Patrick. "God and the Statistical Universe." *Zygon* 16 (December 4, 1981): 345-363.

_____."Insight and the Retrieval of Nature." In *Lonergan Workshop*. Vol. 8. Ed. by Fred Lawrence. Atlanta: Scholars Press, 1990.

_____. *Randomness, Statistics and Emergence*. Notre Dame, IN: University of Notre Dame Press, 1970.

Campbell, Joseph. *Hero with a Thousand Faces*. New York: Pantheon Books, 1949.

Carson, Rachel. *Silent Spring*. Cambridge: Riverside Press, 1962.

Castaneda, Carlos. *Journey to Ixtlan*. New York: Simon and Schuster, 1972.

_____. *Separate Reality*. New York: Simon and Schuster, 1971.

Chenu, M.D. *Nature, Man and Society in the Twelfth Century*. Chicago and London: The University of Chicago Press, 1968.

Clarke, Norris. "Form and Matter." In *The New Dictionary of Theology*. Ed. by Joseph A. Komonchak, Mary Collins and Dermot Lane. Wilmington, DE: Michael Glazier, 1987.

Crites, Stephen. "The Narrative Quality of Experience." In *Why Narrative? Readings in Narrative Theology*. Ed. by Stanley Hauerwas and L. Gregory Jones. Grand Rapids: William B. Eerdmans Publishing Company, 1989. Pp. 65-88.

Crowe, Frederick E. *Appropriating the Lonergan Ideal*. Ed. by Michael Vertin. Washington, DC: The Catholic University of America Press, 1989.

_____. *Lonergan. Outstanding Christian Thinkers Series*. Ed. by Brian Davies. Collegeville, MN: A Michael Glazier Book, Liturgical Press, 1992.

Danesi, Marcel. "Language and the Origin of the Human Imagination: A Vichian Perspective." *New Vico Studies* 4 (1986): 45-56.

Davies, Paul. *The Mind of God*. New York: Simon and Schuster, 1992.

Davis, Charles. "Response by Charles Davis." In *Lonergan's Hermeneutics: Its Development and Application*. Ed. by Sean E. McEvenue and Ben F. Meyer. Washington, DC: The Catholic University of America Press, 1989. Pp. 276-288.

Dawson, Christopher. *The Dynamics of World History*. New York: Sheed and Ward, 1956.

Deloria, Vine. *God Is Red*. New York: Delta Publishing, 1973.

Dillard, Annie. *Pilgrim at Tinker Creek*. New York: Harper and Row, Publishers, Inc., 1974.

Dilthey, Wilhelm. *Pattern and Meaning in History: Thoughts on History and Society*. Ed. and intro. by H.P. Rickman. New York: Harper and Row, Publishers, Inc., 1962.

Dobzhansky, Theodosius. *Mankind Evolving: The Evolution of the Human Species*. New Haven: Yale University Press, 1962.

Dodson, Edward O. *The Phenomenon of Man Revisited: A Biological View-point on Teilhard de Chardin.* New York: Columbia University Press, 1984.

Doran, Robert. "Education for Cosmopolis." *Method: Journal of Lonergan Studies* 1,2 (Fall 1983): 134-157.

_____. *Psychic Conversion and Theological Foundations: Toward a Reorientation of the Human Sciences.* AAR Studies in Religion 25. Chico, CA: Scholars' Press, 1981.

_____. *Theology and the Dialectics of History.* Toronto, Buffalo and London: University of Toronto Press, 1990.

Dubos, René. *The Dreams of Reason: Science and Utopias.* New York: Columbia University Press, 1961.

_____. "Franciscan Conservation versus Benedictine Stewardship." In *A God Within.* Ed. by René Dubos. New York: Charles Scribner, 1972. Pp. 153-174.

_____. *The Wooing of Earth.* New York: Scribner Books, 1980.

Dunn, Stephen, C.P. "Needed: A New Genre for Moral Theology." In *Thomas Berry and the New Cosmology.* Ed. by Anne Lonergan and Caroline Richards. Mystic, CT: Twenty-Third Publications, 1990. Pp. 74-81.

Dyson, Freeman. *Disturbing the Universe.* New York: Harper and Row, Publishers, Inc., 1979.

Ehrenfeld, David. *The Arrogance of Humanism.* New York: Oxford University Press, 1981.

Ehrlich, Paul R., and Anne H. Ehrlich. *Extinction: The Causes and Consequences of the Disappearance of Species.* New York: Random House, 1981.

Eiseley, Loren. *The Immense Journey.* New York: Vintage Books, 1957.

_____. *The Unexpected Universe.* New York and London: Harcourt Brace Jovanovich, 1969, c. 1964.

Eliade, Mircea. *Cosmos and History.* New York: Harper and Row, Publishers, Inc., 1959.

_____. *Mephistopheles and the Androgyne: Studies in Religious Myth and Symbol.* New York: Sheed and Ward, 1965.

_____. *Myth and Reality.* New York: Harper and Row, Publishers, Inc., 1963.

_____. *The Sacred and the Profane.* Trans. by Willard R. Trask. New York and London: Harcourt, Brace, Jovanovich, 1959.

_____ with Willard R. Trask. *Rites and Symbols of Initiation: The Rites and Symbols of Birth and Rebirth.* New York: Harper and Row, Publishers, Inc., 1965, c. 1958.

Fabel, Arthur. *Cosmic Genesis. Teilhard Studies Number 5.* Summer 1981.

_____. *The New Book of Nature. Teilhard Studies Number 8.* Fall 1982.

_____. "The Organic Society: A Search for Synthesis." *Teilhard Perspective* 17,1 (June 1984): 1-7.

Farrer, Austin. *Reflective Faith: Essays in Philosophical Theology.* Ed. by Charles C. Conti. London: SPCK, 1972.

Farris, James. "Redemption: Fundamental to the Story." In *Thomas Berry and the New Cosmology.* Ed. by Anne Lonergan and Caroline Richards. Mystic, CT: Twenty-Third Publications, 1990. Pp. 65-82.

Flint, Robert. *Vico.* Edinburgh: Blackwood and Sons, 1884.

Foerster, Werner. *Gnosis.* Vol. 1. Oxford: Clarendon Press, 1972.

Frohlich, Mary E. *Intersubjectivity and the Mystic.* Missoula, MT: Scholars' Press, 1994.

Furst, Lilian R. *Romanticism.* London: Methuen and Co., 1969.

Gerhart, Mary, and Allan Russell. *Metaphoric Process: The Creation of Religious and Scientific Understanding.* Fort Worth, TX: Texas Christian University Press, 1984.

Gerwin, Jef van. "Root Metaphors of Society: Linking Sociological and Moral-Theological Analysis." *Louvain Studies* (Spring 1986): 41-59.

Gilbert, Felix. "Intellectual History: Its Aims and Methods." In *Historical Studies Today.* Ed. by Felix Gilbert and Stephen R. Graubard. New York: W.W. Norton and Co., Inc., 1972: 141-158.

Gilkey, Langdon. *Religion and the Scientific Future.* New York, Evanston, London: Harper and Row, Publishers, Inc., 1970.

Grau, Joseph A. *Morality and the Human Future in the Thought of Teilhard de Chardin.* London: Associated University Presses, 1976.

Gray, Donald. *The One and the Many.* New York: Herder and Herder, 1969.

Gregson, Vernon. *Lonergan, Spirituality and the Meeting of Religions.* The College Theology Society: Studies in Religion 2. Lanham, MD: University Press of America, 1985.

Gross, Rita M. "Vision and Practicality: A Response to Thomas Berry." In *Pluralism and Oppression: Theology in World Perspective. Annual Publication of the College Theology Society, 1988.* Vol. 34. Ed. by Paul Knitter. Lanham, MD: University Press of America and The College Theology Society, 1991. Pp. 115-124.

Happel, Stephen. "Metaphors and Time Asymmetry: Cosmologies in Physics and Christian Meanings." In *Quantum Cosmology and the Laws of Nature: Scientific Perspectives on Divine Action.* Ed. by Robert John Russell, Nancey Murphy and C.J. Isham. Vatican City State: Vatican Observatory Publications, 1993. Pp. 103-134.

_____. "The Sacraments, Interiority, and Spiritual Direction." In *A Promise of Presence: Festschrift in Honor of David Power, OMI.* Ed. by Michael Downey and Richard Fragomeni. Washington, DC: The Pastoral Press, 1992. Pp. 139-161.

Hauerwas, Stanley, and L. Gregory Jones, eds. *Why Narrative? Readings in Narrative Theology.* Grand Rapids, MI: William B. Eerdmans Publishing Company, 1989.

Haught, John. *Cosmic Adventure: Science, Religion and the Quest for Purpose.* New York: Paulist Press, 1984.

_____. *The Promise of Nature.* Mahwah, NJ: Paulist Press, 1993.

Hawking, Stephen. *A Brief History of Time.* New York: Bantam Books, 1988.

Hefling, Jr., Charles C. "On Understanding Salvation History." In *Lonergan's Hermeneutics: Its Development and Application.* Ed. by Sean E. MacEvenue and Ben F. Meyer. Washington, DC: The Catholic University of America Press, 1989. Pp. 221-275.

_____. "Philosophy, Theology and God." In *Desires of the Human Heart.* Ed. by Vernon Gregson. New York and Mahwah: Paulist Press, 1988. Pp. 120-143.

Henderson, L. [Lawrence] J. *The Order of Nature.* Cambridge: Harvard University Press, 1917.

Horkheimer, Max. "Vico and Mythology." Trans. by Fred Dallmayr. *New Vico Studies* 5 (1987): 63-75.

Hoyle, Fred. *Religion and the Scientists.* London: SCM Press, 1959.

Humboldt, Alexander von. *Aspects of Nature.* New York: AMS Press, 1970.

Hutton, Patrick H. "Vico's Significance for the New Cultural History." *New Vico Studies* 3 (1985): 73-84.

Hyams, Edward. *Soil and Civilization.* London: John Murray, 1976. 1st. publication, 1954.

Hymes, Dell. "From an Anthropologist." *Religion and the Intellectual Life* 6, 2 (Winter 1989): 36-41.

Jantsch, Erich. *The Self-Organizing Universe.* Oxford, New York, Toronto, Sydney, Paris and Frankfurt: Pergamon Press, 1980.

Jaspars, Karl. *The Origins and Goals of History.* Trans. by Michael Bullock. New York: Yale University Press, 1953.

Kafatos, M. and R. Nadeau. *The Conscious Universe: Part and Whole in Modern Physical Theory.* New York: Springer-Verlag, 1990.

Kant, Immanuel. *Critique of Pure Reason.* Trans. by Norman Kemp Smith. New York: St. Martin's Press, 1965.

Keller, Evelyn Fox. *A Feeling for the Organism: The Life and Work of Barbara McClintock.* New York and San Francisco: W.H. Freeman and Co., 1983.

Klemm, David. E. "Toward a Rhetoric of Postmodern Theology," *Journal of the American Academy of Religion* LV, 3 (1987): 443-469.

Koyré, Alexander. *From a Closed World to the Infinite Universe.* Baltimore: Helicon Press, 1957.

Lamb, Matthew. *History, Method and Theology: A Dialectical Comparison of Wilhelm Dilthey's Critique of Historical Reason and Bernard Lonergan's Meta-Methodology.* Missoula, MT: Scholars' Press, 1978.

_____. *Solidarity with Victims: Toward a Theology of Social Transformation.* New York: Crossroad, 1982.

Lawrence, Frederick. "Self-knowledge in History in Gadamer and Lonergan." In *Language, Truth and Meaning.* Ed. by Philip McShane. Notre Dame, IN: University of Notre Dame Press, 1972. Pp. 167-217.

LeDuc, Laurent. "Intellectual Conversion and the Gaia Hypothesis." Ph.D. diss., University of Saint Michael's College, Toronto, 1992.

Leopold, Aldo. *A Sand County Almanac.* New York: Oxford University Press, 1949.

_____. *Round River.* New York: Oxford University Press, 1953.

Levine, Joseph M. "Giambattista Vico and the Quarrel between the Ancients and the Moderns." *Journal of the History of Ideas.* LXX, 1 (Jan.-Mar. 1991): 55-79.

Lewis, C.S. *Miracles.* 8th impression. London: Fontana Press, 1982.

Lilly, John. *Communication between Man and Dolphin: The Possibility of Talking with Other Species.* New York: Crown Publications, 1978.

Loewe, William P. "Lonergan and the Law of the Cross: A Universalist View of Salvation." *Anglican Theological Review* 59 (1977): 162-174.

_____. "Toward a Responsible Contemporary Soteriology." In *Creativity and Method: Essays in Honor of Bernard Lonergan.* Ed. by Matthew Lamb. Milwaukee: Marquette University Press, 1981. Pp. 35-51.

Lonergan, Anne. "Introduction: The Challenge of Thomas Berry." In *Thomas Berry and the New Cosmology.* Ed. by Anne Lonergan and Caroline Richards. Mystic, CT: Twenty-Third Publications, 1990. Pp. 3-5.

Lovejoy, Arthur O. *The Great Chain of Being.* Cambridge, MA and London: Harvard University Press, 1936 and 1964.

_____. "Reflections on the History of Ideas." *Journal of the History of Ideas* 1, 1 (1940): 3-23.

_____. "The Meaning of Romanticism for the Historian of Ideas." *Journal of the History of Ideas* 2, 3 (June 1941): 257-278.

Lovelock, J.E. *The Ages of Gaia.* New York and London: W.W. Norton and Co., Inc., 1988.

_____. "Gaia." In *Gaia 2. Emergence.* Ed. by William Irwin Thompson. Hudson, New York: Lindisfarne Press, 1991.

_____. *Gaia: A New Look at Life on Earth.* New York: Oxford University Press, 1979.

_____ and Sidney Epton. "The Quest for Gaia." *New Science* 65 (1975): 291-320.

Lovin, Robin W., and Frank E. Reynolds, eds. *Cosmogony and Ethical Order.* Chicago and London: University of Chicago Press, 1985.

Lovins, Amory B. *Soft-Energy Paths: Toward a Durable Peace.* New York: Harper Colophon Books, 1979.

Mali, Joseph. "'The Public Grounds of Truth': The Critical Theory of G.B. Vico." *New Vico Studies* 6 (1988): 59-83.

Margulis, L. and J.E. Lovelock, "Biological Modulation of the Earth's Atmosphere." *Icarus* 21 (1974): 471-489.

Marx, Leo. *The Machine in the Garden.* London, Oxford and New York: Oxford University Press, 1964.

McFague, Sallie. *Models of God.* Philadelphia: Fortress Press, 1987.

McMullin, Ernan. "How Should Cosmology Relate to Theology?" In *The Sciences and Theology in the Twentieth Century.* Ed. by Arthur Peacocke. Notre Dame, IN: University of Notre Dame Press, 1981. Pp. 40-53.

McShane, Philip. "*Insight* and the Strategy of Biology." In *Lonergan's Challenge to the University and the Economy.* Lanham, MD: The University Press of America, 1980. Pp. 42-59.

Melchin, Kenneth. *History, Ethics and Emergent Probability.* Lanham, MD: University Press of America, 1987.

Merchant, Carolyn. *The Death of Nature.* San Francisco: Harper and Row, Publishers, Inc., 1980.

Meynell, Hugo. *An Introduction to the Philosophy of Bernard Lonergan.* London and Basingstoke: The Macmillan Press, Ltd., and New York: Harper and Row, Publishers, Inc., 1976.

Mooney, Christopher. "The Anthropic Principle in Cosmology and Theology." *Horizons* 21, 1 (Spring 1994): 105-129.

Moore, Sebastian. *The Fire and the Rose Are One.* New York: Seabury Press, 1981.

Mowat, Farley. *And No Birds Sang.* Toronto: McClelland and Stewart, 1979.

Muir, John. *Ramblings of a Botanist among the Plants and Climates of California.* Los Angeles: Dawson's Book Shop, 1974.

_____. *Yosemite.* New York: Doubleday, 1962.

Myers, Norman, and Gaia Ltd. staff. *Gaia: An Atlas of Planetary Management.* Garden Press, NY: Anchor/Doubleday, 1984.

Nash, Roderick. *Wilderness and the American Mind.* New Haven: Yale University Press, 1976. 1st ed., 1967.

Needham, Joseph, and C.A. Ronan. *A Shorter Science and Civilization in China.* Vol. 1. Cambridge: Cambridge University Press, 1978.

New Catholic Encyclopedia. 2nd ed. S.v. "Romanticism, Philosophical" by A.R. Caponigri.

_____. S.v. "Humanism" by W.J. Ong.

Niebuhr, H. Richard. "The Story of My Life." *Why Narrative ? Readings in Narrative Theology*. Grand Rapids, MI: William B. Eerdmans Publishing Company, 1989. Pp. 43-81.

Orsini, G.N.G. "The Organic Concepts in Aesthetics." *Comparative Literature* 21, 1 (Winter 1969).

Ortolani Calvi, Valerio. *Personalidad Ecológica: Un Modelo del Desarrollo Humano según los Escritos de Thomas Berry*. Puebla: Universidad Iberoamericana, Plantel Golfo Centro, 1984.

Otto, Rudolf. *The Idea of the Holy*. London: Oxford University Press, 1923.

Oyler, David. "Emergence in Complex Systems." *Journal of Lonergan Studies* 1, 1 (Spring 1983): 47-59.

Pepper, Stephen C. "Emergence." *Journal of Philosophy* 23 (1926): 241-245.

_____. *World Hypotheses: A Study in Evidence*. Berkeley and Los Angeles: University of California Press, 1961.

Preuss, J. Samuel. "A 'New Science' of Providence: Giambattista Vico." In *Explaining Religion: Criticism and Theory from Bodin to Freud*. Ed. by J. Samuel Preuss. New Haven and London: Yale University Press, 1987. Pp. 59-69.

Prigogine, Ilya, and Isabel Stengers. *Order Out of Chaos: Man's New Dialogue with Nature*. Toronto, New York, London and Sydney: Bantam Books, 1984.

Rahner, Karl. "The Theology of Symbol." In *Theological Investigations*. Vol. 4. Trans. by David Bourke. London: Darton, Longman and Todd, 1969. Pp. 221-252.

Ramsey, Ian. "Models and Mystery." In *Essays on Metaphor*. Ed. by Warren Shibles. Whitewater, WI: The Language Press, 1972.

Richards, Caroline. "The New Cosmology: What It Really Means." *Thomas Berry and the New Cosmology*. Ed. by Anne Lonergan and Caroline Richards. Mystic, CT: Twenty-Third Publications, 1990. Pp. 98-101.

Ricoeur, Paul. "The Critique of Religion." In *The Philosophy of Paul Ricoeur*. Ed. by Charles E. Reagan and David Stewart. Boston: Beacon Press, 1978. Pp. 213-222.

_____. "Metaphor and Symbol." Trans. by David Pellauer. In *Interpretation Theory: Discourse and the Surplus of Meaning*. Fort Worth, TX: Texas Christian University Press, 1976. Pp. 58-63.

_____. "The Metaphorical Process." *Semeia* 4 (1975): 75-106.

_____. *Time and Narrative*. Vol. 1. Trans. by Kathleen McLaughlin and David Pellauer. Chicago: University of Chicago Press, 1984.

Rockmore, Tom. "A Note on Vico and Antifoundationalism." *Vico Studies* 7 (1989): 18-27.

Ruether, Rosemary Radford. *Gaia and God. An Ecofeminist Theology of Earth Healing*. San Francisco: HarperCollins Publishers, 1992.

Russell, Colin. *Earth, Humanity and God.* London: University College Press, 1994.

Said, Edward. *Culture and Imperialism.* New York: Alfred A. Knopf, 1993.

Sale, Kirkpatrick. "Bioregionalism—A Sense of Place." *The Nation* 241 (October 12, 1985): 326-333.

_____. *Dwellers in the Land: The Bioregional Vision.* San Francisco: Sierra Club Books, 1985.

_____. "How to Bioregion." *The Nation* 252 (September 27, 1986): 269.

Santmire, H. Paul. *The Travail of Nature. The Ambiguous Ecological Promise of Christian Theology.* Minneapolis: Fortress Press, 1985.

Schelling, Friedrich Wilhelm Joseph von. *Ideas for a Philosophy of Nature.* 2nd ed. Trans. by Errol E. Harris and Peter Heath. Cambridge: Cambridge University Press, 1988.

Schenk, H.G. *The Mind of the European Romantics.* London: Constable and Co., Ltd., 1966.

Schick, Edgar B. *Metaphorical Organicism in Herder's Early Works.* The Hague, Netherlands: Mouton and Co., 1971.

Schumacher, Edward. *Small Is Beautiful.* New York: Harper and Row, Publishers, Inc., 1975.

Sheldrake, Rupert. "Is the Universe Alive?" *The Teilhard Review* 25,1 (Spring 1990): 15-24.

Shiva, Vandana. "The Greening of the Global Reach." In *Global Ecology: A New Arena of Political Conflict.* Ed. by Wolfgang Sachs. London and New Jersey: Zed Books, and Halifax, NS: Fernwood Publications, 1993. Pp. 149-156.

Smith, Huston. *The Religions of Man.* New York: Harper and Brothers, 1958.

Snow, C.P. *The Two Cultures and the Scientific Revolution.* The Rede Lecture, 1959. New York: Cambridge University Press, 1959.

Soskice, Janet Martin. *Metaphor and Religious Language.* Oxford: Clarendon Press, 1985.

Spretnak, Charlene. *States of Grace.* San Francisco: Harper, 1991.

Swimme, Brian, and Thomas Berry. *The Universe Story.* San Francisco: HarperCollins Publishers, 1992.

Teale, Edwin May. *The Wilderness World of John Muir.* Boston: Houghton Mifflin Co., 1954.

Thomas, Lewis. *The Lives of a Cell.* New York: Penguin Books, 1974.

Thoreau, Henry David. *The Maine Woods.* New York: Thomas Y. Crowell, 1961.

_____. *The Selected Journals of Henry David Thoreau.* Ed. by Carl Bode. New York: Signet/New American Library, 1967.

_____. *A Week on the Concord and Merrimack Rivers.* New York: Thomas Y. Crowell, 1961.

Topping, Richard R. "Transcendental Method and Private Language." *ARC: The Journal of the Faculty of Religious Studies, McGill University* 21 (Spring 1993): 11-26.

Torrance, Thomas F. *The Ground and Grammar of Theology.* Charlottesville: University Press of Virginia, 1980.

Toulmin, Stephen. *Return to Cosmology.* Berkeley, Los Angeles and London: University of California Press, 1982.

_____. "Nature and Nature's God." *The Journal of Religious Ethics* 13 (1985): 40-53.

Tracy, David. *The Achievement of Bernard Lonergan.* New York: Herder and Herder, 1970.

_____. "Theologies and Praxis." In *Creativity and Method: Essays in Honor of Bernard Lonergan, S.J.* Ed. by Matthew L. Lamb. Milwaukee: Marquette University Press, 1981. Pp. 35-52.

Tresmontant, Claude. *Pierre Teilhard de Chardin—His Thought.* Trans. by Salvator Attanasio. Baltimore: Helicon Press, 1959.

Tuchman, Barbara. *A Distant Mirror: The Calamitous 14th Century.* New York: Alfred A. Knopf, 1978.

Tyrrell, Bernard. *Bernard Lonergan's Philosophy of God.* Notre Dame, IN: University of Notre Dame Press, 1974.

Van Den Hengel, John. "Response by John Van Den Hengel." In *Lonergan's Hermeneutics. Its Development and Application.* Ed. by Sean E. MacEvenue and Ben F. Meyer. Washington, DC: The Catholic University of America Press, 1989. Pp. 294-299.

Vaughan, Frederick. *The Political Philosophy of Giambattista Vico: An Introduction to La Scienza Nuova.* The Hague: Martinus Nijoff, 1972.

Verene, Donald Philip. "The New Art of Narration: Vico and the Muses." *New Vico Studies* 1 (1983): 21-37.

Vickers, Brian. *In Defense of Rhetoric.* Oxford: Clarendon Press, 1988.

Voegelin, Eric. *Order and History, I. Israel and Revelation.* Louisiana State University Press, 1956.

_____. *The Ages of the World.* Trans. by Frederick deWolfe Bolman, Jr. New York: Columbia University Press, 1942.

White, Gilbert. *The Natural History of Shelbourne.* New York: Penguin Books, 1977.

White, Lynn. "The Historical Roots of Our Ecological Crisis." *Science* 155 (March 10, 1967): 1203-1207.

Whitehead, Alfred North. *Process and Reality: An Essay in Cosmology.* Ed. by David Ray Griffin and Donald W. Sherburne. New York: Macmillan Publishing Co., 1978.

_____. *Science and the Modern World*. New York, Toronto and London: Macmillan and Company, 1925.

Wilders, N. Max. *The Theologian and His Universe: Theology and Cosmology from the Middle Ages to the Present*. Trans. by Paul Dunphy. New York: Seabury Press, 1982.

Wilson, Edward O. *The Diversity of Life*. Cambridge, MA: Harvard University Press, 1992.

Winter, Gibson. *Liberating Creation*. New York: Crossroad, 1981.

Wolsky, Alexander. *Teilhard de Chardin's Biological Ideas. Teilhard Studies Number 4*. Spring 1981.

INDEX

The paper used in this publication meets the minimum requirements
of American National Standard for Information Sciences -
Permanence of Paper for Printed Library Materials, ANSI Z39.48-1992.

DANGER

LE
PHOTOCOPILLAGE
TUE LE LIVRE

AGMV MARQUIS
Québec, Canada
1999